The Mystical

Initiations

of Power

The Path to Self-Mastery, vol 3

The Mystical

Initiations

of Power

KIM MICHAELS

MORE TO LIFE PUBLISHING

www.morepublish.com

For foreign and translation rights,

contact info@ morepublish.com

ISBN: 978-87-93297-80-7

The information and insights in this book should not be considered as a form of therapy, advice, direction, diagnosis, and/or treatment of any kind. This information is not a substitute for medical, psychological, or other professional advice, counseling and care. All matters pertaining to your individual health should be supervised by a physician or appropriate health-care practitioner. No guarantee is made by the author or the publisher that the practices described in this book will yield successful results for anyone at any time. They are presented for informational purposes only, as the practice and proof rests with the individual.

For more information: *www.ascendedmasterlight.com and www.transcendencetoolbox.com*

CONTENTS

INTRODUCTION

This book is part of the series *The Path to Self-Mastery*. The purpose of the series is to give you a complete course for knowing and passing the mystical initiations of the seven spiritual rays. The books in the series form a progression, and it is recommended that you start by working through the books in the order of the seven rays.

The purpose of this book is to teach you about the characteristics of the First Ray, which will show you how to free your will to make more aware decisions. If you are new to ascended master teachings, you will benefit greatly from reading the first book in the series, *The Power of Self* because it gives a general introduction to the spiritual path as it is taught by the ascended masters. This will give you a good foundation for taking greater advantage of the teachings in this book.

This book is designed as a workbook in order to help you better integrate and apply the teachings. You will get the best results if you give the invocation that corresponds to the chapter you are studying (Chapter 5 through Chapter 18). It is recommended that you give a specific invocation once a day for nine days and then study part of the corresponding dictation before or after giving the invocation. Each evening, make calls to be taken to Master MORE's retreat, located over Darjeeling, India.

You give an invocation by reading it aloud, thereby invoking high-frequency spiritual energy. For more information about invocations and how to give them, please see the website: *www.transcendencetoolbox.com*. You can also purchase a recording of the invocations and give them along with the recording. The recording is available on *www.morepublish.com*.

In order to learn more about the ascended masters and how they give dictations, see the website *www.ascendedmaster-resources.com*. If you are not familiar with the concepts of the fall and of fallen beings, please read *Cosmology of Evil*. That book gives a profound yet easily understood explanation of why there are some beings who have no respect for the free will (or lives) of human beings. It explains why they are willing to do anything in order to control us or destroy those who will not be controlled.

1 | INTRODUCING THE FIRST RAY

Color of the First Ray: Electric blue
Corresponding chakra: Throat chakra
Elohim of the First Ray: Hercules and Amazonia
Archangel and Archeia of the First Ray: Michael and Faith
Chohan of the First Ray: Master MORE, also known as El Morya, Morya, Master M, M, or Bapu.
Decrees for the First Ray: 1.01 Decree to Elohim Hercules, 1.02 Decree to Archangel Michael, 1.03 Decree to Master MORE.

Pure qualities of the First Ray

Traditionally seen as the ray of power and will, yet from a deeper understanding the First Ray represents the creative drive. This is the desire for self-expression, a willingness to experiment, even when the outcome of the experiment cannot be known ahead of time. Also a willingness to flow with life and learn from every

experience. The First Ray gives rise to the sense that everything matters that life is exciting and that the individual truly
can make a positive difference. The First Ray is also the key
to your willingness to work for raising the whole, instead of
raising only yourself.

Perversions of the First Ray

The perversion of the creative will is a fear of the unknown,
which is expressed as a will to abuse power in order to control
one's circumstances, including other people. There is a fear of
engaging in activities where the outcome cannot be predicted
or guaranteed, which obviously stifles creativity. People with
perverted First Ray qualities are often engaged in a variety of
power games with other people, all based on the desire to control the outcome. They may also be very critical or condemna-
tory towards those who do not conform to their view of life.

A perversion of the First Ray qualities leads to an attempt
to quell the very life force itself, which always points towards
self-transcendence, and instead protect the separate self and
what it thinks it can own in this world. This can lead to a sense
of ownership over other people, which is one of the major
sources of conflict on this planet. In milder cases, people have
a fear of being creative and a sense of powerlessness, feeling
that nothing really matters and that an individual cannot make
a difference—thus, why even bother trying.

2 | INTRODUCING MASTER MORE

When you begin the path under the seven Chohans, Master MORE is the first one you meet. So instead of focusing on how you experience Master MORE, turn it around and imagine how things look from his perspective. Master MORE is the first one to meet students from a wide variety of backgrounds, and it is obvious that many of them still have some rough edges. Some come with various wounds and some come with a desire to have their egos pampered by an ascended master.

Master MORE has to find a way to deal with many types of students, and he, of course, does so by embodying the qualities of the First Ray. If you come to Master MORE with a desire to hide your wounds or your ego games, you will likely find him strict, uncompromising and impersonal. This is due to the First Ray qualities of power and a will that will not bend to human desires. In other words, Master MORE does not play games.

Yet if you are honest and willing to look at your wounds and even see your ego's games, you will find in Master MORE and incredibly loving master, who will support your growth to the utmost degree. Master MORE is looking for one particular quality in hist students, namely the straightforwardness and honesty of being willing to look at yourself in the mirror.

If you are open to having him show you facets of the ego, then he will do so in a way you have never encountered on earth. In his straightforwardness, he will clearly expose an ego game, but he will make it equally clear that you are more than your ego. He will make it clear that he is an unflinching supporter of the real you; in fact, in the beginning he may see and support the real you better than you do yourself.

Nothing compares to the love you will feel from Master MORE, when you consciously see and surrender an aspect of your ego. This is in part due to Master MORE's love for humankind, but also due to the fact that he ascended in 1898 and thus is very much aware of just how difficult it is to walk the spiritual path on this rather turbulent planet of ours. This gives him great insight into the human condition as it manifests in our age, and it gives him infinite patience with those who are willing to work on themselves—and very little patience for those who want to play hide-and-seek with their egos.

Master MORE's primary retreat is over Darjeeling India, and when you – in your finer bodies – come to the retreat, you are greeted by a very rough-looking gatekeeper, who will treat you very impolitely, possibly even by exposing you to verbal abuse. The purpose for this is to quickly sort out lifestreams who are not ready for the initiations offered at Darjeeling. If you come with some unrealistic expectation of how a spiritual master should and should not treat his students, then Master MORE's gatekeeper might just offend your ego so much that you decide to retreat from the retreat. Yet you will always be welcomed, when you come with a willingness to go beyond your expectations, and once you do enter, you will find that Master MORE will exceed your expectations by always surprising you.

Master MORE has had many past embodiments that are known, and in several of them he was a leader, even a king or statesman. Yet in this context, he wants to point out his second-to-last embodiment as the Irish poet Thomas Moore. In that embodiment he showed the gentle tenderness that comes after you have worked your way through the qualities of the First Ray. Once you have expressed enough power and determination, you begin to see that behind the desire to mold the world according to your will, there is a more philosophical, even poetic approach.

Thus, Master MORE is well aware that behind the desire to express your creative powers, there is a gently flowing stream of life that does not use force to bend other people to your will. In fact, Master MORE expressed this quality in several of his earlier embodiments. He also expressed a delightful sense of humor, even joking on his way to the scaffold as Thomas More, who was executed by a king who failed to see anything poetical or humorous in their interactions.

When you come to the point where you can laugh at your ego, you will find that Master MORE will look at you with the most loving glimpse in his eye—only then to crack a joke that exposes the ego in all its ridiculous sense of self-importance. And if you can laugh along with him, you will find that laughing with Master MORE is a most delightful and liberating experience. Master MORE has recently reached the Buddhic level of attainment.

3 | THE FLAME OF MORE

Master MORE I AM, and I come to you with the Flame of More. I come to you on the wings of the Bird of More that flutters its wings and creates a rushing flow of air that causes it to soar aloft where it can see all that happens on the earth. And it can see whether it is more or whether it is less. And so indeed, I too can see all that is more and all that is less, all that is not more. For you see, I am indeed the Being who has embodied the Flame of More that is the very driving force that caused the Creator to start the process of creation. The drive to be more, the desire to be more, the desire to express, the desire to create, even the desire to create self-conscious extensions of itself, and to enjoy watching them unfold, even if they struggle, as many of you on earth struggle. As indeed many of us struggled when we were still in embodiment.

For you who know about the ascended masters need to be aware of the tendency of the ego to build a subtle, or sometimes not so subtle, idolatry of us. You sometimes think we are so far above you and we must have been so special when we were in embodiment on

earth, especially in our last one or several embodiments. You
tend to look at our embodiments as famous beings and you
tend to think that we must have been near perfect in those
embodiments. But dare to look again. Dare to read about our
various lifetimes, both mine, Saint Germain's, Jesus' and other
masters. And see that we were not so perfect after all. We had
our idiosyncrasies, and in many cases we carried with us various
ghosts. And as you see with Jesus hanging on the cross,
giving up the ghost—well we did not give up the last ghost
until right before we ascended, my beloved.

Be humble and do not get discouraged

And so it will be for you, for the simple reason that when you
do give up the last ghost, you can no longer maintain a focus in
the physical octave. And thus, your lifestream begins to stream
beyond the body. And the Conscious You that is the core of
your being sheds the last snake skin of identification with the
outer self, and thus realizes and acknowledges its total oneness
with the Presence. This, my beloved, is a process that is delicate
that is subtle that cannot be completed in five minutes
(as the self-help gurus would have you believe) or even in five
lifetimes as things are on earth today.

Yet it can be completed by all who are willing to continue
to meet the one requirement that is the absolute requirement
for making progress on the path – the willingness to observe
yourself, to look in the mirror, to look in your own psychology,
to look for that which is hidden, the subtle, oh so subtle
layers of the ego that are hidden behind so many beliefs and
justifications that it is beyond belief. And only when you have
seen it in yourself, only when you have unraveled the layers in
your own being, can you truly believe and understand what it

is we are going through as we rise towards that final exit of the ascension.

My beloved, I am not saying this to discourage you from striving to be more. But I am saying it to discourage you from feeling the pride that many ascended master students and many other spiritual people have built up, sometimes over many lifetimes, of thinking that because they always belonged to what they consider the only true church or the only true organization sponsored by the ascended masters or some other higher authority, they were truly superior. They must be special, they must be favored by God, or the ascended masters, or whomever they see as the ultimate Being in heaven.

My beloved, humility is an absolute necessity. For if you are not humble, there will be something that your pride will stop you from looking at. Or you will be afraid of losing that pride. And thus you will define limits for how far you can go towards the ascension. You will create safe zones for the ghosts that are hiding behind the beliefs that your pride will not allow you to look at with openness and honesty. And thus, you are the one who defines your own path back to God, for you were the one who defined the path that led you away from God. And only you can undo what you have done. Only you can un-co-create what you have co-created, using the free will and the self-awareness that God gave you as the ultimate gift of life.

Towards the 96th level of consciousness

I come today to officially release the decree to myself as the Chohan of the First Ray, which is dedicated as the first in a series for all of the Chohans—and, of course, the decrees to the Archangels, to the Elohim and to the Maha Chohan. What we aim to give you here is a complete set of tools that will empower you to walk the Path of the Seven Veils, the seven veils formed by the seven rays that lead you all the way towards the 96th level of consciousness. Where you truly begin to manifest a degree of Christhood that causes you to see the oneness of all life, the oneness of yourself and the Presence. And thus, these decrees, will form a complete toolkit for those who are willing to climb towards the 96th level, whether they start from beneath the 48th level or whether they are somewhere in between the 48th and the 96th.

Indeed, you will see, when you look carefully at this decree that it contains nine verses and that the first seven are dedicated to both the First Ray and one of the other rays. This gives you a double action so that by giving this decree, you are touching upon all of the seven levels of consciousness that are ruled by the First Ray as the Alpha and then by the seven rays as the Omega. And then in the eighth verse we invoke the balancing of all seven rays, which is truly the condition you must meet in order to rise beyond the 96th level and manifest your Christhood. Thus my beloved, it is with great joy that I release this decree, the decree to Archangel Michael and that I give you notice of the others to come.

Truly, it is the joy of spring as we aim for the rest of this year 2012 to take you through a vigil where you each month give the decree for a particular ray. But I can tell you that this is done because so many people have indeed been touched by what the Maha Chohan called the hysteria around 2012. But they have been touched by it in a way where they have been willing to actually consider the possibility that the earth might go through a shift. Of course, this shift will only happen when a critical mass of people change their consciousness. It is by no means guaranteed. It is by no means something that some external force will come to the earth and bring about. It is not something that we the Chohans or the Archangels or the Elohim can bring about, for it can only be brought about by us multiplying what people bring to the altar. So the degree to which people are willing to let go of their old beliefs determines what a shift can happen.

The Darjeeling retreat

Thus my beloved, if you could see the surroundings of my retreat in Darjeeling at the etheric level, you would see the tall pines exuding a very strong fragrance that truly repels all lower spirits. And if you would walk in among the pines (which you can do in safety because there are no ticks, mosquitoes or other lower manifestations), then you would hear the wind gently filtering through the needles of the pines. And then once in a while you would hear the exuberant song of a little blue bird that lives around my retreat. It is what I call the little blue bird of kindness, for it is a bird that counteracts the tendency among some of my best students to become unbalanced on the First Ray.

They sometimes become so focused on doing something to save the world that they begin to express power in an unbalanced manner. Their will becomes so strong that they forget that it is good to have a strong will to clean up your own house, but it is not good to have a will so strong that you think you have to force others to clean up their houses according to your vision. And so, when the students that come to my etheric retreat display this imbalance, I tell them to walk out the door in the back and to walk in among the pines and to keep walking until I tell them to stop. And you see, my beloved, they will not stop until they snap out of their imbalanced state, for until then they will not hear my voice saying stop. So they determine how far they have to walk before they realize that I, Master MORE, will not force their will to turn around. They themselves must decide to turn around.

And that is indeed a thought that you might ponder, for some of you have not been willing to take full responsibility for your own use of your free will. And thus, you tend to want me, as the representative of God's will, to come and force you, to tell you what is God's will for you and what you should do. And those who come to my retreat and have that attitude, will also be sent on a little walk among the tall pines. And they will not turn around until they make a decision to turn around. You see, I cannot reach such people directly. I can only speak to them through the little blue bird of kindness. So if they are so focused on themselves and their own state of mind that they do not have time to stop and listen to the birds, well then, I must allow them to keep walking until they start wondering what might be done differently.

And thus, I will seal this release, which is not meant to be long, but to give you some sense of co-measurement of the Chohan of the First Ray. And I will seal it by giving you an admonishment. Take some time in the spring to go out in the forest and listen to the birds. They sing out of pure joy. When you can approach life out of pure joy, then you are ready for a more direct relationship with the Chohan of the First Ray. For have I not said before that a twinkle of mirth is needed on earth.

I can assure you that those who do not resonate with this statement, will find it difficult to even enter my retreat. For I have a rough gatekeeper, who takes himself very seriously, and therefore, without realizing it, is very good at ruffling the feathers of those students who also take themselves too seriously. And truly, a student will not make it past the gatekeeper until he fulfills one condition: that he no longer takes the gatekeeper seriously. As long as you take my gatekeeper seriously, you cannot enter. But when you stop taking him seriously, then you can pass. He will still stand there in the gate and grumble as he always does, but you will be able to walk past him into the beautiful garden where I will welcome you. And we will then sit down on a bench together, not seeking to solve all the problems of the world. But we will sit there together, you and I, and just listen to the little blue bird of kindness that sings in the top of one of the tall pines. For you see, when you first come to my retreat, you first need to rest. You need to relax. You need to let go of all the pressures of the world, for I am not here to teach you how to exert power and will in the world. I am here to teach you how to transcend worldly power and the will of the separate self.

Transcending the will of the separate self is not something that can be done as a kind of contest where you rush around. Nay, my beloved, it can be done only when you know the point of stillness within you. And what better way to get a taste of that stillness, than by sitting in my aura and listening to the little blue bird of kindness. By the way, my beloved, the little blue bird of kindness has been singing in the background throughout this release. Have you heard it? If not, you might play this release again, and you might continue to do so until you hear the bird with your inner ear. And thus, I bid you a fond and joyful adieu. Master MORE I AM.

4 | BEING TEACHABLE FOR MASTER MORE

Master MORE I AM. Yet, I am more than the name. I am more than any name. For truly, how can a name – given in the words you can understand on earth – capture the fullness of an ascended, God-free being?

What does it mean that I am an ascended being? Does it mean that I am so different from you that you cannot relate to me? Nay, it does not. For truly, I was once embodied on earth as you are today. I have ascended because I have completed the process that you yourself are in the process of completing. And indeed, it is my only desire for the release of these discourses to help you become more consciously aware of the path that you have already been following, likely for many lifetimes.

So, again, I am not so different from you. I am simply further ahead on the path that all self-aware beings have the potential to follow.

The ascension is not evolution

Yet, while I do not want you to see yourself as being fundamentally different from me, it is indeed necessary for you to recognize that there is a fundamental difference between the ascended state of consciousness and the unascended state of consciousness. The ascended state of consciousness is not simply a further evolution of the unascended, or human, state of consciousness. For it is not possible to evolve the human state of consciousness to a point where it smoothly crosses over to the ascended state.

If you know anything about the latest discoveries of modern physics, you might know that there was a point, when scientists developed a branch of science called quantum mechanics. The basis for this science was the discovery that light, although a wave that propagates through space and thus has no fixed location, is not a continuous phenomenon. Light is emitted in discrete units, called quanta, and thus the name "quantum mechanics."

This is important because, as we have explained in the previous two books in this series, human beings have the potential to be at 144 different levels of consciousness. You qualify for your ascension by rising up through these levels, until you reach the 144th level.

Yet the important point here is that this is not a continuous, smooth process. Every time you rise from one level of consciousness to the next, you are not simply going through an evolutionary process. You are, in fact, required to make a quantum leap in consciousness in order to rise from one level to the next. And of course, the greatest of all quantum leaps is when you have reached the 144th level and then take that final leap to the ascended state. Nevertheless, as you rise through the levels and become more consciously aware of the process, you learn to quickly give up the current sense of self and thereby be reborn as a new and more mature sense of self. And the more you are used to this process, the less of a leap it will be for you to leap into the ascended state. Yet it must be recognized that it is still a leap. It will always be a leap. And what does it require to make the quantum leap from one level to the next? It requires a conscious decision.

Master MORE cannot teach everyone

Thus, I start this series of discourses by making you aware that I am a spiritual teacher. But I cannot teach just anyone on earth. There are many people who are not ready for the kind of teaching that I can offer. For naturally, as an ascended being, I offer a teaching that is aimed at taking you towards the ascension.

If you have other goals, as might be perfectly legitimate according to the Law of Free Will, then you may not be ready for me. For you might not be ready to make the decisions that you need to make, in order to take advantage of what I have to offer you.

Thus, you might need to find other teachers for a time, or you may need to spend some time studying in what we have called the School of Hard Knocks where you experience the physical consequences of your frame of mind—what you are projecting out with that frame of mind. And you experience those consequences until you have had enough and cry out: "There must be more to life." And when you cry out that there must be more, then I, Master MORE, can indeed come to your aid. But my ability to help you will be dependent on your willingness to make conscious decisions. And you cannot make conscious decisions without consciously looking at yourself.

Thus, I tell you: Even though I am the first master that people encounter when they start the Path of the Seven Veils – the Path of the Seven Rays – I cannot teach everyone. Yet, I do indeed try to teach as many people as possible. But because people are at different levels of willingness to look at themselves, I have devised different ways to teach people, according to their willingness to look in the mirror and honestly consider their own state of consciousness.

For the purpose of this discussion, I wish to make you aware that in my etheric retreat over Darjeeling, India, I teach at two major levels. I have a part of my retreat that you might compare to one of these large soup kitchens that you see in some cities on earth where people who are homeless or disadvantaged can come in and receive a meal. The facility I have in my retreat is aimed at those who have come to the point where they have cried out: "There must be more to life!" Yet they are not yet willing to truly look at themselves and ask the conscious questions.

So I allow them – during the night in their finer bodies – to come to my retreat and enter the soup kitchen where they stand in a line, coming up to the servers who serve them a bowl of soup—somewhat adapted to their individual needs and state of consciousness. And then they partake of that soup and leave my retreat, sometimes traveling to other places, sometimes going back into their bodies. And in most cases, they have no conscious awareness of having been to my retreat, only retaining certain fragments of the lessons that were, so to speak, built into the soup that they received. I am, of course, here speaking metaphorically—I trust you understand.

After having attended my retreat for some time, then there will come a point when people are ready to not simply eat their soup and then leave but to pause, to look around, and to ask themselves: "Where am I? What is this place? Is there perhaps more for me here than just receiving this bowl of soup and then leaving?"

People who are ready for the path

When people come to that point, then I seek to help them in a different way. For that is when I seek to make them consciously aware of the Path of the Seven Veils. This is where they can start at what ideally would be the 48th level, but regardless of their present level of consciousness, they can start with those initiations that are the first ones you would encounter on a planet like earth where we do not any longer have the ideal scenario for how a new lifestream will be taught at the 48th level. Instead, you encounter these modified instructions that are aimed at taking people on earth through the Path of the Seven Veils.

Naturally, as you can see, this book is not aimed at those who are yet at the level where they only want to receive their bowl of soup and then leave. This book is aimed at those who are ready to step up to the higher level. And thus, let me give you some introductory thoughts on what is required at this level.

My purpose for this book is not to in any way give you instructions that will replace the instructions you will get at my retreat in your finer bodies. For it is a fact that the more consciously aware you are of having attended my retreat and the initiations you go through, the better you will be able to integrate the lesson learned in your daily life, in your waking, conscious state of mind.

This is, of course, important, for, truly, there is an Alpha and Omega to everything. It is one thing that you learn a lesson, but it is another thing that you actually express it in all aspects of your life. For this is how you not only grow individually, but you also become an instrument for helping to raise the collective consciousness. This happens when you dare to express your insights and therefore can surprise others, who might wonder: "I have known this person for some time where did he suddenly come up with this insight? Where did he get this wisdom? How did she become so much more mature than what I remember from the past?"

You are always in the middle of a figure-eight where the upper figure is represented by us, the ascended masters, and the lower figure is represented by those who are tied to you but are below your current level of consciousness. You raise yourself by reaching up to us, who are your ascended brothers and sisters. And then, as you do raise that nexus, you also pull up on the lower part of the figure-eight. And thus, the whole is raised.

This is, of course, the cosmic law that all must fulfill that we of the ascended masters fulfilled. For we, of course, have those above us who are our teachers, our guides towards higher levels of consciousness. Yet, what we receive from our teachers is in direct proportion to how we have multiplied the talents by helping those below. And so it is for you as well.

Cause and effect

What does it take for you to become conscious of the process that I offer at my retreat? It takes that you are willing to consciously look at yourself: Look at your present situation in life, look at your interactions with other people, look at your beliefs, look at your reactions to other people or to your situation in life. And then you need to ask yourself a simple question: "Is my reaction to life getting me where I want to go?"

When you consider the law of action and reaction, you see, of course that everything you do is an action that has a certain result, a certain effect, a certain consequence that you experience in your life. The question is simple: If you do not like what is reflected back to you from the cosmic mirror, are you willing to look at what you are sending out? Are you willing to then say: "If I do not like what is being reflected back by the mirror, then I must be willing to change what I am projecting into the mirror, for I am the one who must take charge of changing my life. I cannot expect that I can continue to project into the mirror what I have always projected, and somehow by magic the mirror will reflect something different back to me."

You see, in order to take advantage of the instructions at my retreat at a conscious level, you need to come to that realization: You are the one that must begin by changing yourself. You cannot expect that the world will change without you first changing yourself.

This is, indeed, the correct understanding of cause and effect. What will it take for students to reach this understanding? Well, there is a range of different reactions. Some actually come to this conclusion after observing what happens to them in the School of Hard Knocks. They eventually begin to see certain patterns. If they behave a certain way, then they always see a certain reaction from the universe. And they begin to wonder whether there might be a deeper reason why they attract negative people to themselves, for example. Could it be that they themselves are sending out something negative that they themselves have an attitude that attracts people with the same attitude to them?

Yet there are also others who can get this through what we call an inner, intuitive experience – a breakthrough experience or Aha experience – where you simply "see it." You see from within that: Of course it is logical that if you truly want to change your circumstances, you must begin by changing yourself.

You can come to see that so many people have it wrong; they have the opposite understanding. They think that when the world treats them better, then they will be happy. But the reality is, of course that consciousness comes before materialization, for matter-realization – what is realized in matter – is a product of what is projected from consciousness.

Which came first, action or reaction?

This is what you intuitively know when you first descend into embodiment at the 48th level. As you go below the 48th level, you actively forget this. And I say that you "actively" forget it because your ego comes up with all kinds of smokescreens to obscure this fact. The ego makes you think – aided of course by the false teachers on this planet – that you are not responsible for everything that comes back to you.

In some sense, there is some truth to this. The fallen beings and the false teachers on earth have, of course, become experts at violating people, thereby dragging them into a negative energy that locks them in this ongoing struggle that the Buddha compared to the Sea of Samsara.

Yet, even so, the devil himself does not have the power to drag you into this struggle. For what drags you into the struggle is not the actions of the devil, it is your reaction to the actions of the devil or other people. Thus, the only way – my beloved, the *only* way – that you can escape this struggle is by consciously looking at your reaction. And wondering whether it is your reaction that now becomes its own action that you are projecting out, therefore creating a reaction from the cosmic mirror.

You have the old question: "Which came first, the chicken or the egg?" Well, which came first, the action or the re-action? Well, you see that it is a question with little meaning, when you understand that even though the devil might have violated you with an action, nothing would have happened – no chain of action-reaction would have started – unless you had reacted to that action. Thus, the moment you reacted, your reaction became a new action—that then created a reaction from the cosmic mirror. And from that moment on, you were trapped in this eternal game of action and reaction.

So really, does it matter which came first? No! What matters is: Do you want to transcend this eternal, ongoing, never-ending human struggle? And if you do, you must then make the quantum leap that will open your mind and heart to the instructions that I offer at Darjeeling. And that quantum leap is that you make the conscious decision that you are willing to look at your own reaction and at least consider what it takes to change that reaction. You must change the reaction so you rise above the chain reaction of being dragged into this never-ending ping-pong match between yourself and the cosmic mirror where the devil no longer needs to violate you. He can just stand by and laugh, as he sees how you are now trapped in reacting to the reactions from the cosmic mirror—that are the result of your own action that started with your reaction.

Because you will not take command of your reaction, you cannot change what comes back from the mirror. But you keep reacting. And in a sense you are reacting to your own previous reaction. This can go on for a very long time.

You see, the quantum leap that I ask you to make, here in this first lesson, is indeed to ponder this. Are you willing to look at yourself and say: "Master MORE, show me how my own reaction keeps me trapped in this endless game. For truly, I have had enough of playing that game, and I want to rise towards the point where I can truly know that there is more to life. Thus, whatever it takes, Master MORE, I am willing to have you show me my reaction."

My beloved, this is when I can help you. And just to make sure that you do not think that I will be harsh or condemning or judgmental towards you, let me tell you a little bit about myself. For as I said, I have certainly been in embodiment as a human being on earth.

Master MORE's embodiments

You may be aware that I have had some embodiments as certain people from history. I can tell you that over the past many decades – now almost a century – where I have expressed myself as an ascended master on earth, I have seen many spiritual students focus on my past embodiments and build up a certain idolatry towards me. They looked at the fact that I am now an ascended master that I am able to give certain messages of a certain content, with a certain energy, a certain power, and they thought I must be far above them in consciousness. Then, they looked at my embodiments and they saw that I had been this or that famous person. And they started building idolatry of me, of how special I was as a human being. Thus, it is no wonder that I could make my ascension when I had all these special embodiments.

But you see, this is not my purpose for having revealed these embodiments. In fact, it is contradictory to my purpose. My purpose for revealing past embodiments is to show you that I have been in embodiment like you that I have wrestled with the difficult situations that come up in the current situation on planet earth and that I have not always made the best possible decision.

You can, of course, take a certain idolatrous view of, for example, my embodiment as Thomas More, when I was the Lord Chancellor of England. You can look at the fact that I took an uncompromising stand against the king, who wanted to compromise the principles of the church. You can see that I was executed by that king and that thereby I took a similar stand to the stand taken by Jesus, who was also willing to let himself be executed by the powers that be in order to bring forth their judgment and demonstrate a stand for higher principles.

Yet, if you cared to look a little closer at that embodiment, you would see that it actually represents a person who wrestled with the difficulties of having power. You will see that I actually abused that power by having several people executed for heresy – for what I considered to be heresy – as a result of my own private inquisition.

I can assure you, my beloved that when I left that embodiment and came to the etheric realm and went through a life review, I not only saw intellectually but I experienced in the fullness of my being, the pain that these people had gone through. I even saw the absolute futility of thinking it can be justified to kill other people in order to take a stand for a higher principle. I even saw that some of these people were indeed the ones who were taking the higher stand, for I was too focused on preserving the doctrines and dogmas of an outer institution.

I even saw with crystal clarity that I was not – as I thought while I was in embodiment – taking the same stand that Jesus took. For I was not taking a stand for the true higher principles of the Christ mind. I was taking a stand based on a watered-down vision and version of those principles, as was embodied in the Catholic teachings at the time—which have, of course, been grossly watered down compared to the purity of the teachings of Christ.

When you come to the etheric realm after an embodiment like that, you experience full force what you actually did. There is no hiding. But you see, there is also no hiding that what caused you to commit certain actions while in embodiment was not the real you, the pure awareness of the Conscious You that you are. It was the outer self, the human self, the separate self that caused you to commit those actions.

When you are given this life review in the etheric realm, you are, of course, together with your ascended teachers. And they show you that they clearly see that you are more than the separate self that made those mistakes. They help you come to the point where you can see this and accept this as well. They help you go through this sometimes difficult process of looking at yourself with full honesty.

Making right decisions

I tell you this to help you see that I am not an ascended master because I had these great embodiments where I never made a mistake. I am indeed an ascended master because I have made just about every possible mistake that one can make as a human being. You might recall – or you might not know – that my beloved brother, Saint Germain, has said that he qualified for his ascension by making one million right decisions.

Yet what is a right decision? My beloved, a right decision is simply this: No matter what you have done, you are willing to look at it honestly. You are willing to learn the lesson. And then you are willing to make the decision to let the self that made the mistake die, so that you can then make the quantum leap to a higher sense of self. Do you see, my beloved?

It is not that you do a certain thing on earth that constitutes a right decision. The right decision is that no matter what you did on earth – whether it seems like a mistake or whether it seems like a good thing to do – you are willing to see that even the so-called right things you did were done based on the separate self. This is a limited self, what the Maha Chohan in his magnificent book has called a separate spirit. And then you are willing to let that spirit die – that separate self die – so that you do not seek to evolve the spirit to a higher self. You, the pure you that you are, make the quantum leap to a higher level.

This – letting a self die and making the quantum leap – this, my beloved, is a right decision. Why did Saint Germain have to make one million decisions to qualify for his ascension? Because during his journey in embodiment, he had created one million spirits that he needed to transcend before he could be free.

My beloved, I myself can go one better, for I had created more than one million such spirits. And that is why it took me longer to qualify for my ascension than it took for Saint Germain. But you see, it is not really a matter of playing a numbers game. It is a matter of being willing to realize that the process whereby you qualify for the ascension is that you look at your current spirit—for it is your current spirit that determines your reaction to life. When you become aware of that spirit, you become aware of how it limits you. And you can make the conscious decision to let it die and rise higher.

This, then, is what we of the ascended masters can help you do. We can help you start this process. We can help you walk it all the way, until you have completed it and let that last spirit die, giving up that last ghost that frees you from the cross of matter.

This is what we aim to do with this and the following books. Of course, we have set a foundation in the previous two books that I trust you will study, for it will indeed help you gain greater benefit from this and the following books.

Nothing is said in vain. Nothing is superfluous. Everything has its place. Everything becomes a stone that you can use to build the spiral staircase as you ascend in consciousness.

Yet remember, ascending a staircase is not an evolutionary, smooth process. You are not sliding up the staircase. You are walking up a series of discreet steps. In order to rise up to the next step, you must take your foot off the previous step and for an interval of time have your foot hovering in the air, while the entire balance of your body rests on the other foot. Unless you are willing to put yourself in this precarious state, you cannot rise from one step to the next.

Thus, I have given you probably more than you can handle in this initial installment. I shall let you ponder this, before I shall return with the next step in my series on the First Ray and the initiations of the First Ray that you receive at Darjeeling.

5 | POWER AND WILL

More I AM. And a master, I AM. Thus, I am a master
of MORE. And I am here to show you how to become
more on the First Ray. Let me begin by giving you an
overview. You are, of course, familiar with the teaching that there are 144 possible levels of consciousness.
You are aware that the purpose of this series of discourses, and the purpose of the books we are bringing
out, is to show you how to rise from the 48th to the 96th
level of consciousness by mastering the initiations of
the seven rays.

Yet, let me now consider what happens when you
first descend to earth. As we have said, when you first
descend to this planet, you descend to the 48th level
of consciousness (if you are a new lifestream that is).
In the ideal scenario, what would happen to such a
lifestream? Well, the lifestream would descend with a
point-like sense of self, a sense of being connected to
something greater – although it has no clear vision of
the I AM Presence – and the lifestream descends with
a desire to experiment with its creative abilities.

Thus, at the 48th level, the most important ability that you naturally have, in the ideal scenario, is the will to experiment. This is the will to try something new, and just see what response you get from the material universe, which we might consider a giant feedback machine. Whatever you send out, will be mirrored back to you by the cosmic mirror.

If you now look at this willingness to experiment from a slightly different perspective, what is this state of consciousness? Well, it is partly what the Buddha talked about when he talked about "beginner's mind." It is what Jesus talked about when he said that unless you become as little children, you cannot enter the kingdom. The state of mind that you have at the 48th level is that of innocence, holy innocence.

The importance of innocence

In the ideal scenario, you could walk up through the initiations of the seven rays without losing this innocence. You would, of course, gain experience, but this would not take away your innocence, although you certainly would become more mature and in some ways more sophisticated. But you would still be innocent in the sense that you would have no impure, self-centered intention about putting down any other form of life. And you would not have been exposed to other lifestreams who had an intention of putting down you and your creative efforts.

Do you see that in the ideal scenario, it is possible to expand your creative abilities, to grow in awareness of your creative abilities, without ever encountering the mindset – the consciousness – that seeks to put you down and judge you according to some relative, dualistic standard, according to which you must be either right or wrong? And if you do something wrong, then there is something wrong with *you*.

Now of course, you have all been exposed to precisely this state of consciousness, even in this lifetime—and, I can assure you, also in many past lifetimes on this planet. For just look back on planet earth and see how this very consciousness of judging, evaluating and putting down has infused life on this planet for as long as you have recorded history—and I can assure you: for much longer than that.

As we have said, you do not have the ideal scenario. The idea that I want to plant as a seed in your mind here is that the goal of walking the Path of the Seven Veils is not to acquire some sophisticated mastery of mind over matter whereby you can produce visible phenomena that will impress other people. It is not even to acquire any specific wisdom or any particular sophistication in doing this or that. The primary goal of walking the path of the seven rays in the current conditions on earth is precisely this: To recapture your innocence, so that you are able to express the creative energies of the seven rays in complete innocence.

This, of course, is a new twist that not many spiritual students have been aware of. We have for now over a century taught openly the teachings of the ascended masters on earth through various messengers and teachings. Yet is has hardly been recognized at all that the real goal of walking the path is to recapture what was lost, namely that innocence that is truly paradise on earth.

The lost paradise

How will you manifest paradise on earth? Did not Jesus say that the kingdom of God is within you? So is it not logical that the way to manifest paradise on earth is to attain a certain state of consciousness? And what is the consciousness you have in

Eden? Well, before you have eaten the forbidden fruit, and therefore cast yourself out of the paradise that was Maitreya's Mystery School, you were in a state of innocence. This was a state of holy innocence where you freely experimented with your creative abilities without evaluating them based on a standard created from the separate, dualistic mind.

You see, what you have encountered here on earth is the standard that was created by the fallen beings, and it was a standard that was created specifically to destroy the innocence of the holy innocent. It was created to make sure that once they had lost that innocence, it would be extremely difficult for them to recapture it.

For how difficult is it to regain your innocence in the current environment on earth, when you are constantly attacked either by other people or by dark forces? Or you are attacked by the many spirits that the Maha Chohan has exposed that are roaming around in the collective consciousness, always seeking to manipulate you into some kind of struggle, some kind of game, to prove something right or prove others wrong.

My beloved, just look at life. Can you not recognize this consciousness and see how it infuses every aspect of society, every aspect of human interactions, and how you have been exposed to it yourself? Well then, let me put it to you that we now have a certain reversal of the original scenario. In the ideal scenario you would start out in innocence, and then you would grow and retain your innocence while becoming more sophisticated and mature. But now, as you come to me and desire to take the initiations on the First Ray, then we have almost the opposite. You are now somewhat sophisticated and mature in the sense that you know many things and have many experiences with life on earth, but you have lost the innocence.

It is not realistic that I can – at the very 48th level of consciousness, as the first initiation – help you regain that innocence. In fact I, as the first Chohan, cannot do so. It is only as you go through all of the seven rays that you have the opportunity to regain that innocence, so that when you reach the 96th level, you will have fully recaptured the innocence with which you first descended.

That is why you can then pass the initiation on the 96th level without going into using your creative abilities in a self-centered way, or even in an aggressive way that is aimed at controlling others or fighting some epic battle or other. This gives you the long-term vision. And it is important for you to keep in mind – as you walk this Path of the Seven Veils – that for each step you move closer and closer to innocence. You need to consider: "What is it that takes away my innocence right now, at my present level of consciousness?"

Learning beyond physical action

This is indeed an important consideration to keep in mind. You may not right now have a clear, conscious sense of what it means to be in a state of innocence. You may not be able to experience even a glimpse of what I mean when I talk about holy innocence. For your mind might be so filled with all of these spirits that are constantly howling at you like hyenas, seeking to pull you out of innocence. And there are the spirits that speak with the subtle tongue of the serpent, seeking to tempt you into partaking of these old patterns that also keep you out of the holy innocence that is your birthright.

Yet I will in this discourse give you the first step. You see, we have talked about the School of Hard Knocks. And truly, while we of the ascended masters can help people to some degree by giving them instructions below the 48th level of consciousness, they are still in the School of Hard Knocks until they reach that 48th level. It is only when they step up from the 47th to the 48th level that they are completely done with the School of Hard Knocks and now enroll themselves in the Path of the Seven Veils. Whereby they can attend our etheric retreats and therefore attain that inner knowing that comes from actually remembering the lessons you have learned, even if you do not remember being given specific instructions.

You can then wake up with an inner knowing, even though you do not remember how the teacher told you or gave you this knowing. But you know something is real, you know something is true and you are willing to implement it in your life. This then shifts your consciousness even at the conscious level.

My point here is simple. In the School of Hard Knocks you primarily learn through action. You take an action, you see a result – or at least you encounter a result, a physical outcome – and then you have the opportunity to learn or not to learn by evaluating the outcome. Yet when you step up to the 48th level, you are no longer primarily learning through physical, external action. Your learning process now happens more within – within your mind – where you evaluate primarily what goes on in your mind and your emotions, but not so much the physical action—even though, of course, you are still acting in the world. Yet the primary concern here is to learn through other ways than through physical action.

Certainly, you can see that learning through physical action is the hard way of learning. For you are sending an impulse into the cosmic mirror, and then it may take some time before that impulse comes back to you in the form of a physical circumstance. If you have forgotten the impulse you sent out, you see no connection to the physical karmic return. And therefore, it may be difficult for you to see how to change your consciousness to avoid a specific karmic return from the universe. What then happens when you graduate from the School of Hard Knocks and enter the School of Inner Direction? Then you begin to have this inner knowing whereby you do not need to take so many physical actions. For you are now able to see, you are able to experience through an "aha" experience: "Yes, this does not work for me. This does not get me where I want to go in life." With this I want to make you aware of the first initiation that you encounter on the 48th level of consciousness.

The first initiation at the 48th level

You have heard that the First Ray is often called the ray of power and the ray of will. So you can see, of course that when you descend at the 48th level as a new lifestream, you must experiment. You must formulate a vision, you must then sum up the will to project that image onto the Ma-ter light in order to then create some kind of return from the Mat-ter light.

It is important for you to express power when you are a new student. But you see, when you are not in the ideal scenario, then it is actually important to hold back your expression of power and to first evaluate before you express yourself. You know, of course that the First Ray corresponds – as do all of the rays – to a certain chakra. And the chakra corresponding to the First Ray is the throat chakra, which is located over your speech center.

Thus, one of the primary ways that you actually express power is through your voice, especially through the spoken word. Below the 48th level you are primarily learning by taking physical action, but at the 48th level, and the first seven levels after that, you need to be primarily concerned with how you express your power through your throat chakra and your spoken word. As Jesus said: "By thy words thou shalt be justified; by thy words thou shalt be condemned." This is an important principle to bear in mind—not that someone is sitting there judging you. I, Master MORE, am not judging you. What I want you to acquire here is a conscious awareness of an ability you already have, and that you have been using in order to come to this level where you are open to my instruction. It is the ability to feel in your heart chakra what happens to energy.

If you will focus your attention on your heart chakra, you will be able to consciously feel whether your energies are raised or whether they are lowered. And you should be able to feel that as you listen to this dictation, then your energies are raised up to a higher level than normal. There is an upward flow, an upward movement. You may even sense it as a spiral that has been building since you started reading or listening to this dictation. And you will, of course, notice the strongest effect from listening to the words, but even by reading it and paying attention, you can feel whether your energies are going up or whether they are going down.

This is an ability that you have already used in many life situations, but you may not have been consciously aware of it. Nevertheless, it is the one essential guiding rod that will carry you through from the 48th to the 96th level: Simply sensing whether something raises or lowers your energy in your heart.

How you use the spoken word

What I need you to do is to become more conscious of applying this ability to your speech, to your spoken word, to what you say and how you say it. You will notice, of course, that you can instantly tell when other people are talking to you in a certain tone of voice that creates a reaction in you that immediately lowers your energy, perhaps into irritation or anger. You may also sometimes feel that other people say things to you that make you feel down, depressed or unworthy and gives you a sense of worthlessness.

You know that what happens here is simple. These people are directing a very specific energy wave at you, and when it enters your forcefield it has an instant effect of either raising or lowering your energies. And then, when you reverse this, you can see that the way you speak to others is also sending out an energy impulse that enters their energy fields and that also creates an effect.

Now there are, of course, many subtle effects that can be created, but at this point I only want you to focus on this simple evaluation: Does it raise my energies or does it lower my energies? For you might see, if you think about and tune in to this that there is an instant effect on yourself as well when you speak to others. It is not only that your words affect them; it is also that your words affect yourself. At first, this will be the initiation at the 48th level. Become aware of how you use the spoken word and how you use your voice as a carrier of energy, a broadcaster of energy waves that are sent to other people and perhaps sent out into the universe.

Of course, we have taught the importance of invoking spiritual energy by using your throat center, your power center, by giving our decrees and invocations. One of the great advantages of doing this is that when you do give our decrees and invocations – and when you do learn to give them in the most efficient way – you are producing, you are broadcasting, energy waves that have an uplifting effect on all life. And it will also have an uplifting effect on you.

Thus, by doing the decrees and invocations, you give yourself a frame of reference for knowing when using your voice raises energy and when it does not. This means that you can now use the effect you feel of the decrees as a very efficient frame of reference for evaluating how you use your power center in other situations in life.

You will instantly begin to be feel how certain things you say, a certain tone of voice you might use, instantly lowers your energy. And this is where you need to become aware of this consciously. And as I said in my first release, there comes a point when you have to make conscious choices: "Does this get me where I want to go or does it hinder my progress?" Of course, anything that lowers your own energies or that sends out an energy impulse that lowers the energies of other people, will not get you where you want to go—if you want to rise from the 48th to the 96th level.

The circular pattern of action-reaction

If you want to transcend your current level of consciousness, you do not want to stay in the School of Hard Knocks where you only learn by projecting your current state of consciousness into the cosmic mirror and seeing what is returned from the mirror. You want to get into a positive spiral where you can start acting and reacting based on a higher state of consciousness than your current level.

Do you see the simple natural law here? The universe is a mirror. If you send out an energy impulse at a certain vibratory level, corresponding to a certain level of consciousness, what is it that will come back to you? Well, it is a reaction that is at the same vibratory level. And then, what happens when this reaction comes back from the universe? Well, as I said, you then react to that return based on your current level of consciousness, which means you create another impulse at the same level of consciousness. How will you ever escape this treadmill of actually reacting constantly to your own previous reactions to your previous reactions, to your previous reactions—that may, some time long ago, have started out as an action. But since then, it has been all *reaction*.

You have to find a way to break this, and how do you break it? Well, you must take conscious control of your mind, so that the next time you receive a return from the cosmic mirror, you do not react with the same level of consciousness that created the impulse. Instead, you are able to react at a higher level, which means you now produce an impulse at a higher level of consciousness—and that becomes what you send out, so that the return will also be higher. How else will you ever break this circular pattern of reaction to reaction?

You see, in order to change the reaction, you have to actually stop reacting and instead act at a higher level. But you can do this only by reaching for a higher level of consciousness. And what is the first step towards starting this process? It is, as I have said, to evaluate everything that you send out, but especially the spoken word, based on this simple consideration: Does it raise the energy or does it lower the energy?

This is where we must begin when you come and apply yourself at my Darjeeling retreat. I do, in fact, have a certain room at my retreat where I have the ability to make visible the energy impulses you are sending out with your voice. You have, of course, seen on earth certain computer programs where you can play music and the program displays colored patterns on the computer monitor.

Well, I have a room that has a spherical shape and half of that sphere is a giant screen that then displays certain patterns based on the sounds that you send at the screen. Thereby, you can see the visible effect of the sounds that you send out with your voice. This can be very instructional for people who have never thought about this before and have never considered how much damage you can actually do with the human voice by sending out discordant and inharmonious impulses, or even impulses that are directly disruptive to other forms of life.

The power of the human voice

You will, of course, know the different studies that have been done on how certain types of music can have specific effects on plants, or children's ability to learn, or on the patterns formed in water. You know there is power in sound, and there is no more powerful way to produce sound for you than by using the human voice.

You, of course, all take it for granted. You go around talking all day, and you think that the only effect is that which is visible or audible. Does it have any direct effect on other people, in terms of how they react and how they talk back to you? But do you see, an energy impulse that is sent out will spread like rings in the water, and it will go very, very far into the cosmos, having far-ranging effects.

If you were to rise up with me high into the atmosphere above the earth, and if you were to see, as I can, the sound waves produced by humankind, you would see a map that is not dissimilar to the maps that you have seen where satellites have taken pictures at night and show how all areas, especially around the big cities, are like filigrees of light. Well, likewise you would see that the sound waves produced by human beings are like these intricate patterns, and they are, of course, concentrated around the bigger cities with a greater concentration of people.

If you could then see the different colors and shapes of these energy waves, you would see how much of a destructive effect is produced every day through people's speech. It is simply amazing. And if you could see the effect of this, you would see that you are literally walking around in an energy soup, which is being constantly created and reinforced by people talking.

You would see how there are certain forms of talk that create these downward spirals of energy, which then tap into the planetary vortexes of negative energy. Therefore, they become two-way streets, for the people producing the speech are not only sending out energy, they are also receiving energy back from the vortexes in the collective consciousness. This becomes an inroad for the spirits in the collective consciousness to now come into people's energy fields.

Have you not experienced yourself, or seen in others that people can become trapped in a pattern where they simply cannot stop talking about certain topics? It is almost like they have no control; they *must* say something. They must talk about this. And every day they have to go around to that topic, and they have to reinforce it even though there is nothing new to say. They still have to talk about it over and over and over again because it stirs up the energy.

The influence of aggressive spirits

I can assure you that any time – and I mean, truly, *any* time – that you feel compelled to talk about things, especially things that are not entirely positive, it is because your energy field has been invaded by an aggressive spirit that wants you to talk about this because by doing so you feed energy to that spirit. This is something you can also learn to recognize, by evaluating whether the energies are raised or lowered in your heart. Any time they are lowered, you know that lowered energy goes somewhere. And you can actually learn to feel that it is being sucked or drained out of your heart, and you know that this is because there is an aggressive spirit that is sucking that energy out of your field.

This is why you can sometimes feel this pattern where you can actually – by talking about something, or even by talking to someone in an angry or derogatory way – you can feel a temporary sense of empowerment where it is almost as if your anger or your agitation gives you more power, more power to your voice than you normally have. And this is because you have been invaded by an aggressive spirit, who is using you to create this outburst where you speak to another person with this greater energy that actually comes from this spirit. But the price you pay is that once the outburst stops, then the high – the artificial high that you feel – now disappears. Then you will, as always happens when you have an artificial high, crash into a low.

You can learn to recognize this pattern of highs and lows and realize that even when you are in the so-called high – and even when you are speaking with this empowerment of this aggressive spirit – it is not actually raising your energies. You can learn to feel that even though there is a certain power flowing through you, it is not a high energy flowing through you. Thus, even though it is giving you more output, more aggressive outgoing energy, it is not raising the energies in your heart—for it is not raising the vibration of the energy.

You will see, my beloved that when it comes to sound, there is a difference between the frequency of the sound waves and the volume of the sound. A low sound that has a low frequency can still be loud. But the frequency does not become higher when you raise the volume.

Self-awareness without guilt

I need you to gently start looking at your speech, looking at how you use your voice, and become aware of whether it lowers or raises your energy. Then, I do not need you – and I do not *want* you – to condemn yourself, to criticize yourself, to come down upon yourself. Do you now understand, my beloved, that we who are your spiritual teachers walk a delicate balance? We cannot help you unless we make you aware of what needs to change. Yet, in the beginning when you are new to our instructions, it may be that when we expose to you what needs to change, you tie into certain patterns you have in your psychology. As I said, you cannot be alive on this planet without having been exposed to this very aggressive, accusatory energy.

It is possible that you have certain patterns in your energy field, so that when I talk to you about the need to evaluate how you use your voice, you may become aware that you have not used your voice in the highest possible way. This may tie in to some emotional wounds where you now think you have to feel bad about this. You have to condemn yourself, you have to feel angry with yourself, you have to be afraid of what will happen, perhaps even afraid that I, Master MORE, will condemn you. But you see, I condemn you not. I judge you not. I have no need to judge you. This is not a quality of the First Ray or any other ray.

I only seek to make you more aware, so that you can decide whether you want to continue a pattern or whether you want to consciously transcend it by recognizing: "This is not for me anymore. This is no longer an expression of who I am. This is no longer a reflection of how I see myself. For I have experienced the presence of Master MORE, and I know that

Master MORE does not condemn me, criticize me, or put me down."

Thus, you see my beloved, I only want to raise you up. I am an ascended master. I have no desire to put down any part of life. I only desire to raise up all life. You are worthy to be raised up. You are ready to be raised up or you would not be reading or listening to this teaching. It is that simple.

The equation of worthiness

Do you understand the simple equation? If you are willing to listen to my teaching, you are worthy of transcending your current level of consciousness, you are capable of transcending you current level of consciousness. There is only one question left. Are you *willing* to transcend you current level of consciousness? Let me tell you the simple answer.

If you have the willingness to listen to the teaching, you also have the power to implement the teaching. All you need is the conscious willingness to implement the teaching and to leave behind that old sense of self that old spirit, at your present level of consciousness.

I do not expect that most people will be able to leave behind that spirit by reading or listening to these words. That is why these words are only meant to help you attune your consciousness to my Presence, so that you can attend my retreat at night. For it is there that I will help you do the work of coming to see the spirit, and then separating yourself from it. For you realize, my beloved, it is not so difficult to transcend the spirit. You simply need to come to see it from the outside, so that you see that the spirit is not you. And when you know that the spirit is not you, you know that you can let the spirit die and you will not die. You will be reborn into a higher sense of self.

This is a process that I have great experience with. I have much experience in helping people go through this process. You may not be consciously aware of going through it, but I can assure you that when you apply yourself to me – give the invocations in this book and ask to be taken to my Darjeeling retreat at night – then you will be going through this process.

I will help you. I am already helping you. I have already helped you. For how else do you think you would be ready to even tune in to this teaching with the outer mind? Cause comes before effect. If you are not ready in the higher levels of your mind – in your identity, mental and emotional level – you would not have been able to find and study this teaching at the conscious level.

All that is needed is that you tune in to that readiness that willingness, at your higher levels and realize, as we have said before, that when the student is ready the teacher appears. Meaning that now that I have appeared to you at the conscious level, you will know that I have already been working with you at the three higher levels for some time before you were able to recognize me. Therefore, you are ready to bring that attainment you have gained at the three higher levels into your conscious awareness and become aware that you are a student – you are a chela, as we say – of Master MORE.

You are worthy to be my chela. You are already worthy, or you would not be receiving this teaching. So put aside all need to criticize or put yourself down. Apply the practical approach: Does it work or does it not work? Does it raise my energies or does it lower my energies? Does my speech get me where I want to go or does it not?

If you find that certain patterns of speech do not get you where you want to go, then ask me – ask me with your conscious awareness – to take you to my retreat over Darjeeling and help you overcome it. You will be surprised – if you will make this simple prayer and give the invocations as well – then you will be surprised at the effects of how easy it will be to let go of these old patterns, and how you will begin to transform your speech within a short period of time. Truly, there is a reason why you will see that many spiritual adepts talk very little. For when it comes right down to it, there is not so much to say.

I am not thereby saying that I want my students to remain silent. But there is not nearly as much to say as is being said every day. For much of what is being said is not actually human beings talking to each other; it is the aggressive spirits talking to each other through human beings. And this, I trust, is not a game that you want to play any longer.

I am the master who can help you start the process of breaking this spiral, so that you can build a positive spiral where your voice only raises up your own energies and the energies of all life around you. Where your voice suddenly becomes the open door whereby the energies of the seven rays can be expressed in the material realm where they will accelerate the vibrations of the energies here until you obtain that mastery.

You can use your voice to be a completely uplifting force, more powerful than anything else available to human beings, for radiating the light that will transform this planet and bring into physical manifestation the Golden Age of my illustrious brother, Saint Germain. Yes, this is the highest potential for the use of the human voice. You have that potential, and I AM the master who can teach you, as you are willing. And willing I trust you will be, when you begin to see the true power of the human voice, which is truly the open door for the voice of God, until you may say: "For the mouth of the Lord has spoken it. Amen."

6 | INVOKING POWER AND WILL

In the name I AM THAT I AM, Jesus Christ, I call to my I AM Presence to flow through the I Will Be Presence that I AM and give this invocation with full power. I call to beloved Elohim Hercules and Amazonia, Archangel Michael and Faith and Master MORE to help me overcome all abuses of power, especially as it relates to how I use my voice. Help me see and surrender all patterns that block my oneness with Master MORE and my oneness with my I AM Presence, including ...

[Make personal calls]

Part 1

1. Master MORE, help me experience the sense of being connected to something greater and have a vision of my I AM Presence.

O Hercules Blue, we're one with your will,
all space in our beings with Blue Flame you fill,
a beacon that radiates light to the earth,
bringing about our planet's rebirth.

O Hercules Blue, all life you defend,
giving us power to always transcend,
in you the expansion of self has no end,
as we in God's infinite spirals ascend.

2. Master MORE, help me experience my desire to experiment
with my creative abilities.

O Hercules Blue, your wisdom so great,
within us a sense of knowing create,
a new frame of reference we suddenly gain,
for going beyond duality's pain.

O Hercules Blue, all life you defend,
giving us power to always transcend,
in you the expansion of self has no end,
as we in God's infinite spirals ascend.

3. Master MORE, I have the will to experiment, the will to
try something new, and just see what response I get from the
material universe.

O Hercules Blue, we lovingly raise,
our voices in giving God infinite praise,
in feeling your flame, so clearly we see,
transcending the self is the true alchemy.

**O Hercules Blue, all life you defend,
giving us power to always transcend,
in you the expansion of self has no end,
as we in God's infinite spirals ascend.**

4. Master MORE, help me accept that the material universe is a giant feedback machine. Whatever I send out, will be mirrored back to me by the cosmic mirror.

O Hercules Blue, all life now you heal,
enveloping all in your Blue-flame Seal,
we're grateful for playing a personal part,
In God's infinitely intricate work of art.

**O Hercules Blue, all life you defend,
giving us power to always transcend,
in you the expansion of self has no end,
as we in God's infinite spirals ascend.**

5. Master MORE, help me see that the willingness to experiment is what the Buddha called "beginner's mind." It is what Jesus talked about when he said that unless we become as little children, we cannot enter the kingdom.

O Hercules Blue, your Temple of Light,
revealed to us all through our inner sight,
your power allows us to forge on until,
we pierce every veil and climb every hill.

**O Hercules Blue, all life you defend,
giving us power to always transcend,
in you the expansion of self has no end,
as we in God's infinite spirals ascend.**

6. Master MORE, help me see that the state of mind that I had when I descended to earth at the 48th level was that of innocence, holy innocence.

O Hercules Blue, I pledge now my life,
in helping this planet transcend human strife,
duality's lies are pierced by your light,
restoring the fullness of our inner sight.

**O Hercules Blue, all life you defend,
giving us power to always transcend,
in you the expansion of self has no end,
as we in God's infinite spirals ascend.**

7. Master MORE, help me see that in the ideal scenario, it is possible to expand my creative abilities, to grow in awareness of my creative abilities, without ever encountering the consciousness that seeks to put me down and judge me.

O Hercules Blue, we set all life free,
from the subtlest lies of duality,
the prince of this world no more has a bond,
for with you we go completely beyond.

**O Hercules Blue, all life you defend,
giving us power to always transcend,
in you the expansion of self has no end,
as we in God's infinite spirals ascend.**

8. Master MORE, help me see that over many lifetimes, I have been judged according to a relative, dualistic standard, according to which I must be either right or wrong. And when I do something wrong, then there is something wrong with *me*.

O Hercules Blue, in oneness with thee,
we open our hearts to your reality,
your electric-blue fire within us reveal,
our innermost longing for all that is real.

**O Hercules Blue, all life you defend,
giving us power to always transcend,
in you the expansion of self has no end,
as we in God's infinite spirals ascend.**

9. Master MORE, help me see that the goal of walking the Path of the Seven Veils is not to acquire some sophisticated mastery of mind over matter whereby I can produce visible phenomena that will impress other people.

O Hercules Blue, you fill every space,
with infinite Power and infinite Grace,
you embody the key to creativity,
the will to transcend into Infinity.

**O Hercules Blue, all life you defend,
giving us power to always transcend,
in you the expansion of self has no end,
as we in God's infinite spirals ascend.**

Part 2

1. Master MORE, help me see that the goal of the path is not to acquire any specific wisdom or any particular sophistication in doing this or that.

O Hercules Blue, we're one with your will,
all space in our beings with Blue Flame you fill,
a beacon that radiates light to the earth,
bringing about our planet's rebirth.

O Hercules Blue, all life you defend,
giving us power to always transcend,
in you the expansion of self has no end,
as we in God's infinite spirals ascend.

2. Master MORE, help me see that the primary goal of walking the path of the seven rays in the current conditions on earth is to recapture my innocence, so that I am able to express the creative energies of the seven rays in complete innocence.

O Hercules Blue, your wisdom so great,
within us a sense of knowing create,
a new frame of reference we suddenly gain,
for going beyond duality's pain.

O Hercules Blue, all life you defend,
giving us power to always transcend,
in you the expansion of self has no end,
as we in God's infinite spirals ascend.

3. Master MORE, help me see that the real goal of walking the path is to recapture what was lost, namely the innocence that is truly paradise on earth.

O Hercules Blue, we lovingly raise,
our voices in giving God infinite praise,
in feeling your flame, so clearly we see,
transcending the self is the true alchemy.

**O Hercules Blue, all life you defend,
giving us power to always transcend,
in you the expansion of self has no end,
as we in God's infinite spirals ascend.**

4. Master MORE, help me see that Jesus said that the kingdom of God is within me, so the way to manifest paradise on earth is to attain a certain state of consciousness.

O Hercules Blue, all life now you heal,
enveloping all in your Blue-flame Seal,
we're grateful for playing a personal part,
In God's infinitely intricate work of art.

**O Hercules Blue, all life you defend,
giving us power to always transcend,
in you the expansion of self has no end,
as we in God's infinite spirals ascend.**

5. Master MORE, help me see that before I had eaten the forbidden fruit, and therefore cast myself out of the paradise that was Maitreya's Mystery School, I was in a state of innocence.

O Hercules Blue, your Temple of Light,
revealed to us all through our inner sight,
your power allows us to forge on until,
we pierce every veil and climb every hill.

**O Hercules Blue, all life you defend,
giving us power to always transcend,
in you the expansion of self has no end,
as we in God's infinite spirals ascend.**

6. Master MORE, help me see that this was a state of holy innocence where I freely experimented with my creative abilities without evaluating them based on a standard created from the separate, dualistic mind.

O Hercules Blue, I pledge now my life,
in helping this planet transcend human strife,
duality's lies are pierced by your light,
restoring the fullness of our inner sight.

**O Hercules Blue, all life you defend,
giving us power to always transcend,
in you the expansion of self has no end,
as we in God's infinite spirals ascend.**

7. Master MORE, help me see that what I have encountered here on earth is the standard that was created by the fallen beings, and it is a standard that was created specifically to destroy the innocence of the holy innocent. It was created to make sure that once I had lost that innocence, it would be difficult for me to recapture it.

O Hercules Blue, we set all life free,
from the subtlest lies of duality,
the prince of this world no more has a bond,
for with you we go completely beyond.

**O Hercules Blue, all life you defend,
giving us power to always transcend,
in you the expansion of self has no end,
as we in God's infinite spirals ascend.**

8. Master MORE, help me recognize this consciousness and see how it infuses every aspect of society, every aspect of human interactions, and how I have been exposed to it myself.

O Hercules Blue, in oneness with thee,
we open our hearts to your reality,
your electric-blue fire within us reveal,
our innermost longing for all that is real.

O Hercules Blue, all life you defend,
giving us power to always transcend,
in you the expansion of self has no end,
as we in God's infinite spirals ascend.

9. Master MORE, help me see that we now have a reversal of the original scenario. I am now somewhat sophisticated and mature in the sense that I know many things and have many experiences with life on earth, but I have lost the innocence.

O Hercules Blue, you fill every space,
with infinite Power and infinite Grace,
you embody the key to creativity,
the will to transcend into Infinity.

O Hercules Blue, all life you defend,
giving us power to always transcend,
in you the expansion of self has no end,
as we in God's infinite spirals ascend.

Part 3

1. Master MORE, help me see that it is only as I go through all of the seven rays that I have the opportunity to regain my innocence, so that when I reach the 96th level, I will have fully recaptured the innocence with which I first descended.

> Michael Archangel, in your flame so blue,
> there is no more night, there is only you.
> In oneness with you, we're filled with your light,
> what glorious wonder, revealed to our sight.

> **Michael Archangel, your Knowing so strong,**
> **Michael Archangel, oh sweep us along.**
> **Michael Archangel, we're singing your song,**
> **Michael Archangel, with you we belong.**

2. Master MORE, help me see that this is the only way I can pass the initiation on the 96th level without going into using my creative abilities in a self-centered way, or even in an aggressive way that is aimed at controlling others or fighting some epic battle.

> Michael Archangel, protection you give,
> within your blue shield, we ever shall live.
> Sealed from all creatures, roaming the night,
> we remain in your sphere, of electric blue light.

> **Michael Archangel, your Knowing so strong,**
> **Michael Archangel, oh sweep us along.**
> **Michael Archangel, we're singing your song,**
> **Michael Archangel, with you we belong.**

3. Master MORE, help me always remember that as I walk the path, for each step I move closer to innocence, I need to consider: "What is it that takes away my innocence right now, at my present level of consciousness?"

Michael Archangel, what power you bring,
as millions of angels, praises will sing.
Consuming the demons, of doubt and of fear,
we know that your Presence, will always be near.

Michael Archangel, your Knowing so strong,
Michael Archangel, oh sweep us along.
Michael Archangel, we're singing your song,
Michael Archangel, with you we belong.

4. Master MORE, help me see the spirits that speak with the subtle tongue of the serpent, seeking to tempt me into partaking of these old patterns that keep me out of the holy innocence that is my birthright.

Michael Archangel, God's will is your love,
you bring to us all, God's light from Above.
God's will is to see, all life taking flight,
transcendence of self, our most sacred right.

Michael Archangel, your Knowing so strong,
Michael Archangel, oh sweep us along.
Michael Archangel, we're singing your song,
Michael Archangel, with you we belong.

5. Master MORE, help me graduate from the School of Hard Knocks so I can remember the impulse I sent out and see the connection to the physical karmic return.

Michael Archangel, you are the best friend,
from all worldly dangers you do us defend,
the devil no match for your power of light,
and therefore our souls can freely take flight.

Michael Archangel, your Knowing so strong,
Michael Archangel, oh sweep us along.
Michael Archangel, we're singing your song,
Michael Archangel, with you we belong.

6. Master MORE, help me see how to change my consciousness to avoid a specific karmic return from the universe.

Michael Archangel, as children we play,
we're bringing the earth into a new day,
we raise it from all of the patterns so old,
our planet's life story is by us retold.

Michael Archangel, your Knowing so strong,
Michael Archangel, oh sweep us along.
Michael Archangel, we're singing your song,
Michael Archangel, with you we belong.

7. Master MORE, help me become aware of the inner knowing whereby I do not need to take so many physical actions. Help me see, help me *experience* through an "aha" experience what works and what does not work.

Michael Archangel, God's power you show,
that you are invincible, this we do know,
you are undivided and thus can withstand,
anything coming from serpentine band.

**Michael Archangel, your Knowing so strong,
Michael Archangel, oh sweep us along.
Michael Archangel, we're singing your song,
Michael Archangel, with you we belong.**

8. Master MORE, help me hold back my expression of power
and first evaluate before I express myself, especially when it
comes to using my voice and throat chakra.

Michael Archangel, come raise now the earth,
giving her thus a complete rebirth,
collective the mind that we do now raise,
for this we do give our infinite praise.

**Michael Archangel, your Knowing so strong,
Michael Archangel, oh sweep us along.
Michael Archangel, we're singing your song,
Michael Archangel, with you we belong.**

9. Master MORE, help me develop the conscious awareness of
my ability to feel in my heart chakra what happens to energy,
to feel whether my energies are raised or whether they are
lowered.

Michael Archangel, the earth is now new,
covered in Blue-flame as the morning dew,
our planet now sparkles throughout all of space,
as we are receiving your infinite Grace.

**Michael Archangel, your Knowing so strong,
Michael Archangel, oh sweep us along.
Michael Archangel, we're singing your song,
Michael Archangel, with you we belong.**

Part 4

1. Master MORE, help me become more conscious of applying this ability to my speech, to my spoken word, to what I say and how I say it.

> Michael Archangel, in your flame so blue,
> there is no more night, there is only you.
> In oneness with you, we're filled with your light,
> what glorious wonder, revealed to our sight.
>
> **Michael Archangel, your Knowing so strong,**
> **Michael Archangel, oh sweep us along.**
> **Michael Archangel, we're singing your song,**
> **Michael Archangel, with you we belong.**

2. Master MORE, help me notice when other people are talking in a certain tone of voice that lowers my energy into irritation or anger, or makes me feel down, depressed or unworthy.

> Michael Archangel, protection you give,
> within your blue shield, we ever shall live.
> Sealed from all creatures, roaming the night,
> we remain in your sphere, of electric blue light.
>
> **Michael Archangel, your Knowing so strong,**
> **Michael Archangel, oh sweep us along.**
> **Michael Archangel, we're singing your song,**
> **Michael Archangel, with you we belong.**

3. Master MORE, help me see when other people are directing an energy wave at me, and help me see when I am sending out an energy impulse that enters other people's energy fields.

Michael Archangel, what power you bring,
as millions of angels, praises will sing.
Consuming the demons, of doubt and of fear,
we know that your Presence, will always be near.

Michael Archangel, your Knowing so strong,
Michael Archangel, oh sweep us along.
Michael Archangel, we're singing your song,
Michael Archangel, with you we belong.

4. Master MORE, help me see that there is an instant effect on myself when I speak to others. It is not only that my words affect them; it is also that my words affect myself.

Michael Archangel, God's will is your love,
you bring to us all, God's light from Above.
God's will is to see, all life taking flight,
transcendence of self, our most sacred right.

Michael Archangel, your Knowing so strong,
Michael Archangel, oh sweep us along.
Michael Archangel, we're singing your song,
Michael Archangel, with you we belong.

5. Master MORE, help me become aware of how I use the spoken word and how I use my voice as a carrier of energy, a broadcaster of energy waves that are sent to other people and perhaps sent into the universe.

Michael Archangel, you are the best friend,
from all worldly dangers you do us defend,
the devil no match for your power of light,
and therefore our souls can freely take flight.

Michael Archangel, your Knowing so strong,
Michael Archangel, oh sweep us along.
Michael Archangel, we're singing your song,
Michael Archangel, with you we belong.

6. Master MORE, help me see how my use of decrees and invocations gives me a frame of reference for knowing when using my voice raises energy and when it does not.

Michael Archangel, as children we play,
we're bringing the earth into a new day,
we raise it from all of the patterns so old,
our planet's life story is by us retold.

Michael Archangel, your Knowing so strong,
Michael Archangel, oh sweep us along.
Michael Archangel, we're singing your song,
Michael Archangel, with you we belong.

7. Master MORE, help me feel how certain things I say, a certain tone of voice, instantly lowers my energy. Help me evaluate: "Does this get me where I want to go or does it hinder my progress?"

Michael Archangel, God's power you show,
that you are invincible, this we do know,
you are undivided and thus can withstand,
anything coming from serpentine band.

Michael Archangel, your Knowing so strong,
Michael Archangel, oh sweep us along.
Michael Archangel, we're singing your song,
Michael Archangel, with you we belong.

8. Master MORE, help me get into a positive spiral where I can start acting and reacting based on a higher state of consciousness than my current level.

Michael Archangel, come raise now the earth,
giving her thus a complete rebirth,
collective the mind that we do now raise,
for this we do give our infinite praise.

Michael Archangel, your Knowing so strong,
Michael Archangel, oh sweep us along.
Michael Archangel, we're singing your song,
Michael Archangel, with you we belong.

9. Master MORE, help me see the natural law that if I send out an energy impulse at a certain vibratory level, corresponding to a certain level of consciousness, what will come back to me is a reaction that is at the same vibratory level.

Michael Archangel, the earth is now new,
covered in Blue-flame as the morning dew,
our planet now sparkles throughout all of space,
as we are receiving your infinite Grace.

Michael Archangel, your Knowing so strong,
Michael Archangel, oh sweep us along.
Michael Archangel, we're singing your song,
Michael Archangel, with you we belong.

Part 5

1. Master MORE, help me see that when the reaction comes back from the universe, I react to it based on my current level of consciousness, which means I create another impulse at the same level of consciousness.

Master MORE, come to the fore,
we will absorb your flame of MORE.
Master MORE, our will so strong,
our power centers cleared by song.

**Master MORE, your Sacred Heart,
from this we will no more depart,
we are forever in your flow,
of Diamond Will that you bestow.**

2. Master MORE, help me see how to escape the treadmill of reacting constantly to my own previous reactions to my previous reactions to my previous reactions—that may, some time long ago, have started out as an action. But since then, it has been all reaction.

Master MORE, your wisdom flows,
as our attunement ever grows.
Master MORE, we have a tie,
that helps us see through Serpent's lie.

**Master MORE, your Sacred Heart,
from this we will no more depart,
we are forever in your flow,
of Diamond Will that you bestow.**

3. Master MORE, help me break this by taking conscious control of my mind, so that the next time I receive a return from the cosmic mirror, I do not react with the same level of consciousness that created the impulse.

Master MORE, your love so pink,
there is no purer love, we think.
Master MORE, you set us free,
from all conditionality.

**Master MORE, your Sacred Heart,
from this we will no more depart,
we are forever in your flow,
of Diamond Will that you bestow.**

4. Master MORE, help me react at a higher level, which means I produce an impulse at a higher level of consciousness—and that becomes what I send out, so that the return will also be higher, breaking the circular pattern of reaction to reaction.

Master MORE, we will endure,
your discipline that makes us pure.
Master MORE, intentions true,
as we are always one with you.

**Master MORE, your Sacred Heart,
from this we will no more depart,
we are forever in your flow,
of Diamond Will that you bestow.**

5. Master MORE, help me see that in order to change the reaction, I have to stop reacting and instead act at a higher

level. But I can do this only by reaching for a higher level of consciousness.

> Master MORE, our vision raised,
> the will of God is always praised.
> Master MORE, creative will,
> raising all life higher still.

> **Master MORE, your Sacred Heart,**
> **from this we will no more depart,**
> **we are forever in your flow,**
> **of Diamond Will that you bestow.**

6. Master MORE, help me see that the first step is to evaluate everything that I send out, but especially the spoken word, based on the consideration: Does it raise the energy or does it lower the energy?

> Master MORE, your peace is power,
> the demons of war it will devour.
> Master MORE, we serve all life,
> our flames consuming war and strife.

> **Master MORE, your Sacred Heart,**
> **from this we will no more depart,**
> **we are forever in your flow,**
> **of Diamond Will that you bestow.**

7. Master MORE, help me see if I engage in certain forms of talk that create downward spirals of energy, which then tap into the planetary vortexes of negative energy, creating an inroad for the spirits in the collective consciousness to enter my energy field.

Master MORE, we are so free,
eternal bond from you we see.
Master MORE, we find rebirth,
in flow of your eternal mirth.

**Master MORE, your Sacred Heart,
from this we will no more depart,
we are forever in your flow,
of Diamond Will that you bestow.**

8. Master MORE, help me see if I am trapped in a pattern where I cannot stop talking about certain topics where I have no control; I *must* talk about it over and over because it stirs up the energy.

Master MORE, you balance all,
the seven rays upon our call.
Master MORE, forever MORE,
we are the Spirit's open door.

**Master MORE, your Sacred Heart,
from this we will no more depart,
we are forever in your flow,
of Diamond Will that you bestow.**

9. Master MORE, help me see that any time I feel compelled to talk about things, especially things that are not entirely positive, it is because my energy field has been invaded by an aggressive spirit that wants me to talk about this because by doing so I feed energy to that spirit.

Master MORE, your Presence here,
filling up the inner sphere.

Life is now a sacred flow,
God Power we on all bestow.

**Master MORE, your Sacred Heart,
from this we will no more depart,
we are forever in your flow,
of Diamond Will that you bestow.**

Part 6

1. Master MORE, help me learn to feel when energy is being sucked or drained out of my chakras. Help me know that this is because there is an aggressive spirit that is sucking the energy out of my field.

Master MORE, come to the fore,
we will absorb your flame of MORE.
Master MORE, our will so strong,
our power centers cleared by song.

**Master MORE, your Sacred Heart,
from this we will no more depart,
we are forever in your flow,
of Diamond Will that you bestow.**

2. Master MORE, help me see the pattern where, by talking in an angry or derogatory way, I can feel a temporary sense of empowerment where my anger or agitation gives more power to my voice than I normally have.

Master MORE, your wisdom flows,
as our attunement ever grows.
Master MORE, we have a tie,
that helps us see through Serpent's lie.

Master MORE, your Sacred Heart,
from this we will no more depart,
we are forever in your flow,
of Diamond Will that you bestow.

3. Master MORE, help me see that this is because I have been
invaded by an aggressive spirit, who is using me to create this
outburst where I speak with this greater energy that actually
comes from the spirit.

Master MORE, your love so pink,
there is no purer love, we think.
Master MORE, you set us free,
from all conditionality.

Master MORE, your Sacred Heart,
from this we will no more depart,
we are forever in your flow,
of Diamond Will that you bestow.

4. Master MORE, help me see that the price I pay is that once
the outburst stops, then the artificial high I feel disappears, and
I will crash into a low.

Master MORE, we will endure,
your discipline that makes us pure.
Master MORE, intentions true,
as we are always one with you.

Master MORE, your Sacred Heart,
from this we will no more depart,
we are forever in your flow,
of Diamond Will that you bestow.

5. Master MORE, help me recognize this pattern of highs and lows and realize that even when I am in the so-called high, it is not raising my energies, it is not a high energy flowing through me.

Master MORE, our vision raised,
the will of God is always praised.
Master MORE, creative will,
raising all life higher still.

Master MORE, your Sacred Heart,
from this we will no more depart,
we are forever in your flow,
of Diamond Will that you bestow.

6. Master MORE, help me see that even though it is giving me more output, more aggressive outgoing energy, it is not raising the energies in my heart—for it is not raising the vibration of the energy.

Master MORE, your peace is power,
the demons of war it will devour.
Master MORE, we serve all life,
our flames consuming war and strife.

Master MORE, your Sacred Heart,
from this we will no more depart,

we are forever in your flow,
of Diamond Will that you bestow.

7. Master MORE, help me see that there is a difference between the frequency of the sound waves and the volume of the sound. A low sound that has a low frequency can still be loud. But the frequency does not become higher when I raise the volume.

Master MORE, we are so free,
eternal bond from you we see.
Master MORE, we find rebirth,
in flow of your eternal mirth.

Master MORE, your Sacred Heart,
from this we will no more depart,
we are forever in your flow,
of Diamond Will that you bestow.

8. Master MORE, help me become aware of whether my speech lowers or raises my energy without condemning myself, criticizing myself or coming down upon myself.

Master MORE, you balance all,
the seven rays upon our call.
Master MORE, forever MORE,
we are the Spirit's open door.

Master MORE, your Sacred Heart,
from this we will no more depart,
we are forever in your flow,
of Diamond Will that you bestow.

9. Master MORE, help me see that you can help me only by making me aware of what needs to change. Yet this can cause me to feel guilty because I have been exposed to this very aggressive, accusatory energy.

Master MORE, your Presence here,
filling up the inner sphere.
Life is now a sacred flow,
God Power we on all bestow.

**Master MORE, your Sacred Heart,
from this we will no more depart,
we are forever in your flow,
of Diamond Will that you bestow.**

Part 7

1. Master MORE, help me see that even though I may have emotional wounds that make me think I have to feel bad about this, you will *not* condemn me. You have no need to judge me because this is not a quality of the First Ray or any other ray.

Master MORE, come to the fore,
we will absorb your flame of MORE.
Master MORE, our will so strong,
our power centers cleared by song.

**Master MORE, your Sacred Heart,
from this we will no more depart,
we are forever in your flow,
of Diamond Will that you bestow.**

2. Master MORE, help me see that you only seek to make me more aware, so that I can decide whether I want to continue a pattern or whether I want to consciously transcend it.

Master MORE, your wisdom flows,
as our attunement ever grows.
Master MORE, we have a tie,
that helps us see through Serpent's lie.

Master MORE, your Sacred Heart,
from this we will no more depart,
we are forever in your flow,
of Diamond Will that you bestow.

3. Master MORE, help me recognize: "This is not for me anymore. This is no longer an expression of who I am. This is no longer a reflection of how I see myself. For I have experienced the presence of Master MORE, and I know that Master MORE does not condemn me, criticize me, or put me down."

Master MORE, your love so pink,
there is no purer love, we think.
Master MORE, you set us free,
from all conditionality.

Master MORE, your Sacred Heart,
from this we will no more depart,
we are forever in your flow,
of Diamond Will that you bestow.

4. Master MORE, help me see the equation that when I am willing to listen to your teaching, I am worthy of transcending my current level of consciousness, I am capable of transcending

my current level of consciousness. And I am *willing* to transcend my current level of consciousness.

> Master MORE, we will endure,
> your discipline that makes us pure.
> Master MORE, intentions true,
> as we are always one with you.

> **Master MORE, your Sacred Heart,**
> **from this we will no more depart,**
> **we are forever in your flow,**
> **of Diamond Will that you bestow.**

5. Master MORE, I have the conscious willingness to implement the teaching and leave behind the old sense of self that old spirit, at my present level of consciousness. I am willing to do the work of coming to see the spirit, and then separating myself from it.

> Master MORE, our vision raised,
> the will of God is always praised.
> Master MORE, creative will,
> raising all life higher still.

> **Master MORE, your Sacred Heart,**
> **from this we will no more depart,**
> **we are forever in your flow,**
> **of Diamond Will that you bestow.**

6. Master MORE, help me come to see the spirit from the outside, so that I see that the spirit is not me. Help me know that the spirit is not me, so I can let the spirit die and I will not die. I will be reborn into a higher sense of self.

Master MORE, your peace is power,
the demons of war it will devour.
Master MORE, we serve all life,
our flames consuming war and strife.

Master MORE, your Sacred Heart,
from this we will no more depart,
we are forever in your flow,
of Diamond Will that you bestow.

7. Master MORE, help me tune in to the readiness, the willingness that I have at the higher levels of my mind. Help me bring the attainment I have gained at the three higher levels into my conscious awareness and become aware that I am a student of Master MORE.

Master MORE, we are so free,
eternal bond from you we see.
Master MORE, we find rebirth,
in flow of your eternal mirth.

Master MORE, your Sacred Heart,
from this we will no more depart,
we are forever in your flow,
of Diamond Will that you bestow.

8. Master MORE, help me see any patterns of speech that do not get me where I want to go. Take me to your retreat over Darjeeling and help me overcome it.

Master MORE, you balance all,
the seven rays upon our call.

Master MORE, forever MORE,
we are the Spirit's open door.

**Master MORE, your Sacred Heart,
from this we will no more depart,
we are forever in your flow,
of Diamond Will that you bestow.**

9. Master MORE, help me break this spiral, so that I can build a positive spiral where my voice only raises up my own energies and becomes the open door whereby the energies of the seven rays can be expressed in the material realm.

Master MORE, your Presence here,
filling up the inner sphere.
Life is now a sacred flow,
God Power we on all bestow.

**Master MORE, your Sacred Heart,
from this we will no more depart,
we are forever in your flow,
of Diamond Will that you bestow.**

Sealing:

In the name of the Divine Mother, I fully accept that the power of these calls is used to set free the Ma-ter light, so it can outpicture the perfect vision of Christ for my own life, for all people and for the planet. In the name I AM THAT I AM, it is done! Amen.

7 | POWER AND WISDOM

Master MORE I AM. And I am the master of power. Thus, in this discourse, I will talk to you about the abuses of power and of wise uses of power. The trouble here is that, in your sojourn on planet earth, you have mostly encountered abuses of power and you have rarely seen a wise use of power. Thus, you have come to accept a false frame of reference where it has often been portrayed on earth that the key to evaluating whether something is successful or powerful is the physical outcome, the physical result that is produced.

You tend to think that a person who is powerful is a person who can get things done, regardless of the human cost and the human consequences. You may, for example, look at a general who can defeat the enemy; but yet the cost in human lives and suffering is very high. You may look at leaders of nations who have achieved certain outer results but at what cost to the people of those nations or other nations.

You see I, as the Chohan of Power, do not evaluate power based on the physical outcome on earth. For to me, the physical outcome is not important at all. This is a statement that might startle some spiritual students. But it is because they have come to look at the First Ray of power through the filter of the earthly standard, the false standard of power.

Life's purpose is your growth

What have we said many times? The material universe is a schoolroom, a learning environment. The universe is the cosmic mirror. What you send out will be reflected back in the form of physical circumstances. But what is the purpose of reflecting back to you what you are sending out? It is simply this: To make visible in a way that is difficult to deny that which you do not see in your own subconscious mind, or sometimes even in the conscious. And why does the universe do this? Because the purpose of life is your growth in consciousness.

You might consider the technology you have where you wear these virtual reality goggles. You put on a pair of goggles and then you do not see the room around you. You only see what is projected in front of your eyes on a screen that is inside the goggles. What you are seeing is not the actual environment; what you are seeing is an environment that is created by a computer program—in other words a virtual, an unreal, environment. Yet I can assure you that if you could see as I see, you would see that the physical environment on planet earth is just as unreal as the virtual environment you see in these virtual reality goggles.

Outer results are irrelevant

Planet earth is simply a projection of consciousness. We have talked about the fact that there are spheres that have not ascended, but you are living in the latest unascended sphere. In an unascended sphere nothing is ultimately real, nothing has ultimate permanence, for it is an experimental environment. And as such, nothing will be permanent – nothing will gain ultimate reality – until the sphere ascends. Given that you live in an environment that is not ultimately real, why would I, or any other ascended being, be concerned about the physical results that you produce or fail to produce? It is irrelevant to us.

Do you not see that we have consistently taught that there is an outer false path to salvation and an inner true path? The outer false path is where you think, in its most primitive version that by being a member of a particular outer religion, you are guaranteed to be saved. In the more sophisticated versions, you may think that if you are an ascended master student, and if you do all of these outer things right and produce certain outer results, then you are guaranteed to be saved.

But what we have said over and over again is this: It is your state of consciousness that determines whether you can be saved, whether you can ascend, whether you can enter the spiritual realm. You will not enter the spiritual realm until you reach the 144th level of consciousness. You will not reach that level if you think it is a matter of producing specific outer results. In fact, you will not rise from the 48th to the 49th level of consciousness if you think that all that matters is the outer results you produce.

The consequence of abusing power

What I would like to give you is the vision that in order to go below the 48th level of consciousness, there is only really one way to do so and that is to start abusing power. The way you start abusing power is that you use your momentum, your attainment, on the seven rays to formulate an intent that aggressively seeks to produce a specific outer result by seeking to control or force other people. This is how you descend below the 48th level of consciousness.

Whether you descend at the 48th level or at any level above that, the only way to really fall in consciousness is to become attached to a specific outer result to the point where you are willing to use force – and with force I include deception – in order to get other people to comply with your vision of what should or should not happen. This is how beings fall.

This is how the original beings fell in the fourth sphere. This is how they have continued, some of them, to fall through the fifth, the sixth, and now into the seventh sphere. This is how they have managed to drag many of the beings who took embodiment for the first time in the seventh sphere into their downward spiral, and therefore they have followed them into the fallen consciousness.

The fallen consciousness is, in its essence, the abuse of power in order to get other people to use their free will according to your vision—even though it is not their vision. Or you may seek to force them to adopt your vision over what should be their individual vision, based on their divine individuality. This is the fallen mindset. There is no two ways about it.

Knowing you are part of a whole

You are an individual being. You have been given an individual free will. You have the right to experiment with that free will and with your creative ability. As I have said in the first two discourses here, what you are meant to do at the 48th level is to experiment with your creative powers. But you see, experimenting with your creative powers does not mean that you can do anything you want, for there is a subtle consideration to be made.

You see, even though you are an individual being with free will, you do not come into existence as an individual being in an environment where you are alone. You are always coexisting, sharing a certain environment with other self-aware individual beings. Thus, you are never in a situation where you can do anything you want without considering the effect that it has.

Now, I am aware that when I say this, many students will be so influenced by the consciousness of separation that they do not at first fully comprehend what I am saying. For in the ideal scenario, when a being first descends at the 48th level of consciousness on a planet like earth, you are an individual being, but you do not see yourself as a separate being. You know you are connected to something greater than yourself. You are aware that there are other beings in your environment and that there is, also, some sense of being connected to them. Thus, you are part of a whole, and whatever you do affects the whole—and therefore, the whole will affect you. Therefore, whatever you do also affects yourself.

When you descend at the 48th level, you do not see this as, in any way, being a limitation of your free will or your creative power. You take it for granted that you are existing in an environment and that you express your creative powers in that environment—not as a separate being who can do whatever you want. This is part of what I, in my last discourse, called holy innocence where you simply know intuitively that you are part of a whole. Whatever you do affects the whole and all who are part of that whole, including yourself. For you see yourself as an expression of the whole.

Seeing yourself as a separate being

There is a fundamental difference between this ideal scenario and what happens when students come to me at my retreat in Darjeeling and apply to the initiations of the First Ray. For when you come into embodiment on a planet like earth where we have descended below the ideal scenario, you do not see yourself as a connected being. You see yourself as a separate being. As a separate being you tend to think that you can disconnect cause and effect. You tend to think that it is possible for you to act without affecting yourself.

You think it is possible to do something which you see has a clear effect on other people or your environment; but it will somehow not have an effect on yourself. This is the illusion of separation in its essence. What we have called the duality consciousness has the effect of justifying this illusion, therefore justifying the actions you take based on this illusion. The illusion is where you, as I said earlier, can come to believe that because of some greater cause – of saving the world or spreading a certain ideology throughout the world – it is justified to force other people.

But you see, the flaw in this reasoning is the very concept that there are "other people." For when you descend in holy innocence, you do not see the other self-aware beings in your environment as other people, meaning they are separated from you. You see them as part of the whole and you see yourself as part of the whole. It is obvious to you that what you do has an effect on others and that while you are allowed to affect other people, you are not allowed to force them.

When I say allowed, I mean according to the universal law expressed by Jesus in the saying: Do unto others what you want them to do unto you. That universal law is simply this: What is best for me and what is best for you is what is best for the whole. Yet, there is another subtle distinction here because at the 48th level – when you descend as a new co-creator – you have no experience with your creative powers. So how will you gain that experience? Well, only by experimenting, and that is why a new being that descends at this level, descends into a protected environment, which is what we have called a Mystery School.

The purpose of a Mystery School

This Mystery School is overseen by an ascended master. You may know that the Garden of Eden story from the book of Genesis depicts such a Mystery School in a symbolic form. You may even know that the Mystery School that was called Eden was overseen by an ascended master called Lord Maitreya. Yet, the point here is this: In a Mystery School, in the protected environment, you can literally do anything you want with your creative powers. You can experiment with them freely because the ascended master that oversees the Mystery School has created what is literally a virtual environment within the greater virtual environment of the material universe.

In this environment you can do whatever you want without creating long-term consequences, without creating long-term karma, for yourself. This is what the master of the Mystery School does for you: He gives you a safe environment that is like a sandbox where you can do anything you want. But you cannot really hurt the sand, you cannot really hurt yourself, you cannot really hurt the other children playing in the sandbox. For at the end of the day, when you all have exercised your creative abilities as you saw fit, then the master will set everything right and the sand will be returned to its pure state. And all of you will be healed of whatever wounds you may have received.

You learn without creating long-term consequences for yourself. You learn without actually creating karma that will come back and hurt you later. The reason for this is that you are under the direct guidance of the ascended teacher. And the reason why he will erase your karma at the end of the day is that he makes you look at the results of your creative actions, so that you can learn the lesson of that day's creation right then and there. Once you have learned the lesson, what is the point in having the karma that will come back later to haunt you? For the purpose of karma is, of course, as everything else: your learning.

The purpose of karma

The karma is only necessary when you are not willing to look at the consequences of your actions at the end of the day under the guidance of the teacher. Thus, there is no karma in the Mystery School. But once the students decide that they are not willing to let the teacher show them the results of their creative efforts – but instead they will hide from the teacher – well then, they cannot remain in the Mystery School. Then, how will they learn, unless their actions have consequences? Yet, if their action had an immediate consequence, how would they learn because in many cases they would destroy themselves? That is why the material universe is set up in such a way that when you perform an action that action may have an immediate physical consequence upon your environment and upon other people; but it may not have an immediate physical consequence on you. Instead, you send a karmic impulse, an energy impulse, into the higher levels of the material universe: the identity, mental and emotional. The impulses go through those three higher levels, before they eventually come back to the physical, manifest as a physical circumstance.

The reason for this delay is that you now have the opportunity to raise your consciousness in the time interval, before your karma comes back. When the karmic return comes back to you, you can do what I talked about in my last discourse: You can respond from a higher level of consciousness than the consciousness at which you sent out the impulse. That way your reaction to your own karma coming back will be from a higher level, which means you will now create a new karmic impulse that is at a higher level. When that one comes back to you, you are at a higher level than originally. And thus, you still progress, albeit very slowly and with somewhat great difficulty, and also often with great suffering. Yet, this is your choice to leave the Mystery School.

Reentering Maitreya's Mystery School

There is hardly anyone on earth who has not left the Mystery School. Clearly, what you are doing now – in coming here and applying yourself to the Chohan of the First Ray – is that you are applying to reenter Maitreya's Mystery School. But in order to reenter, in order to qualify yourself for reentry into Maitreya's Mystery School, you must qualify yourself by walking the Path of the Seven Veils, the Path of the Seven Rays under the seven Chohans. And then, when you reach that 96th level, you can apply to the Maha Chohan. And when you pass his initiation, then you can reenter the Mystery School under Maitreya, who will then take you the rest of the way towards the 144th level of consciousness.

Of course, in order to pass that initiation at the 96th level and above, you must be willing to no longer hide anything from the teacher. For if you seek to hide, you will fall again. And then, you will have to start all over, walking through the School of Hard Knocks until you again come to the 48th level where you can apply to the Chohan of the First Ray and start working your way up.

There are lifestreams who have done this several times. They fall to the lowest level of consciousness or close to it. They eventually create a downward spiral that is so intense that they simply cannot stand it. Thus, they begin to gradually raise their consciousness until they reach that 48th level. Then, they apply themselves to the Chohans and they work their way up through the seven rays. When they come to that level where they need to stop hiding from the teacher, there is – once again – something they will not expose to the teacher. So, they fall again and have to start all over.

I would like to see that those of you who have applied yourself to follow this course – that we release now for the first time in the physical through this and the following books – will not follow this pattern. I would like to see that you will break this pattern, if you have been in it, or that you will not go into it—that you will, indeed, come to the 96th level and be fully prepared for the initiation. That is why I give you an instruction here that is actually beyond your present level of consciousness for most students. Nevertheless, even that which is beyond your present level of consciousness to implement is not beyond your present level of ability to understand, to grasp, to reason about.

Intuition goes hand in hand with reasoning

Even though we have often talked about the need to sharpen your intuition – your inner sense, your innocence – intuition goes hand in hand with reasoning. Reasoning is not the enemy of spiritual growth; for if you could not reason, you could grow in only one way and that is by experiencing everything. Do you understand, my beloved that when you look at life on earth as it is currently manifest, you can see any number of things that people do that are unspiritual that are not helpful to their spiritual growth? Yet, how will you know that a certain activity is detrimental to your spiritual growth?

In my last discourse, I told you to apply the simple measure: "Does it raise my energies; does it lower my energies?" This is an intuitive faculty, but it is an experiential faculty. Until you are actually in a certain situation, you will not feel whether it lowers or raises your energy. So this would mean that in order to know, for example, whether stealing from other people raises or lowers your energies, you would have to try it. You would have to try to be at war and be killed. You would have to try to kill other people. You would have to try every activity that is possible on earth. And do you realize how many lifetimes it would take to experience everything that is possible on earth?

Of course, you see that as time goes by people develop more and more activities. Look at how many activities are possible that were unthinkable a century ago when you did not have computer technology, for example. You can see that you can spend almost an unlimited amount of lifetimes experiencing everything. Thus, the only way to avoid having to experience everything is to use the higher reasoning faculty, which is actually what my illustrious brother, Saint Germain, brought forth to this planet earth in his embodiments. For example, as Sir Francis Bacon where he set the foundation for the scientific method. This is where you say that by conducting certain experiments that always give the same result, we can make an inference about what will happen in all similar situations. Thus, you might say that if you have had one or several embodiments where you embodied as a poor person who had to steal for a living, you could say that after having embodied in two or three different countries, you do not have to embody in every country on earth but you can use the inductive ability to say: "Yes, embodying in this kind of environment will not increase my spiritual growth, and thus I do not need to experience all of them. I can reason: This is enough. And therefore, I can leave a certain level of consciousness behind."

In order to take this to a different level, let us look at the fact that a person at the 48th level could potentially embody in tens of thousands of different actual situations here on earth but still live through those situations at the 48th level. But would you really have to embody in tens of thousands of different lifetimes in order to figure out that you do not want to anymore be at the 48th level, you want to rise to the 49th level? Well, you don't if you use your reasoning ability, the higher reasoning of the Christ mind. Then you can say: "Yes, I have now had enough. I have now had enough of a feel for the 48th level of consciousness. I have explored this level of the building. I am ready to find the staircase and ascend to the next level where I have a greater view of the surroundings and more freedom to create."

When it comes to power and the abuse of power, do you really have to experience – whether on the giving end or the receiving end – every form of the abuse of power? Or can you use your reasoning ability to say: "Master MORE, show me how power is abused. Show me the mechanism whereby I can rise beyond this abuse of power and rise to the next level."

Learning below the 48ᵗʰ level

What I have given you here is simple: another frame of reference. You are allowed, even on earth, to abuse power in the sense that you do something that forces other people to react. You are allowed to do this in the School of Hard Knocks. Do you understand?

We of the ascended masters do not apply the normal moral and ethical concerns that you have on earth. We are not saying it is morally right to kill another human being, but what we are saying is that for those who are below the 48ᵗʰ level of consciousness, it is really meaningless to apply this measure of what is morally right according to some higher standard.

In order to apply such a standard successfully, you have to be able to use your reasoning faculties. And many of the people who are below the 48ᵗʰ level of consciousness are not able to use their reasoning faculties in a higher way. They only look at what is good for me, seen from their present level of consciousness. They are not able to ask themselves what is good for themselves based on a higher consideration than their present level of consciousness.

What I am trying to explain to you here is this: When people have not acquired or activated their higher reasoning faculties, it is really meaningless to say what is right and wrong and what they should do or should not do. Because the only concern that is valid for us is: How will they learn at their present level of consciousness? And my point here is this: If they are not using their reasoning faculties – which you do have, even at the lowest level of consciousness – then there is only one way they can learn. And that is by doing whatever they want, based on their present level of consciousness, and then experiencing the physical, karmic return from the cosmic mirror.

Do you see here that if a person is at such a low level of consciousness that he thinks he has a right to kill another human being in order to get something – money or property – from that person, then it does not do any good that someone comes in and raises the finger and says: "You are not allowed to do this?" The person is not going to learn, for you have nothing to reason with. So the person can learn in only one way, and that is to kill that other person and then experience the karmic return.

Do you understand that even though the act of killing is wrong from a higher perspective, nevertheless, at a certain level of consciousness, this is the only way people can learn? I can assure you that karma works out very accurately, so that if a person is killed by someone who is at, say, the tenth level of consciousness; then it is because the person who is killed is also at a very low level of consciousness. That person has killed others in a past life and thus, in a sense, what is happening now is the outplaying of a karmic return. Do you see, again: Both the person who killed and the person who was killed are simply learning the only way they can learn: through seeing a physical karmic return of their own state of consciousness?

That is why you do, indeed, see people on earth who are trapped in repeating the same patterns over and over and over again. They have not activated their reasoning ability that allows them to say: "I have had enough of this. There must be a better way. There must be more to life. There must be a higher way to learn." And then, you can use your reasoning ability to look for some teaching that gives you the understanding that there is a higher way to react than the way dictated by your current level of consciousness and the spirit at that level of consciousness, which can only react that way.

The spirit you create cannot transcend itself

Do you see, as we have said before, once you descend below the 48th level, you become a self-fulfilling prophecy because your mind is a closed system? You send out a certain impulse. When it comes back through the cosmic mirror, you react with the same level of consciousness, creating another impulse—and so on and so forth. The reason for this is that you are creating the impulse through a certain spirit, and you are reacting to the return through that same spirit. And the spirit cannot transcend itself.

This is one of the important points, the absolutely essential teaching, given by the Maha Chohan in his book. *[Flowing with the River of Life]* The spirit you create cannot transcend itself, for it does not have the ability to reason beyond its level of consciousness and beyond the thought matrix that defines it. But you, the Conscious You, have the ability to reason beyond that spirit. So that – even though you may be at a certain level of consciousness, such as the very lowest level – you still maintain some ability to draw yourself out from the spirit through which you are seeing life.

Therefore, you can connect – not necessarily to the highest expression of the Christ mind – but you can connect to the next level up and see that there is something higher than your current level of consciousness. And if you acknowledge this, if you act upon it, then you will be able, at least gradually, to break the stranglehold that your current spirit has on your vision and your attention, so that you can rise to that next level. This is the essential ability, the saving grace that allows you to escape the downward spiral that you create by abusing power at any level.

You can reason that what has gotten you into your current situation is the way you have used power. And the only thing that will get you out of your current situation is to learn to use power in a higher way. This will, then, help you ascend to the next step up. Then you can reason again, after having experimented with using power at that level.

You can then come to that point, eventually where you are at the 48th level. Now you are able to tune in to me and learn to use power through your reasoning ability, by having me teach you about the uses and abuses of power. This, of course, is part of my purpose for this series of discourses.

Thus, I will end this installment by, again, asking you to activate your ability to sense whether something raises or lowers your energy. Spend a little time looking at the world, perhaps reading books about history, about certain intense periods, such as wars or revolutions and their abuse or use of power. Then, consider this: Did it raise or lower the energies in my heart when I looked at a particular expression of power? When I look at how, for example, Napoleon or Hitler or other famous people in history expressed power, what happens to the energies in my heart? Are they raised or are they lowered? This, then, will give you some sense of co-measurement, which will then prepare you for my next level of instruction.

8 | INVOKING POWER AND WISDOM

In the name I AM THAT I AM, Jesus Christ, I call to my I AM Presence to flow through the I Will Be Presence that I AM and give this invocation with full power. I call to beloved Elohim Hercules and Amazonia and Apollo and Lumina, Archangel Michael and Faith and Archangel Jophiel and Christine, Master MORE and Lanto to help me activate my higher reasoning ability. Help me see and surrender all patterns that block my oneness with Master MORE and my oneness with my I AM Presence, including ...

[Make personal calls]

Part 1

1. Master MORE, help me see the false frame of reference that says something is powerful based on the physical outcome, the physical result that is produced.

O Hercules Blue, we're one with your will,
all space in our beings with Blue Flame you fill,
a beacon that radiates light to the earth,
bringing about our planet's rebirth.

O Hercules Blue, all life you defend,
giving us power to always transcend,
in you the expansion of self has no end,
as we in God's infinite spirals ascend.

2. Master MORE, help me see through the false ideal that a person who is powerful, is a person who can get things done, regardless of the human cost and consequences.

O Hercules Blue, your wisdom so great,
within us a sense of knowing create,
a new frame of reference we suddenly gain,
for going beyond duality's pain.

O Hercules Blue, all life you defend,
giving us power to always transcend,
in you the expansion of self has no end,
as we in God's infinite spirals ascend.

3. Master MORE, help me see that as the Chohan of Power, you do not evaluate power based on the physical outcome on earth. For to you, the physical outcome is not important at all.

O Hercules Blue, we lovingly raise,
our voices in giving God infinite praise,
in feeling your flame, so clearly we see,
transcending the self is the true alchemy.

**O Hercules Blue, all life you defend,
giving us power to always transcend,
in you the expansion of self has no end,
as we in God's infinite spirals ascend.**

4. Master MORE, help me avoid looking at the First Ray of power through the filter of the earthly standard, the false standard of power.

O Hercules Blue, all life now you heal,
enveloping all in your Blue-flame Seal,
we're grateful for playing a personal part,
In God's infinitely intricate work of art.

**O Hercules Blue, all life you defend,
giving us power to always transcend,
in you the expansion of self has no end,
as we in God's infinite spirals ascend.**

5. Master MORE, help me see that the material universe is a schoolroom, a learning environment. The universe is the cosmic mirror. What I send out, will be reflected back in the form of physical circumstances.

O Hercules Blue, your Temple of Light,
revealed to us all through our inner sight,
your power allows us to forge on until,
we pierce every veil and climb every hill.

**O Hercules Blue, all life you defend,
giving us power to always transcend,
in you the expansion of self has no end,
as we in God's infinite spirals ascend.**

6. Master MORE, help me see that the purpose of reflecting back to me what I am sending out, is to make visible in a way that is difficult to deny that which I do not see in my own sub-conscious or conscious mind.

O Hercules Blue, I pledge now my life,
in helping this planet transcend human strife,
duality's lies are pierced by your light,
restoring the fullness of our inner sight.

O Hercules Blue, all life you defend,
giving us power to always transcend,
in you the expansion of self has no end,
as we in God's infinite spirals ascend.

7. Master MORE, help me see that the purpose of life is my growth in consciousness. Help me see that the physical environment on planet earth is just as unreal as the environment in virtual reality goggles.

O Hercules Blue, we set all life free,
from the subtlest lies of duality,
the prince of this world no more has a bond,
for with you we go completely beyond.

O Hercules Blue, all life you defend,
giving us power to always transcend,
in you the expansion of self has no end,
as we in God's infinite spirals ascend.

8. Master MORE, help me see that planet earth is simply a projection of consciousness. Nothing is ultimately real, nothing has permanence, for it is an experimental environment.

O Hercules Blue, in oneness with thee,
we open our hearts to your reality,
your electric-blue fire within us reveal,
our innermost longing for all that is real.

O Hercules Blue, all life you defend,
giving us power to always transcend,
in you the expansion of self has no end,
as we in God's infinite spirals ascend.

9. Master MORE, help me see that nothing will be permanent until the sphere ascends. That is why you are not concerned about the physical results that I produce or fail to produce.

O Hercules Blue, you fill every space,
with infinite Power and infinite Grace,
you embody the key to creativity,
the will to transcend into Infinity.

O Hercules Blue, all life you defend,
giving us power to always transcend,
in you the expansion of self has no end,
as we in God's infinite spirals ascend.

Part 2

1. Master MORE, help me see that it is my state of consciousness that determines whether I can ascend, whether I can enter the spiritual realm.

Beloved Apollo, with your second ray,
you open our eyes to see a new day,
We see through duality's lies and deceit,
transcending the mindset producing defeat.

**Beloved Apollo, thou Elohim Gold,
your radiant light our eyes now behold,
as pages of wisdom you gently unfold,
our planet is free from all that is old.**

2. Master MORE, help me see that I will not enter the spiritual realm until I reach the 144th level of consciousness. I will not reach that level if I think it is a matter of producing specific outer results.

Beloved Apollo, in your flame we know,
that your living wisdom is always a flow,
in your light we see our own highest will,
immersed in the stream that never stands still.

**Beloved Apollo, thou Elohim Gold,
your radiant light our eyes now behold,
as pages of wisdom you gently unfold,
our planet is free from all that is old.**

3. Master MORE, help me see that in order to go below the 48th level of consciousness, there is only one way to do so and that is to start abusing power.

Beloved Apollo, your light makes it clear,
why we have taken embodiment here,
exposing all lies causing the fall,
you help us reclaim the oneness of all.

**Beloved Apollo, thou Elohim Gold,
your radiant light our eyes now behold,
as pages of wisdom you gently unfold,
our planet is free from all that is old.**

4. Master MORE, help me see that abusing power is when I use my momentum, my attainment, to formulate an intent that aggressively seeks to produce a specific outer result by seeking to control or force other people. This is how I descend below the 48th level of consciousness.

Beloved Apollo, exposing all lies,
we hereby surrender all ego-based ties,
we know our perception is truly the key,
to transcending the serpentine duality.

**Beloved Apollo, thou Elohim Gold,
your radiant light our eyes now behold,
as pages of wisdom you gently unfold,
our planet is free from all that is old.**

5. Master MORE, help me see that the only way to fall in consciousness is to become attached to a specific outer result, so that I am willing to use force in order to get other people to comply with my vision.

Beloved Apollo, we heed now your call,
drawing us into Wisdom's Great Hall,
working to raise our own cosmic sphere,
together we form the tip of the spear.

**Beloved Apollo, thou Elohim Gold,
your radiant light our eyes now behold,**

**as pages of wisdom you gently unfold,
our planet is free from all that is old.**

6. Master MORE, help me see that the fallen consciousness is the abuse of power in order to get other people to use their free will according to my vision—even though it is not their vision.

Beloved Apollo, your wisdom so clear,
in oneness with you, no serpent we fear,
the beam in our eye we willingly see,
we're free from the serpent's own duality.

**Beloved Apollo, thou Elohim Gold,
your radiant light our eyes now behold,
as pages of wisdom you gently unfold,
our planet is free from all that is old.**

7. Master MORE, help me see that I have been given an individual free will. I have the right to experiment with that free will and with my creative ability. Experimenting with my creative powers does not mean that I can do anything I want.

Beloved Apollo, you help us to see
through your knowing eyes we truly are free,
we willingly stand in your piercing gaze,
empowered, we exit duality's maze.

**Beloved Apollo, thou Elohim Gold,
your radiant light our eyes now behold,
as pages of wisdom you gently unfold,
our planet is free from all that is old.**

8. Master MORE, help me see that I do not come into existence as an individual being in an environment where I am alone. I am always sharing a certain environment with other individual beings. Thus, I am never in a situation where I can do anything I want without considering the effect it has.

Beloved Apollo, our vision we raise,
we see that the earth is in a new phase,
for nothing can stop the knowledge you bring,
exposing that there's no separate thing.

**Beloved Apollo, thou Elohim Gold,
your radiant light our eyes now behold,
as pages of wisdom you gently unfold,
our planet is free from all that is old.**

9. Master MORE, help me see that I am part of a whole, and whatever I do affects the whole—and therefore, the whole will affect me. Therefore, whatever I do also affects myself.

Beloved Apollo, in wisdom's great mirth,
we all are together uplifting the earth,
as you now the true Flame of Wisdom reveal,
all of earth's people can see what is real.

**Beloved Apollo, thou Elohim Gold,
your radiant light our eyes now behold,
as pages of wisdom you gently unfold,
our planet is free from all that is old.**

Part 3

1. Master MORE, help me see that this is not a limitation of my free will or my creative power because I am part of a whole. Whatever I do affects the whole and all who are part of that whole, including myself.

> Michael Archangel, in your flame so blue,
> there is no more night, there is only you.
> In oneness with you, we're filled with your light,
> what glorious wonder, revealed to our sight.

> **Michael Archangel, your Knowing so strong,**
> **Michael Archangel, oh sweep us along.**
> **Michael Archangel, we're singing your song,**
> **Michael Archangel, with you we belong.**

2. Master MORE, help me see that on earth we do not see ourselves as connected beings. We see ourselves as separate beings and think we can disconnect cause and effect. We tend to think it is possible for us to act without affecting ourselves.

> Michael Archangel, protection you give,
> within your blue shield, we ever shall live.
> Sealed from all creatures, roaming the night,
> we remain in your sphere, of electric blue light.

> **Michael Archangel, your Knowing so strong,**
> **Michael Archangel, oh sweep us along.**
> **Michael Archangel, we're singing your song,**
> **Michael Archangel, with you we belong.**

3. Master MORE, help me see through the illusion that it is possible to do something, which has a clear effect on other people or my environment, but I think it will not have an effect on myself.

Michael Archangel, what power you bring,
as millions of angels, praises will sing.
Consuming the demons, of doubt and of fear,
we know that your Presence, will always be near.

**Michael Archangel, your Knowing so strong,
Michael Archangel, oh sweep us along.
Michael Archangel, we're singing your song,
Michael Archangel, with you we belong.**

4. Master MORE, help me see that this is the illusion of separation in its essence. The duality consciousness has the effect of justifying this illusion, therefore justifying the actions we take based on this illusion.

Michael Archangel, God's will is your love,
you bring to us all, God's light from Above.
God's will is to see, all life taking flight,
transcendence of self, our most sacred right.

**Michael Archangel, your Knowing so strong,
Michael Archangel, oh sweep us along.
Michael Archangel, we're singing your song,
Michael Archangel, with you we belong.**

5. Master MORE, help me see through the illusion that because of some greater cause – of saving the world or spreading a certain ideology – it is justified to force other people.

Michael Archangel, you are the best friend,
from all worldly dangers you do us defend,
the devil no match for your power of light,
and therefore our souls can freely take flight.

Michael Archangel, your Knowing so strong,
Michael Archangel, oh sweep us along.
Michael Archangel, we're singing your song,
Michael Archangel, with you we belong.

6. Master MORE, help me see that the flaw in this reasoning is the very concept that there are "other people." When we descend in holy innocence, we do not see the other self-aware beings in our environment as other people, meaning they are separated from us.

Michael Archangel, as children we play,
we're bringing the earth into a new day,
we raise it from all of the patterns so old,
our planet's life story is by us retold.

Michael Archangel, your Knowing so strong,
Michael Archangel, oh sweep us along.
Michael Archangel, we're singing your song,
Michael Archangel, with you we belong.

7. Master MORE, help me see people as part of the whole and see myself as part of the whole, making it obvious that what I do has an effect on others. While I am allowed to affect other people, I am not allowed to force them.

Michael Archangel, God's power you show,
that you are invincible, this we do know,

you are undivided and thus can withstand,
anything coming from serpentine band.

Michael Archangel, your Knowing so strong,
Michael Archangel, oh sweep us along.
Michael Archangel, we're singing your song,
Michael Archangel, with you we belong.

8. Master MORE, help me see the universal law that what is best for me and what is best for others is what is best for the whole.

Michael Archangel, come raise now the earth,
giving her thus a complete rebirth,
collective the mind that we do now raise,
for this we do give our infinite praise.

Michael Archangel, your Knowing so strong,
Michael Archangel, oh sweep us along.
Michael Archangel, we're singing your song,
Michael Archangel, with you we belong.

9. Master MORE, help me see that when I descend as a new co-creator, I have no experience with my creative powers. I gain that experience only by experimenting, and that is why I descend into a protected environment, a Mystery School.

Michael Archangel, the earth is now new,
covered in Blue-flame as the morning dew,
our planet now sparkles throughout all of space,
as we are receiving your infinite Grace.

Michael Archangel, your Knowing so strong,
Michael Archangel, oh sweep us along.
Michael Archangel, we're singing your song,
Michael Archangel, with you we belong.

Part 4

1. Master MORE, help me see that in a Mystery School, I can do anything I want with my creative powers. I can experiment with them freely because the ascended master that oversees the Mystery School has created a virtual environment within the greater virtual environment of the material universe.

Jophiel Archangel, in wisdom's great light,
all serpentine lies exposed to our sight.
So subtle the lies that creep through the mind,
yet you are the greatest teacher we find.

Jophiel Archangel, exposing all lies,
Jophiel Archangel, cutting all ties.
Jophiel Archangel, clearing the skies,
Jophiel Archangel, the mind truly flies.

2. Master MORE, help me see that in such an environment I can do whatever I want without creating long-term consequences, without creating long-term karma, for myself.

Jophiel Archangel, your wisdom we hail,
your sword cutting through duality's veil.
As you show the way, we know what is real,
from serpentine doubt, we instantly heal.

**Jophiel Archangel, exposing all lies,
Jophiel Archangel, cutting all ties.
Jophiel Archangel, clearing the skies,
Jophiel Archangel, the mind truly flies.**

3. Master MORE, help me see that the master of the Mystery School gives me a safe environment that is like a sandbox where I can do anything I want. I cannot really hurt the sand, I cannot really hurt myself, I cannot really hurt the other children playing in the sandbox.

Jophiel Archangel, your reality,
the best antidote to duality.
No lie can remain in your Presence so clear,
with you on our side, no serpent we fear.

**Jophiel Archangel, exposing all lies,
Jophiel Archangel, cutting all ties.
Jophiel Archangel, clearing the skies,
Jophiel Archangel, the mind truly flies.**

4. Master MORE, help me see that when I am under the direct guidance of the ascended teacher, I look at the results of my creative actions, and I learn the lesson of that day's creation.

Jophiel Archangel, God's mind is in me,
and through your clear light, its wisdom we see.
Divisions all vanish, as we see the One,
and truly, the wholeness of mind we have won.

**Jophiel Archangel, exposing all lies,
Jophiel Archangel, cutting all ties.**

Jophiel Archangel, clearing the skies,
Jophiel Archangel, the mind truly flies.

5. Master MORE, help me see that once I have learned the lesson, what is the point in having the karma that will come back later to haunt me? For the purpose of karma is my learning.

Jophiel Archangel, now show us the way,
that leads us beyond duality's fray,
we long to discern the truth and the lie,
so we the serpentine knots can untie.

Jophiel Archangel, exposing all lies,
Jophiel Archangel, cutting all ties.
Jophiel Archangel, clearing the skies,
Jophiel Archangel, the mind truly flies.

6. Master MORE, help me see that karma is only necessary when I am not willing to look at the consequences of my actions under the guidance of the teacher.

Jophiel Archangel, your Presence is here,
and therefore our minds are perfectly clear,
in wisdom's great fount we do take a bath,
and now we withstand the devil's own wrath.

Jophiel Archangel, exposing all lies,
Jophiel Archangel, cutting all ties.
Jophiel Archangel, clearing the skies,
Jophiel Archangel, the mind truly flies.

7. Master MORE, help me see that once students decide that they are not willing to let the teacher show them the results

of their creative efforts, they cannot remain in the Mystery School.

> Jophiel Archangel, it is your great task,
> to raise all mankind, if only we ask,
> so now on behalf of those who are blind,
> we ask for your help in wisdom to find.

> **Jophiel Archangel, exposing all lies,**
> **Jophiel Archangel, cutting all ties.**
> **Jophiel Archangel, clearing the skies,**
> **Jophiel Archangel, the mind truly flies.**

8. Master MORE, help me see that outside the Mystery School we cannot learn unless our actions have consequences. Yet, if our actions had immediate consequences, in many cases we would destroy ourselves.

> Jophiel Archangel, your Presence we hail,
> your Light cutting through the serpentine veil,
> the serpents can no longer people deceive,
> for all now your Flame of Wisdom receive.

> **Jophiel Archangel, exposing all lies,**
> **Jophiel Archangel, cutting all ties.**
> **Jophiel Archangel, clearing the skies,**
> **Jophiel Archangel, the mind truly flies.**

9. Master MORE, help me see that the material universe is set up in such a way that when I perform an action that action may have an immediate physical consequence upon my environment and other people; but it may not have an immediate physical consequence on me.

Jophiel Archangel where else can we go,
when we long the highest wisdom to know?
You share with us gladly all that you are,
and now our vision goes ever so far.

Jophiel Archangel, exposing all lies,
Jophiel Archangel, cutting all ties.
Jophiel Archangel, clearing the skies,
Jophiel Archangel, the mind truly flies.

Part 5

1. Master MORE, help me see that instead, I send a karmic impulse, an energy impulse, into the identity, mental and emotional levels. The impulses go through those levels, before they come back to me, manifest as a physical circumstance.

Master MORE, come to the fore,
we will absorb your flame of MORE.
Master MORE, our will so strong,
our power centers cleared by song.

Master MORE, your Sacred Heart,
from this we will no more depart,
we are forever in your flow,
of Diamond Will that you bestow.

2. Master MORE, help me see that the reason for this delay is that I have the opportunity to raise my consciousness in the time interval, before my karma comes back.

Master MORE, your wisdom flows,
as our attunement ever grows.
Master MORE, we have a tie,
that helps us see through Serpent's lie.

Master MORE, your Sacred Heart,
from this we will no more depart,
we are forever in your flow,
of Diamond Will that you bestow.

3. Master MORE, help me see that when the karmic return comes back to me, I can respond from a higher level of consciousness than the consciousness at which I sent out the impulse.

Master MORE, your love so pink,
there is no purer love, we think.
Master MORE, you set us free,
from all conditionality.

Master MORE, your Sacred Heart,
from this we will no more depart,
we are forever in your flow,
of Diamond Will that you bestow.

4. Master MORE, help me see that in this way, my reaction to my own karma coming back will be from a higher level, which means I will now create a new karmic impulse that is at a higher level.

Master MORE, we will endure,
your discipline that makes us pure.

Master MORE, intentions true,
as we are always one with you.

**Master MORE, your Sacred Heart,
from this we will no more depart,
we are forever in your flow,
of Diamond Will that you bestow.**

5. Master MORE, help me see that when the next impulse comes back to me, I am at a higher level than originally. I still progress, although slowly and with difficulty, and also often with suffering. Yet, it was *my* choice to leave the Mystery School.

Master MORE, our vision raised,
the will of God is always praised.
Master MORE, creative will,
raising all life higher still.

**Master MORE, your Sacred Heart,
from this we will no more depart,
we are forever in your flow,
of Diamond Will that you bestow.**

6. Master MORE, I am applying myself to the Chohan of the First Ray because I am applying to reenter Maitreya's Mystery School. I am willing to qualify myself by walking the Path of the Seven Rays under the seven Chohans.

Master MORE, your peace is power,
the demons of war it will devour.
Master MORE, we serve all life,
our flames consuming war and strife.

**Master MORE, your Sacred Heart,
from this we will no more depart,
we are forever in your flow,
of Diamond Will that you bestow.**

7. Master MORE, help me see that intuition goes hand in hand with reasoning. Reasoning is not the enemy of spiritual growth; for if I could not reason, I could grow in only one way and that is by experiencing everything.

Master MORE, we are so free,
eternal bond from you we see.
Master MORE, we find rebirth,
in flow of your eternal mirth.

**Master MORE, your Sacred Heart,
from this we will no more depart,
we are forever in your flow,
of Diamond Will that you bestow.**

8. Master MORE, help me see that the only way to know whether a certain activity is detrimental to my spiritual growth is to sense: "Does it raise my energies; does it lower my energies?"

Master MORE, you balance all,
the seven rays upon our call.
Master MORE, forever MORE,
we are the Spirit's open door.

**Master MORE, your Sacred Heart,
from this we will no more depart,**

we are forever in your flow,
of Diamond Will that you bestow.

9. Master MORE, help me see that this is an intuitive faculty, and it is an experiential faculty. Until I am in a certain situation, I will not feel whether it lowers or raises my energy. This means I would have to experience everything in order to know.

Master MORE, your Presence here,
filling up the inner sphere.
Life is now a sacred flow,
God Power we on all bestow.

Master MORE, your Sacred Heart,
from this we will no more depart,
we are forever in your flow,
of Diamond Will that you bestow.

Part 6

1. Master MORE, help me see that the only way to avoid having to experience everything is to use the higher reasoning faculty. By conducting experiments that always give the same result, I can make an inference about what will happen in all similar situations so I do not have to experience them all.

Master Lanto, golden wise,
expose in us the ego's lies.
Master Lanto, will to be,
we will to win our mastery.

**Master Lanto, Wisdom's Fount,
with blessings we can hardly count,
you are for earth a shining light,
your Golden Wisdom oh so bright.**

2. Master MORE, help me see that by using the higher reasoning of the Christ mind, I can say: "I now have enough of a feel for the 48th level of consciousness. I have explored this level of the building. I am ready to find the staircase and ascend to the next level where I have a greater view of the surroundings and more freedom to create."

Master Lanto, balance all,
for wisdom's balance we do call.
Master Lanto, help us see,
that balance is the Golden Key.

**Master Lanto, Wisdom's Fount,
with blessings we can hardly count,
you are for earth a shining light,
your Golden Wisdom oh so bright.**

3. Master MORE, help me see that I do not have to experience – whether on the giving end or the receiving end – every form of the abuse of power. I use my reasoning ability to say: "Master MORE, show me how power is abused. Show me the mechanism whereby I can rise beyond this abuse of power and rise to the next level."

Master Lanto, from Above,
we call forth discerning love.
Master Lanto, love's not blind,
through love, God vision we do find.

**Master Lanto, Wisdom's Fount,
with blessings we can hardly count,
you are for earth a shining light,
your Golden Wisdom oh so bright.**

4. Master MORE, help me see that once I descend below the 48th level, I become a self-fulfilling prophecy because my mind is a closed system. I send out a certain impulse, and when it comes back through the cosmic mirror, I react with the same level of consciousness, creating another impulse—and so on and so forth.

Master Lanto, we are sure
as Christic lamb intentions pure.
Master Lanto, we'll transcend,
acceleration is our truest friend.

**Master Lanto, Wisdom's Fount,
with blessings we can hardly count,
you are for earth a shining light,
your Golden Wisdom oh so bright.**

5. Master MORE, help me see that I am creating the impulse through a certain spirit, and I am reacting to the return through that same spirit. The spirit I create cannot transcend itself, for it does not have the ability to reason beyond its level of consciousness and beyond the thought matrix that defines it.

Master Lanto, we are whole,
no more division in the soul.
Master Lanto, healing flame,
all balance in your sacred name.

Master Lanto, Wisdom's Fount,
with blessings we can hardly count,
you are for earth a shining light,
your Golden Wisdom oh so bright.

6. Master MORE, help me see that I, the Conscious You, have the ability to reason beyond that spirit. Even though I am at a certain level of consciousness, I still maintain some ability to draw myself out from the spirit through which I am seeing life.

Master Lanto, serve all life,
as we transcend all inner strife.
Master Lanto, peace you give,
to all who want to truly live.

Master Lanto, Wisdom's Fount,
with blessings we can hardly count,
you are for earth a shining light,
your Golden Wisdom oh so bright.

7. Master MORE, help me connect to the next level of the Christ mind and see that there is something higher than my current level of consciousness. Help me break the stranglehold that my current spirit has on my vision and my attention, so that I can rise to the next level.

Master Lanto, free to be,
in balanced creativity.
Master Lanto, we employ,
your balance as the key to joy.

Master Lanto, Wisdom's Fount,
with blessings we can hardly count,

you are for earth a shining light,
your Golden Wisdom oh so bright.

8. Master MORE, help me reason that what has gotten me into my current situation is the way I have used power. And the only thing that will get me out of my current situation is to learn how to use power in a higher way, so I ascend to the next step up.

Master Lanto, balance all,
the seven rays upon our call.
Master Lanto, we take flight,
the threefold flame a blazing light.

Master Lanto, Wisdom's Fount,
with blessings we can hardly count,
you are for earth a shining light,
your Golden Wisdom oh so bright.

9. Master MORE, help me tune in to you and learn how to use power through my reasoning ability, by having you teach me about the uses and abuses of power.

Lanto dear, your Presence here,
filling up the inner sphere.
Life is now a sacred flow,
God Wisdom we on all bestow.

Master Lanto, Wisdom's Fount,
with blessings we can hardly count,
you are for earth a shining light,
your Golden Wisdom oh so bright.

Sealing:

In the name of the Divine Mother, I fully accept that the power of these calls is used to set free the Ma-ter light, so it can outpicture the perfect vision of Christ for my own life, for all people and for the planet. In the name I AM THAT I AM, it is done! Amen.

9 | POWER AND LOVE

Master MORE, I AM. Let me give you another layer of understanding of your higher reasoning faculties. As we have said, earth is far below the ideal scenario. Thus, when you come to the Path of the Seven Veils and apply to me as the first Chohan, you do not come with a clean slate; you come with a certain amount of baggage.

This baggage has been picked up on your sojourn here on earth, which is a heavily polluted environment. It is heavily polluted not only by what humankind has co-created over the millennia, but it is especially polluted by the ideas and teachings of what we might call the false teachers, who have been allowed to embody on this planet now for a very long time—and who have therefore had an impact on every aspect of life on earth. There is no aspect of life on earth that has not been affected by the mindset of these false teachers, which is what we have also called the fallen beings. This mindset is the duality consciousness, the dualistic consciousness, which is represented in a symbolic form as the serpent in the Garden of Eden.

The lie of becoming as a god

Now, the serpent told Eve that if she ate the forbidden fruit she would not "surely die" but she would become as a god "knowing good and evil." The explanation of this is, as we have explained in more detail before, simply this: When you become as a god, you think that you have the ability and the right to define what is good and evil. In other words, the essence of the serpentine mind is that it creates a false standard for what is good and what is evil, and then it says that if you live up to this outer standard – seeking to avoid the evil and act on the good – you are guaranteed to enter heaven.

When students come to me at my retreat at Darjeeling, they come with varying degrees of this fallen mindset. They all come having accepted some standard or other, and they now think that they can come into my retreat and, so to speak, impose their standard upon me.

My beloved, there are those who actually come to my retreat in their finer bodies, and they are so attached to their standard – so intent on imposing their standard upon me – that when I will not conform to their standard, they immediately reason that I must be a false teacher or not an advanced enough teacher for them—and they leave in a huff.

They leave feeling fully justified in rejecting me, even though their rejection is based on a complete illusion— whereas I am indeed real. For I have transcended the fallen mindset, in which the students are so trapped that they cannot even see that I offer them a frame of reference from outside that fallen mindset. They cannot even see the need for them to reach beyond the closed, mental box of their own minds. They cannot see the value of a teacher that offers them a frame of reference from beyond the fallen mindset. For they are only looking for a teacher that will validate a standard that is based on the serpentine mind.

Using your reasoning ability

Do you see that I cannot help such students? And that is why the first point I want to get across in this discourse is that in order for you to become teachable by an ascended master, you have to be willing to use your reasoning ability at whatever level of consciousness you are at. You have to be able to use your reasoning ability to realize one simple fact: Your current level of awareness forms a box around your mind, a mental box. The only way to rise from your current level of consciousness to the next level up is to reach for something beyond your current mental box. This is the only way that anyone has ever risen to a higher level of consciousness. It is the only way that anyone ever will rise to a higher level of consciousness. There is no way of cheating here.

Do you realize that this is one of the lessons of science and the laws of nature? You cannot cheat gravity. If you step out into thin air from a tall building or a tall cliff, you will fall down. How many times would you have to step out from a tall building in order to prove to your own satisfaction that gravity will turn you into a red dot on the pavement below? How many times do you then have to go through an entire embodiment being trapped in a certain mental box in order to prove to yourself that the false paths to salvation offered by the false teachers will not automatically get you to heaven after that lifetime?

What I am saying here is this: No matter what level of consciousness you are at, you have the reasoning ability to see that it forms a closed system – a closed mental box – and that the only way to rise to the next level is that you must reach up for a teacher who can give you something from beyond your mental box, from beyond your current level. Then, by grasping that lifeline, you can use it to pull yourself up to the next level of the path.

You see, when you are below the 48th level of consciousness, your current level of consciousness is like quicksand, and you know that the more your struggle the faster you sink. There is only one way to escape, and that is to stop struggling and let your mind fall still, so you can see that there is indeed someone who is offering a rope. When you grasp that rope, then you have a fixed point by which you can pull yourself up.

I am asking you to use your reasoning ability to see that I am a real teacher. I am offering you a rope. But if you allow some attachment to some false standard or false teaching to cause you to reject me or reject specific aspects of my instruction, then of course I cannot help you. I must simply respect the Law of Free Will, which I do with great love, and I must allow you to let go of the rope and therefore fall back into the quicksand of your current level of consciousness.

I am, however, an unconditionally loving teacher—because I have transcended conditions. So even if you do reject me, I will always be there if you desire to reach for me again and ask for my help. So for those who are willing to use their reasoning ability to realize that Master MORE must offer you something beyond your current mental box, let us look at how you can make the best possible use of what I offer you.

The higher and the lower reaction

It begins with realizing that when you receive a certain instruction from a spiritual teacher, there will be two reactions in you. You may wonder why this is so, but if you think about it logically, you will realize that until you ascend, there will always be a certain division in your being. For there will be some element – whether we call it ego or human consciousness – that keeps you in embodiment on earth.

As I have said, earth is a very dense planet. There are many, many planets in this material universe that have a higher level of consciousness than earth. Earth is a very dense planet, my beloved. And that means that as long as you are in embodiment here, there needs to be a certain element of human consciousness – a certain element of ego – that keeps you in a physical body.

If you were to let go of all of it in this instant, you simply could not maintain your focus inside the body, and thus you would ascend, leaving the body behind. So my point here is this: Regardless of your level of consciousness, when you receive an instruction from the next level of consciousness up, there will always be two reactions in your being. One will be a higher reaction of longing for that which is more, longing for that which is higher than your present level. And the other will be a lower reaction of wanting to reject that which is higher in order to justify why you cling to your current level, your current view of life, your current view of the spiritual path.

Again, this is simply a matter of using the reasoning ability that you have, regardless of your current level of consciousness. You can, as I have said now several times, learn to tune in to your heart, but you can also tune in to other aspects of your being, including your other chakras. You will then learn to distinguish between the reaction that lifts you up and the reaction that resists the instruction you are given. There is a reaction that wants to come into oneness with the teacher who gives the instruction, and there is the reaction that wants to reject and run away from and continue to hide from the teacher. This reaction will want to justify why you continue to run from the teacher, instead of accepting the teacher's instruction and using it to transcend you current level of consciousness.

The reaction of rejecting the teacher

Let us now look at this reaction that seeks to get you to reject the teacher and the instruction given. What is this reaction based on? Well, it is always based on some kind of standard that you have accepted with the outer mind, and this standard is always – *always*, my beloved – designed by the serpentine mind.

Yes, I am deliberately seeking to shock you because I want to give you the opportunity to feel the reactions, the two reactions within you, to this statement. Regardless of what standard you have accepted here on earth that standard is *always* based on or influenced by the serpentine mind.

I know that when spiritual students first come to my retreat, they have a very hard time accepting this. I have seen them so many times come to me with a standard – that they believe is valid and has some ultimate authority – and they expect me to either conform to that standard or validate that standard. But you see, if your standard could get you to heaven, you would not need my instructions, would you?

Therefore, I know that since you have come to my retreat, you are not ready to enter heaven. For if you were, you would not have come to me in the first place. By the very fact that you have come to my retreat, I know that your standard will not get you to heaven. Which means that I cannot help you rise to a higher level of consciousness by validating or conforming to your standard. I must challenge your standard—if I am to help you at all.

Do you see this? This is, again, just a matter of using the reasoning faculties you have. No teacher can help you rise to a higher level by validating the standard you have at the current level. It is really that simple.

A religious or spiritual standard

I would like to point out that when students come to my retreat, most of them have been in some kind of spiritual or religious movement or organization. Most of them have used that movement and its teachings to build a certain standard for evaluating their actions, their creative efforts. We have even in the past given teachings through various messengers where we openly presented ourselves as the ascended masters. We have even given, in some cases, certain outer rules and regulations for what people should do or not do. Yet, in some cases we have given so many rules that it was impossible to follow all of them. The purpose of this was very simple: If people will not listen to the inner instruction, if they will not let go of their attachments to an outer standard, then how can we help them?

Do you not see that one of the typical outcomes of having an outer standard is that you want to define rules for everything? You want to have a rule, and when you follow the rule, you are okay and God must then accept you into heaven. Those who do not follow the rule will be condemned to an eternity of torment in hell. It is a simple, binary logic. Yes or no. Good or evil. On or off. And this is the dualistic mind. What do we do, when students want to have rules so that they think that by following all of the outer rules on earth, they will automatically qualify for their ascension? How can we get them beyond this mindset? Well, we can by giving them teachings about it. But what about the students who will not listen to the teaching? Well, our only other option is to give them so many rules that they take their desire for defining rules to such an extreme that they can no longer follow the rules. Or if they try to, they can no longer move because they paralyze themselves. They confine themselves to such a small box that they suddenly realize how confining this is, and something in their being cries out for freedom from the rules.

Why the ego cannot give you freedom

Let me now give you what might be a startling teaching. What is it within you that cries out for freedom? There is a common understanding on earth of what it means to be egotistical. You see many egotistical people who do anything they want regardless of the consequences for others. You will, for example, see some of the greatest dictators in history who had absolute power. They could do anything they wanted, they could kill any amount of people that stood in their way or that opposed their power—and they did kill, in some cases, millions of people. You might look at this and think that this is freedom, but it is not freedom, as I will shortly explain.

The ego cannot give you freedom. In fact, if you take a closer look at the psychology of such dictators, you will see that even though they may have what seems like freedom at the level of action – because they can do anything they want and get away with it – they do not actually have true freedom. They do not have freedom of mind because in their minds they are so boxed in by the self-created rules that they use to judge others. You may say that, in a certain sense, the ego wants freedom to do whatever it wants, but what I am trying to help you see here is that even though the ego wants to be able to do whatever it wants and get away with it, the ego does not actually long for freedom—because it does not know what freedom is. And it never can.

You see, the ego's definition of freedom is not actually beyond rules. The ego seeks to set up freedom for itself by defining a set of rules that creates a double standard. There is one standard that applies to other people and there is one standard that applies to you, so that you can do whatever you want and get away with it but other people cannot; other people have to accept that you do whatever you want.

Do you see – for again, this is just a matter of applying reason – that the ego may have freedom to act any way it wants, but it does not have freedom of mind? Because in your mind you have this set of rules that defines the double standard, and you must live up to that standard in order to have the freedom defined by the standard. So even if your ego has managed to define a standard that gives you the right to do seemingly anything you want, you are still trapped by the standard. And there will come a point when you begin to feel that you are imprisoned by your own standard.

You will even see this in the psychology of some of the people that have attained seemingly absolute power on earth. They came to a point where they began to realize how trapped they actually were in the system they had created. For they could not allow themselves to violate the standard that defined their absolute powers. They could not allow themselves to be seen as having certain weaknesses, or even as being human beings. They had to live up to the image of an absolute ruler that they created. And there came a point where it started to dawn on them that they had created a gilded cage for themselves, and that the cage was beginning to seem more and more narrow, to the point where they could hardly move.

Which part of you longs for freedom?

What is it in you that truly yearns for freedom? It is what we have called the Conscious You because it is an extension of your I AM Presence. It is Spirit. And Spirit will always feel confined when it has to conform to matter. It cannot be any other way. But why is this so? Because Spirit has creative freedom.

Creative freedom is not the same as having the freedom to do anything you want according to a set of rules defined in the world of form. For do you not see that the rules are defined by a certain form, and once you accept them as rules, you cannot change the form? The form is locked in a matrix, and as long as you believe in the rule, the form cannot be transcended. But Spirit is not created to be locked in form. Spirit is created to create form and to continue to create form by learning from its previous expressions of its creative powers to create a form that is more than what it created previously.

Do you not see that creativity – the creative drive of Spirit – is to create form but then not to be locked in that form for an extended period of time, but to use the experience it gained creating the first form to create a form that is more? And it is in doing this – in creating, learning, and then creating more – it is in doing this that you grow in self-awareness. This is the purpose of life. This is how life progresses: through the creative process.

What the false teachers have done is make people believe that they should kill their creative drive. When you are seeking to conform to rules, you are not being creative. You cannot be creative by conforming to rules that are defined based on form because then you cannot transcend the form. And how can you be creative without transcending the form that exists now? It cannot be done. It is not creativity.

The false teachers have created this false standard – this false belief – that says that in order to enter heaven you must conform to a set of rules that are defined by this ultimate authority, such as the angry god in the sky promoted by the three monotheistic religions now for thousands of years. Even the very similar image promoted by materialistic science that there are invariable laws of nature.

Yes, there are laws of nature. There are creative principles used by the Creator. But you can learn to use those principles in ever more creative ways to create something that raises the whole. This is creativity whereas defining the laws of nature or the laws of God as a straightjacket that shuts down your creativity—well, this is not creativity. This is the consciousness of death that Jesus talked about. It is not the consciousness of Life, the Christ Consciousness that seeks to raise all life.

Creative use of the laws of nature

How can you raise all life? Just look at this in a very linear way. Look at the problem of poverty on earth. From a certain linear, superficial viewpoint you might say that the problem with poverty is the lack of money. So if we could have more money, then everybody could have enough money to buy whatever they need. But how will you increase the money supply? Yes, you can do it in an artificial way, such as many governments and institutions have attempted to do. But the inevitable consequence will be what you call inflation, so that the value of the money will be less. Therefore, even though you have more money, you cannot buy more with it.

What would be the way to overcome poverty? It is to actually increase the total amount of abundance on earth. But abundance is not the same as money. Abundance does not come from running the printing presses and printing more money. Abundance comes through creativity, so that you learn to make better use of natural resources and the laws of nature.

I earlier talked about the law of gravity and said that if you step out from the top of a tall building, you will fall down. And this is true. Look at how, for thousands of years, human beings thought that flying like the birds was an unattainable thing. Yet look at how you have learned to use certain laws of nature to neutralize the law of gravity, so that you can now fly through the air. And look how this creative discovery – this creative use of the laws of nature – has opened up an entire new industry that has created new wealth, new abundance.

This was done though a creative application of the laws of nature, not by blindly following rules. For if nobody had dared to think creatively, then you human beings would still be walking around on the ground, looking with envy at the birds, thinking that flight was an unattainable dream.

Disconnecting creativity from physical results

My beloved, when students first come to my retreat, the biggest challenge I face is to get them to the point where they are willing to let me take them beyond their current standard. For do you not see that the standard you have – the standard you have accepted on earth – has one purpose only, and that is to limit your creativity so that you cannot use your creative abilities to rise to the next level of consciousness?

It is not a matter, my beloved, of using your creative abilities to produce certain results on earth. Yes, we of the ascended masters do indeed seek to help people use their creativity to raise society to a higher level, as we have done through science and technology and in other ways. But our primary concern, as I have already said, is not the outer results. Our primary concern is that you learn to use your creative abilities to rise to the next level of consciousness. It is not so much the outer things that we want to see changed. It is your sense of self that we want to see changed because it is only by changing your sense of self that you can rise from the 49th to 50th level of consciousness.

Do you not see this? You do not need to produce certain outer results in order to rise to a higher level. But you do need to produce the result of changing your sense of self. And this cannot be done by following the rules of your current standard, for that standard will keep your sense of self at the present level of consciousness. Thus, the only way to recreate your sense of self is to use your creative abilities.

When students first come to my retreat, my first task is to get them to set aside their standards – their rules – so much that they can get back in touch with their creative abilities. For I can assure you that there is no one on earth that is fully in touch with their creative abilities. And certainly, there is no student who comes to my retreat having the full awareness of his or her creative abilities. Thus, my first task is always to get people so in touch with their creative abilities that they can even grasp the fact that there is more than their current level of consciousness, and that they have the potential to rise to that level. Not by me doing it for them, but by them using the abilities they have within them, their own creative abilities.

For do you not see that many of the spiritual and religious people on earth have come to accept a standard that says that they need a teacher or an external savior to do something for them? And thus, when they come to my retreat they think that

I, Master MORE, am going to give them some magical potion or some magical formula whereby they suddenly – puff – are at a higher level of consciousness.

Burying your talents in the ground

But you see, here is again one of these subtle points where you can use your reasoning ability. For it is true that you need something from outside your current level of consciousness. You need that rope hanging down that you can grasp and use to pull yourself above the quicksand. So yes, you do need a teacher who is above your level of consciousness and who can offer you a frame of reference from beyond your current level. But this does not mean that the teacher will do it for you. The teacher will give you what you need, but you must internalize it. You must, as Jesus illustrated in his parable, multiply the talents given to you instead of burying them in the ground.

What does it mean to bury the talents in the ground? It means taking the teaching I give you and then forcing it to conform to your current standard, your current set of rules. So that you turn the teaching into another rule, thinking that if only you do this and don't do that, then you must rise to a higher level.

But you see, the teaching is not given to be turned into a rule. The teaching is given to challenge a certain rule and free up your creative abilities. It is not by following rules that you will get into heaven—this is the fatal misunderstanding of most religions and certain spiritual teachings as well. It is by co-creating a higher sense of self that you will get into heaven, and continuing to do so until you reach the 144th level—and can let go of the last ghost of the self that keeps you tied to a physical body.

The love-fear equation

Let me give you another way to look at this. I earlier talked about the dictators who have absolute power and can do anything they want at the level of action. But if you take Jesus' rule: "Do onto others what you would have them do onto you," what is the deeper meaning of this rule? What is the deeper meaning of this principle? It is simply this: What you do onto others, you have already done to yourself in consciousness.

How can you force another human being? Only when you have already forced yourself to conform to a certain standard held in your own mind. So you see, a dictator cannot enslave other people without having first enslaved himself. He may not be enslaved physically, as the other people are, but he is enslaved in a much more powerful way, for he is enslaved in the three higher levels of his mind. He is enslaved in his emotions, in his thoughts, and in his sense of identity.

I can tell you that psychic thralldom is far more powerful than physical thralldom. For when you are physically enslaved, you realize you are enslaved and you yearn for freedom. But when you are enslaved by the mind, you may be so blinded by your own standard that you do not even realize that there is an alternative that there is a life outside the standard. Thus, you do not consciously yearn for freedom, even though there will be a part of you that yearns for it. And eventually, you may consciously tune in to it, and you will realize that you are Spirit and that your Spirit is entrapped by your own mind. And then you may tune in to this.

Thus, I will give you, again, a relatively simple standard. I have spoken now about tuning in to your heart and seeing whether something raises your energies or lowers your energies. Let me now add a consideration to this. What does it actually mean that something raises your energies or lowers your energies? Well, what raises the energies is love and what lowers the energies is fear.

Thus, you see a simple measure for evaluating everything in life. Look at yourself and how you feel about your life; how you feel about certain conditions in your life. Realize that any condition which limits you has a cause. You are often so used to thinking that the outer condition itself is the cause and the inner feeling of being limited is the effect. But in reality, as we have attempted to explain many times, it is the other way around. It is the inner feeling that is the original cause and the outer conditions are simply an outpicturing of what is going on in your consciousness.

The trouble here is that you are not consciously aware of what is going on in the emotional, mental and identity levels of your mind, so you do not see that it is the conditions in the three higher levels of the mind that have created your outer situation. Thus, you do not see that when you react to your outer situation, you are reacting to what you have created. But the standard I want to give you – and I say "standard" in order to trick your mind, for now I am asking you to distinguish between the lower standard, the outer standard, and a higher, absolute guiding rod – so the standard, so to speak that I am asking you to adopt here is that anything that limits you is created by you by using your creative abilities through fear.

You have, really, numerous ways to express your creative abilities. But beyond the specific ways of expressing your creative abilities, the overall consideration is this: Are you expressing your creative abilities through the overall attitude of love or the overall attitude of fear? You see, in the specifics there may not be an easily discernible difference in terms of the outer results. You may, for example, look at two people who paint pictures and you may not see any difference in how they paint their pictures, but one is painting from a state of fear and the other from a state of love. Likewise with any other activity on earth.

You will of course – when you begin to tune in to this – you will begin to see that there are many activities on earth that entirely spring from fear. And you will be able to discern this by again asking yourself: "Does it raise my energies or does it lower my energies?" When you see a certain activity on earth, you will know, you will feel that this lowers your energies. Then, you will be able to reason that it is because the activity is based on fear.

Creativity beyond fear

Here is what you need to see next. Fear is the inevitable companion of applying a certain standard to how you use your creative abilities. The moment you adopt a standard, you go into a dualistic evaluation where you can either be in compliance with the standard or you can be in violation of the standard. But the overall effect of this is that it induces an inevitable fear in your being, the fear of violating the standard and the dire consequences that this has according to the standard. For a standard does not simply say: "Do this, don't do that." A standard always has the duality of the reward for following the standard and the punishment for violating it.

Do you see this, my beloved? Do you then see that in the ideal scenario, when a new lifestream comes into embodiment, there is no dualistic standard? The lifestream is given complete freedom to do whatever it wants, and then it is given the love and guidance of an ascended master so that it can see the consequences of its actions, of its co-creative efforts. And then it evaluates those consequences and says: "I do not want that, I want more of this." And then it refines its use of its creative abilities. But in doing so there is no fear. Why would there be fear when you know you can transcend any past choice you have made? Will you please consider this sentence again: Why would there be fear when you know you can transcend any past choice by making a better choice?

This is how it is in the Mystery School. This is how it is when you walk the Path of the Seven Rays without having the false standard of the false teachers. You would never have fear. You can walk from the 48th to the 96th level without even encountering fear. Of course, we do not have the ideal scenario on earth, so you do have fear, you do have to deal with this standard.

That is why, when students come to my retreat, the first thing I have to do is to help them question their own standard. I have to help them try to step outside of their standard, look at it from the outside, and see that even though this standard offers certain advantages to their egos – by making their egos feels secure – they themselves feel imprisoned by this standard. Their Conscious You, the Spirit, feels imprisoned by this standard.

And that is when you can begin to see that if you can leave that level of ego behind, you can rise to a new level of consciousness where you are free from your previous standard. You may still have some standard, but at least you are free from some limitation that you have come to see as truly imprisoning you.

The false dualistic standard

Do you see that what the standard of the dualistic consciousness, the serpentine mind, does is that it imposes this very, very subtle lie that you are confined by – trapped in – your past choices? The very creation of a standard implies that there are some choices you have made that were wrong in an ultimate sense. They violated the standard, and thus what caused you to violate the standard was that you used your free will in a creative way.

This is the lie imposed by the serpent. Therefore, the underlying promise that is made is that if you will stop using your free will in a creative way – but instead confine your free will to the outer standard – then you will be guaranteed to go to heaven. Because God must accept you when you live up to this standard defined by the serpent here on earth.

This is the underlying lie behind the false path. They say: You got into trouble – you made a mistake – by using your creativity. And therefore, the only way to avoid hell is to stop being creative and follow the rules that will get you to heaven. But do you not see the lie, my beloved?

Can you not at least begin to have a glimpse of reasoning here that the entire purpose of life is for you to learn how to use your creative abilities to constantly transcend yourself and become more? And can you not see that what the serpent is saying is that you cannot transcend yourself, you cannot transcend your past choices? Thus, the serpent is saying that you can enter heaven by following rules instead of by transcending your sense of self. The serpent is saying that by following the outer rules, you can perfect your current sense of self.

The only way to enter heaven is to transcend your current sense of self, and the only way to transcend your current sense of self is to use your creative abilities to re-create your sense of self, to create a higher sense of self. You do this by learning from your past choices and then making better choices. You do not do this by refusing to make choices, by refusing to learn, by thinking you can follow outer rules or an outer standard. This you are able to reason about. I am telling you with absolute certainty. I am Master MORE. I have seen millions of students come to my retreat. And I know that you cannot come to my retreat without having the ability to reason as I have explained it to you. Therefore, you can begin the process of fundamentally changing your outlook on life to where you realize that you will not grow – you will not enter heaven, you will not ascend – through fear, but only through love. And therefore, your first task here – your primary task – is to free your creative abilities so that you can use them in love instead of using them in fear.

Being creative through love

So many people today because of the outer standard, are using their creative abilities in fear because they are constantly reacting to the standard. They are constantly seeking to avoid something, they are constantly seeking to compensate for what was done in the past.

But you do not need to compensate for your past choices. You need to learn from those choices and transcend the level of consciousness through which you made those choices. What is there to compensate for in the sandbox of earth? Transcend the sense of self instead of continuing to co-create through that sense of self. This is the requirement of a spiritual student.

Thus, again, use your ability to sense what lowers or raises the energies. Begin to apply it to how you look at life, your own standard. And then realize that the standard you have – certain elements of it at least, you should be able to see – is based on fear. And then begin to consider what it is you fear. Get in touch with those fears. Feel how even just thinking about this lowers your energies. Then realize that whatever lowers your energies comes from fear, and whatever comes from fear hinders, restrains, kills your creativity.

I am Master MORE. I am the Chohan of the First Ray. It has been called the ray of power and will, but what you see on earth is the abuse of power based on a certain standard, a double standard that applies one set of rules to the elite and another set of rules to the people.

Then there is, of course, the concept of the will of God, which many people see as a straightjacket. For when you follow the will of God, you have to give up your free will. But my beloved, it is the will of God that you have free will! It is *free*. God gave you *free* will and it is God's will that you exercise it freely.

But exercising your will freely means simply this: That you freely look at the result of your choice, your past choice. And then you evaluate: Do I want more of this result or do I want something more than this result? And if you want more, you use your past choice to learn to re-create yourself so that you can co-create the more. And this is how you gradually raise your free will so that it becomes truly free. For you now know that no matter what you have chosen before, you can transcend that level of consciousness and chose something higher. You are not bound by your past choices. You are not bound by rules. You are not bound by an outer standard on earth.

It is my hope that by the end of these discourses, you will begin to understand what free will really is. And for now I have given you enough and probably more than you can handle, so I will now seal this release until I return with the next installment.

But for now consider your fears, and then realize that the key to making progress on the spiritual path is to move away from fear and move into love. It cannot be any other way. For did not Jesus say that the most important point of the law was to love your God with all your mind, heart and soul? And how can you love a god whom you think is a tyrant that seeks to restrict the will that he supposedly gave you?

It is not possible to love a god that you fear. You can love God only by transcending and coming to the point where your consciousness has only love in it. For the prince of this world comes and has no fear in you whereby he can pull you into seeking to conform to the serpentine standard. For you have only the love of knowing that you can transcend any past choice. And thus, you are free—always free to be more.

10 | INVOKING POWER AND LOVE

In the name I AM THAT I AM, Jesus Christ, I call to my I AM Presence to flow through the I Will Be Presence that I AM and give this invocation with full power. I call to beloved Elohim Hercules and Amazonia and Heros and Amora, Archangel Michael and Faith and Archangel Chamuel and Charity, Master MORE and Paul the Venetian to help me experience and accept unconditional love. Help me see and surrender all patterns that block my oneness with Master MORE and my oneness with my I AM Presence, including ...

[Make personal calls]

Part 1

1. Master MORE, help me see that the essence of the serpentine mind is that it creates a false standard for what is good and what is evil, and then it says that if I

live up to this outer standard – seeking to avoid the evil and act on the good – I am guaranteed to enter heaven.

> O Hercules Blue, we're one with your will,
> all space in our beings with Blue Flame you fill,
> a beacon that radiates light to the earth,
> bringing about our planet's rebirth.

> **O Hercules Blue, all life you defend,**
> **giving us power to always transcend,**
> **in you the expansion of self has no end,**
> **as we in God's infinite spirals ascend.**

2. Master MORE, help me see that by living on earth I have picked up some degree of this fallen mindset, some standard or other. Help me see if I think that I can come into your retreat and impose my standard upon you.

> O Hercules Blue, your wisdom so great,
> within us a sense of knowing create,
> a new frame of reference we suddenly gain,
> for going beyond duality's pain.

> **O Hercules Blue, all life you defend,**
> **giving us power to always transcend,**
> **in you the expansion of self has no end,**
> **as we in God's infinite spirals ascend.**

3. Master MORE, I am not attached to my standard and I am willing to have you expose it so I can overcome it. When you will not conform to my standard, I will not reason that you must be a false teacher or not an advanced enough teacher for me.

O Hercules Blue, we lovingly raise,
our voices in giving God infinite praise,
in feeling your flame, so clearly we see,
transcending the self is the true alchemy.

**O Hercules Blue, all life you defend,
giving us power to always transcend,
in you the expansion of self has no end,
as we in God's infinite spirals ascend.**

4. Master MORE, help me see that my standard is based on a complete illusion—whereas you are indeed real. For you have transcended the fallen mindset, and you offer me a frame of reference from outside that fallen mindset.

O Hercules Blue, all life now you heal,
enveloping all in your Blue-flame Seal,
we're grateful for playing a personal part,
In God's infinitely intricate work of art.

**O Hercules Blue, all life you defend,
giving us power to always transcend,
in you the expansion of self has no end,
as we in God's infinite spirals ascend.**

5. Master MORE, help me reach beyond the closed, mental box of my own mind for a teacher that offers me a frame of reference from beyond the fallen mindset. Help me become teachable by an ascended master.

O Hercules Blue, your Temple of Light,
revealed to us all through our inner sight,

your power allows us to forge on until,
we pierce every veil and climb every hill.

O Hercules Blue, all life you defend,
giving us power to always transcend,
in you the expansion of self has no end,
as we in God's infinite spirals ascend.

6. Master MORE, help me use my reasoning ability to realize that my current level of awareness forms a box around my mind, a mental box. The only way to rise from my current level of consciousness to the next level up is to reach for something beyond my current mental box.

O Hercules Blue, I pledge now my life,
in helping this planet transcend human strife,
duality's lies are pierced by your light,
restoring the fullness of our inner sight.

O Hercules Blue, all life you defend,
giving us power to always transcend,
in you the expansion of self has no end,
as we in God's infinite spirals ascend.

7. Master MORE, help me see that this is the only way that anyone has ever risen to a higher level of consciousness. It is the only way that anyone ever will rise to a higher level of consciousness. There is no way of cheating here.

O Hercules Blue, we set all life free,
from the subtlest lies of duality,
the prince of this world no more has a bond,
for with you we go completely beyond.

O Hercules Blue, all life you defend,
giving us power to always transcend,
in you the expansion of self has no end,
as we in God's infinite spirals ascend.

8. Master MORE, I do not want to go through an entire embodiment being trapped in a certain mental box. I see that the false paths to salvation offered by the false teachers will not automatically get me to heaven after this lifetime.

O Hercules Blue, in oneness with thee,
we open our hearts to your reality,
your electric-blue fire within us reveal,
our innermost longing for all that is real.

O Hercules Blue, all life you defend,
giving us power to always transcend,
in you the expansion of self has no end,
as we in God's infinite spirals ascend.

9. Master MORE, help me see that no matter what level of consciousness I am at, I have the reasoning ability to see that it forms a closed system and that the only way to rise to the next level is to reach for a teacher who can give me something from beyond my mental box.

O Hercules Blue, you fill every space,
with infinite Power and infinite Grace,
you embody the key to creativity,
the will to transcend into Infinity.

O Hercules Blue, all life you defend,
giving us power to always transcend,

**in you the expansion of self has no end,
as we in God's infinite spirals ascend.**

Part 2

1. Master MORE, help me see that my current level of consciousness is like quicksand, and that the more I struggle, the
faster I sink. There is only one way to escape, and that is to
stop struggling and let my mind fall still, so I can see that you
are offering a rope.

O Heros-Amora, in your love so pink,
we care not what others about us may think,
in oneness with you, we claim a new day,
as innocent children, we frolic and play.

**O Heros-Amora, we reap what we sow,
yet this is Plan B for helping us grow,
for truly, Plan A is that we join the flow,
immersed in the Infinite Love you bestow.**

2. Master MORE, help me see the fixed point that you offer
me, which is how I can pull myself up.

O Heros-Amora, a new life begun,
we laugh at the devil, the serious one,
the serpent is stuck in his duality,
but we are set free by Love's reality.

**O Heros-Amora, we reap what we sow,
yet this is Plan B for helping us grow,**

**for truly, Plan A is that we join the flow,
immersed in the Infinite Love you bestow.**

3. Master MORE, help me use my reasoning ability to see that
you are a real teacher. You are offering me a rope. But if I allow
an attachment to a false standard or false teaching to cause me
to reject you or reject specific aspects of your instruction, then
you cannot help me.

O Heros-Amora, awakened we see,
in true love is no conditionality,
we bathe in your glorious Ruby-Pink Sun,
knowing our God allows life to be fun.

**O Heros-Amora, we reap what we sow,
yet this is Plan B for helping us grow,
for truly, Plan A is that we join the flow,
immersed in the Infinite Love you bestow.**

4. Master MORE, I realize that you offer me something beyond
my current mental box. Help me make the best possible use of
what you offer me.

O Heros-Amora, life is such a joy,
we see that the world is like a great toy,
whatever the mind into it projects,
the mirror of life exactly reflects.

**O Heros-Amora, we reap what we sow,
yet this is Plan B for helping us grow,
for truly, Plan A is that we join the flow,
immersed in the Infinite Love you bestow.**

5. Master MORE, help me see that when I receive a certain instruction from a spiritual teacher, there will be two reactions in me. Until I ascend, there will always be a division in my being, for there will be some element of ego that keeps me in embodiment on earth.

O Heros-Amora, conditions you burn,
we know we are free to take a new turn,
Immersed in the stream of infinite Love,
we know that the Spirit came from Above.

O Heros-Amora, we reap what we sow,
yet this is Plan B for helping us grow,
for truly, Plan A is that we join the flow,
immersed in the Infinite Love you bestow.

6. Master MORE, help me see that because earth is a very dense planet, as long as I am in embodiment here, there needs to be a certain element of human consciousness that keeps me in a physical body.

O Heros-Amora, we feel that at last,
we've risen above the trap of the past,
in true love we claim our freedom to grow,
forever we're one with Love's Infinite Flow.

O Heros-Amora, we reap what we sow,
yet this is Plan B for helping us grow,
for truly, Plan A is that we join the flow,
immersed in the Infinite Love you bestow.

7. Master MORE, help me see that regardless of my level of consciousness, when I receive an instruction from the next

level of consciousness up, there will always be two reactions in my being.

> O Heros-Amora, conditions are ties,
> forming a net of serpentine lies,
> but you have the antidote setting us free,
> you take us beyond conditionality.

> **O Heros-Amora, we reap what we sow,**
> **yet this is Plan B for helping us grow,**
> **for truly, Plan A is that we join the flow,**
> **immersed in the Infinite Love you bestow.**

8. Master MORE, help me see that one will be a higher reaction of longing for that which is higher than my present level. The other will be a lower reaction of wanting to reject that which is higher in order to justify why I cling to my current level.

> O Heros-Amora, your love is no bond,
> for love only wants to take us beyond,
> your love has no bounds, forever it flies,
> raising all life into Ruby-Pink skies.

> **O Heros-Amora, we reap what we sow,**
> **yet this is Plan B for helping us grow,**
> **for truly, Plan A is that we join the flow,**
> **immersed in the Infinite Love you bestow.**

9. Master MORE, help me learn to distinguish between the reaction that lifts me up and the reaction that resists the instruction I am given.

O Heros-Amora, love bathing the earth,
filling all people with infinite mirth,
for fear and despair there is no more room,
as all are awakened by love's sonic boom.

O Heros-Amora, we reap what we sow,
yet this is Plan B for helping us grow,
for truly, Plan A is that we join the flow,
immersed in the Infinite Love you bestow.

Part 3

1. Master MORE, help me see that there is a reaction that wants
to come into oneness with the teacher who gives the instruction, and there is a reaction that wants to reject the teacher.
This reaction will want to justify why I run from the teacher,
instead of accepting the teacher's instruction and using it to
transcend my current level of consciousness.

Michael Archangel, in your flame so blue,
there is no more night, there is only you.
In oneness with you, we're filled with your light,
what glorious wonder, revealed to our sight.

Michael Archangel, your Knowing so strong,
Michael Archangel, oh sweep us along.
Michael Archangel, we're singing your song,
Michael Archangel, with you we belong.

2. Master MORE, help me see that the reaction that seeks to
get me to reject the teacher and the instruction given is always

based on some kind of standard that I have accepted with the outer mind, and this standard is always designed by the serpentine mind.

Michael Archangel, protection you give,
within your blue shield, we ever shall live.
Sealed from all creatures, roaming the night,
we remain in your sphere, of electric blue light.

Michael Archangel, your Knowing so strong,
Michael Archangel, oh sweep us along.
Michael Archangel, we're singing your song,
Michael Archangel, with you we belong.

3. Master MORE, help me feel the two reactions within me to the statement that regardless of what standard I have accepted here on earth that standard is *always* based on or influenced by the serpentine mind.

Michael Archangel, what power you bring,
as millions of angels, praises will sing.
Consuming the demons, of doubt and of fear,
we know that your Presence, will always be near.

Michael Archangel, your Knowing so strong,
Michael Archangel, oh sweep us along.
Michael Archangel, we're singing your song,
Michael Archangel, with you we belong.

4. Master MORE, help me see the simple fact that if my standard could get me to heaven, I would not need your instructions.

Michael Archangel, God's will is your love,
you bring to us all, God's light from Above.
God's will is to see, all life taking flight,
transcendence of self, our most sacred right.

Michael Archangel, your Knowing so strong,
Michael Archangel, oh sweep us along.
Michael Archangel, we're singing your song,
Michael Archangel, with you we belong.

5. Master MORE, help me see that by the very fact that I have come to your retreat, my standard will not get me to heaven. Therefore, you cannot help me rise to a higher level of consciousness by validating or conforming to my standard. You must challenge my standard—if you are to help me at all.

Michael Archangel, you are the best friend,
from all worldly dangers you do us defend,
the devil no match for your power of light,
and therefore our souls can freely take flight.

Michael Archangel, your Knowing so strong,
Michael Archangel, oh sweep us along.
Michael Archangel, we're singing your song,
Michael Archangel, with you we belong.

6. Master MORE, help me see that no teacher can help me rise to a higher level by validating the standard I have at the current level.

Michael Archangel, as children we play,
we're bringing the earth into a new day,

we raise it from all of the patterns so old,
our planet's life story is by us retold.

Michael Archangel, your Knowing so strong,
Michael Archangel, oh sweep us along.
Michael Archangel, we're singing your song,
Michael Archangel, with you we belong.

7. Master MORE, help me see if I have used a spiritual or religious movement and its teachings to build a certain standard for evaluating my actions, my creative efforts.

Michael Archangel, God's power you show,
that you are invincible, this we do know,
you are undivided and thus can withstand,
anything coming from serpentine band.

Michael Archangel, your Knowing so strong,
Michael Archangel, oh sweep us along.
Michael Archangel, we're singing your song,
Michael Archangel, with you we belong.

8. Master MORE, help me see that one of the typical outcomes of having an outer standard is that I want to define rules for everything. I want to have a rule, and when I follow the rule, God must accept me into heaven.

Michael Archangel, come raise now the earth,
giving her thus a complete rebirth,
collective the mind that we do now raise,
for this we do give our infinite praise.

Michael Archangel, your Knowing so strong,
Michael Archangel, oh sweep us along.
Michael Archangel, we're singing your song,
Michael Archangel, with you we belong.

9. Master MORE, help me see that my standard says that those who do not follow the rule will be condemned to an eternity of torment in hell. It is a simple binary logic. Yes or no. Good or evil. On or off. And this is the dualistic mind.

Michael Archangel, the earth is now new,
covered in Blue-flame as the morning dew,
our planet now sparkles throughout all of space,
as we are receiving your infinite Grace.

Michael Archangel, your Knowing so strong,
Michael Archangel, oh sweep us along.
Michael Archangel, we're singing your song,
Michael Archangel, with you we belong.

Part 4

1. Master MORE, help me see that many people think freedom is when we can do anything we want. Dictators may seem to have freedom at the level of action, but they do not have freedom of mind because in their minds they are so boxed in by the self-created rules that they use to judge others.

Chamuel Archangel, in ruby ray power,
we know we are taking a life-giving shower.

Love burning away all perversions of will,
we suddenly feel our desires falling still.

Chamuel Archangel, descend from Above,
Chamuel Archangel, with ruby-pink love,
Chamuel Archangel, so often thought-of,
Chamuel Archangel, o come Holy Dove.

2. Master MORE, help me see that the ego wants to be able
to do whatever it wants and get away with it, but the ego does
not actually long for freedom—because it does not know what
freedom is and it never can.

Chamuel Archangel, a spiral of light,
as ruby ray fire now pierces the night.
All forces of darkness consumed by your fire,
consuming all those who will not rise higher.

Chamuel Archangel, descend from Above,
Chamuel Archangel, with ruby-pink love,
Chamuel Archangel, so often thought-of,
Chamuel Archangel, o come Holy Dove.

3. Master MORE, help me see that the ego's definition of freedom is not beyond rules. The ego seeks to set up freedom for
itself by defining a set of rules that creates a double standard.
There is one standard that applies to other people and there is
one standard that applies to me, so that I can do whatever I
want and get away with it but other people cannot.

Chamuel Archangel, your love so immense,
with clarified vision, our lives now make sense.

The purpose of life you so clearly reveal,
immersed in your love, God's oneness we feel.

Chamuel Archangel, descend from Above,
Chamuel Archangel, with ruby-pink love,
Chamuel Archangel, so often thought-of,
Chamuel Archangel, o come Holy Dove.

4. Master MORE, help me see that when I have this set of rules that defines the double standard, I must live up to that standard in order to have the freedom defined by the standard.

Chamuel Archangel, what calmness you bring,
we see now that even death has no sting.
For truly, in love there can be no decay,
as love is transcendence into a new day.

Chamuel Archangel, descend from Above,
Chamuel Archangel, with ruby-pink love,
Chamuel Archangel, so often thought-of,
Chamuel Archangel, o come Holy Dove.

5. Master MORE, help me see that even if my ego has managed to define a standard that gives me the right to do seemingly anything I want, I am still trapped by the standard, I am imprisoned by my own standard.

Chamuel Archangel, God's Love Flame bestow,
on all those longing God's true love to know,
conditions we know can never be real,
and this is the love you always reveal.

Chamuel Archangel, descend from Above,
Chamuel Archangel, with ruby-pink love,
Chamuel Archangel, so often thought-of,
Chamuel Archangel, o come Holy Dove.

6. Master MORE, help me see that what truly yearns for freedom is the Conscious You because it is an extension of my I AM Presence. It is Spirit, and Spirit will always feel confined when it has to conform to matter because Spirit has creative freedom.

Chamuel Archangel, love's seed you have sown,
in hearts of all those who don't seek to own,
for love that possesses is nothing but fear,
that pierces the heart with duality's spear.

Chamuel Archangel, descend from Above,
Chamuel Archangel, with ruby-pink love,
Chamuel Archangel, so often thought-of,
Chamuel Archangel, o come Holy Dove.

7. Master MORE, help me see that creative freedom is not the same as having the freedom to do anything I want according to a set of rules defined in the world of form.

Chamuel Archangel, we don't want control,
for this is the devil's hold on the soul,
your love will now break the serpentine chain,
so we are set free God's love to reclaim.

Chamuel Archangel, descend from Above,
Chamuel Archangel, with ruby-pink love,

Chamuel Archangel, so often thought-of,
Chamuel Archangel, o come Holy Dove.

8. Master MORE, help me see that the rules are defined by a certain form, and once I accept them as rules, I cannot change the form. The form is locked in a matrix, and as long as I believe in the rule, the form cannot be transcended.

Chamuel Archangel, you are so adept,
at helping us God's true love to accept,
we know that the love for which we so yearn,
is not something we on earth have to earn.

Chamuel Archangel, descend from Above,
Chamuel Archangel, with ruby-pink love,
Chamuel Archangel, so often thought-of,
Chamuel Archangel, o come Holy Dove.

9. Master MORE, help me see that Spirit is not created to be locked in form. Spirit is created to create form by learning from its previous expressions of its creative powers to create a form that is more than what it created previously.

Chamuel Archangel, for love to accept,
we do not need to be so perfect,
for love is not static but always a flow,
demanding only we're willing to grow.

Chamuel Archangel, descend from Above,
Chamuel Archangel, with ruby-pink love,
Chamuel Archangel, so often thought-of,
Chamuel Archangel, o come Holy Dove.

Part 5

1. Master MORE, help me see that creativity – the creative drive of Spirit – is to create form but then not to be locked in that form for an extended period of time, but to use the experience it gained to create a form that is more.

> Master MORE, come to the fore,
> we will absorb your flame of MORE.
> Master MORE, our will so strong,
> our power centers cleared by song.

> **Master MORE, your Sacred Heart,**
> **from this we will no more depart,**
> **we are forever in your flow,**
> **of Diamond Will that you bestow.**

2. Master MORE, help me see that it is in doing this – in creating, learning, and then creating more – that I grow in self-awareness. This is the purpose of life. This is how life progresses: through the creative process.

> Master MORE, your wisdom flows,
> as our attunement ever grows.
> Master MORE, we have a tie,
> that helps us see through Serpent's lie.

> **Master MORE, your Sacred Heart,**
> **from this we will no more depart,**
> **we are forever in your flow,**
> **of Diamond Will that you bestow.**

3. Master MORE, help me see that the false teachers have made people believe that they should kill their creative drive. When I am seeking to conform to rules, I am not being creative.

Master MORE, your love so pink,
there is no purer love, we think.
Master MORE, you set us free,
from all conditionality.

**Master MORE, your Sacred Heart,
from this we will no more depart,
we are forever in your flow,
of Diamond Will that you bestow.**

4. Master MORE, help me see that I cannot be creative by conforming to rules that are defined based on form because then I cannot transcend the form. How can I be creative without transcending the form that exists now?

Master MORE, we will endure,
your discipline that makes us pure.
Master MORE, intentions true,
as we are always one with you.

**Master MORE, your Sacred Heart,
from this we will no more depart,
we are forever in your flow,
of Diamond Will that you bestow.**

5. Master MORE, help me see that the false teachers have created a false standard that says I must conform to a set of rules that are defined by this ultimate authority, such as the angry god in the sky.

Master MORE, our vision raised,
the will of God is always praised.
Master MORE, creative will,
raising all life higher still.

**Master MORE, your Sacred Heart,
from this we will no more depart,
we are forever in your flow,
of Diamond Will that you bestow.**

6. Master MORE, help me see that there are laws of nature.
There are creative principles used by the Creator. I can learn
to use those principles in ever more creative ways to create
something that raises the whole.

Master MORE, your peace is power,
the demons of war it will devour.
Master MORE, we serve all life,
our flames consuming war and strife.

**Master MORE, your Sacred Heart,
from this we will no more depart,
we are forever in your flow,
of Diamond Will that you bestow.**

7. Master MORE, help me see that this is creativity whereas
defining the laws of nature or the laws of God as a straightjacket that shuts down creativity, this is not creativity. This is
the consciousness of death. It is not the consciousness of Life,
the Christ Consciousness that seeks to raise all life.

Master MORE, we are so free,
eternal bond from you we see.

Master MORE, we find rebirth,
in flow of your eternal mirth.

**Master MORE, your Sacred Heart,
from this we will no more depart,
we are forever in your flow,
of Diamond Will that you bestow.**

8. Master MORE, I am willing to let you take me beyond my current standard. Help me see that the standard I have accepted on earth, has one purpose only, and that is to limit my creativity so that I cannot use my creative abilities to rise to the next level of consciousness.

Master MORE, you balance all,
the seven rays upon our call.
Master MORE, forever MORE,
we are the Spirit's open door.

**Master MORE, your Sacred Heart,
from this we will no more depart,
we are forever in your flow,
of Diamond Will that you bestow.**

9. Master MORE, help me see that it is not a matter of using my creative abilities to produce certain results on earth. Help me learn to use my creative abilities to rise to the next level of consciousness. Help me change my sense of self because it is only by changing my sense of self that I can rise to the next level of consciousness.

Master MORE, your Presence here,
filling up the inner sphere.

Life is now a sacred flow,
God Power we on all bestow.

Master MORE, your Sacred Heart,
from this we will no more depart,
we are forever in your flow,
of Diamond Will that you bestow.

Part 6

1. Master MORE, help me see that I do not need to produce certain outer results in order to rise to a higher level. I need to change my sense of self. This cannot be done by following the rules of my current standard, for that standard will keep my sense of self at the present level. The only way to recreate my sense of self is to use my creative abilities.

Master Paul, venetian dream,
your love for beauty's flowing stream.
Master Paul, in love's own womb,
your power shatters ego's tomb.

Master Paul, your love so true,
and therefore we apply to you,
to set all free in the great love,
that you are shining from Above.

2. Master MORE, help me set aside my standard so I can get back in touch with my creative abilities. Help me grasp the fact that there is more than my current level of consciousness,

and I have the potential to rise to that level by using my own creative abilities.

> Master Paul, your counsel wise,
> our minds are raised to lofty skies.
> Master Paul, in wisdom's love,
> such beauty flowing from Above.

> **Master Paul, your love so true,**
> **and therefore we apply to you,**
> **to set all free in the great love,**
> **that you are shining from Above.**

3. Master MORE, help me see that many religious people have come to accept a standard that says they need a teacher or an external savior to do something for them. Yet I see that you, Master MORE, will not do it all for me.

> Master Paul, love is an art,
> it opens up the secret heart.
> Master Paul, love's rushing flow,
> our hearts awash in sacred glow.

> **Master Paul, your love so true,**
> **and therefore we apply to you,**
> **to set all free in the great love,**
> **that you are shining from Above.**

4. Master MORE, help me see that I need a teacher who is above my level of consciousness and who can offer me a frame of reference from beyond my current level. But this does not mean that the teacher will do it for me.

Master Paul, accelerate,
upon pure love we meditate.
Master Paul, intentions pure,
our self-transcendence will ensure.

Master Paul, your love so true,
and therefore we apply to you,
to set all free in the great love,
that you are shining from Above.

5. Master MORE, help me see that he teacher will give me what
I need, but I must internalize it. I will not take the teaching you
give me and force it to conform to my current standard. I will
not turn the teaching into another rule.

Master Paul, your love will heal,
our inner light you do reveal.
Master Paul, all life console,
with you we're being truly whole.

Master Paul, your love so true,
and therefore we apply to you,
to set all free in the great love,
that you are shining from Above.

6. Master MORE, help me see that the teaching is not given
to be turned into a rule. The teaching is given to challenge a
certain rule and free up my creative abilities. It is not by following rules that I will get to heaven. It is by co-creating a higher
sense of self.

Master Paul, you serve the All,
by helping us transcend the fall.

Master Paul, in peace we rise,
as ego meets its sure demise.

**Master Paul, your love so true,
and therefore we apply to you,
to set all free in the great love,
that you are shining from Above.**

7. Master MORE, help me see that what I do onto others,
I have already done to myself in consciousness. I can force
another human being only when I have already forced myself
to conform to a standard held in my own mind.

Master Paul, love all life free,
your love is for eternity.
Master Paul, you are the One,
to help us make the journey fun.

**Master Paul, your love so true,
and therefore we apply to you,
to set all free in the great love,
that you are shining from Above.**

8. Master MORE, help me see that what raises my energies is
love and what lowers the energies is fear.

Master Paul, you balance all,
the seven rays upon our call.
Master Paul, you paint the sky,
with colors that delight the I.

**Master Paul, your love so true,
and therefore we apply to you,**

to set all free in the great love,
that you are shining from Above.

9. Master MORE, help me see that any condition which limits me has a cause, but the cause is not an outer condition. It is the inner feeling that is the original cause, and the outer condition is simply an outpicturing of what is going on in my consciousness.

Master Paul, your Presence here,
filling up the inner sphere.
Life is now a sacred flow,
God Love we do on all bestow.

Master Paul, your love so true,
and therefore we apply to you,
to set all free in the great love,
that you are shining from Above.

Part 7

1. Master MORE, help me become more consciously aware of what is going on in the emotional, mental and identity levels of my mind, so I can see that it is the conditions in the three higher levels of the mind that have created my outer situation.

Master MORE, come to the fore,
we will absorb your flame of MORE.
Master MORE, our will so strong,
our power centers cleared by song.

Master MORE, your Sacred Heart,
from this we will no more depart,
we are forever in your flow,
of Diamond Will that you bestow.

2. Master MORE, help me see that when I react to my outer situation, I am reacting to what I have created. Help me see that anything that limits me is created by me, by using my creative abilities through fear.

Master MORE, your wisdom flows,
as our attunement ever grows.
Master MORE, we have a tie,
that helps us see through Serpent's lie.

Master MORE, your Sacred Heart,
from this we will no more depart,
we are forever in your flow,
of Diamond Will that you bestow.

3. Master MORE, help me see if I am expressing my creative abilities through the overall attitude of love or the overall attitude of fear.

Master MORE, your love so pink,
there is no purer love, we think.
Master MORE, you set us free,
from all conditionality.

Master MORE, your Sacred Heart,
from this we will no more depart,
we are forever in your flow,
of Diamond Will that you bestow.

4. Master MORE, help me see that fear is the inevitable companion of applying a certain standard to how I use my creative abilities. The moment I adopt a standard, I go into a dualistic evaluation where I can either be in compliance with the standard or I can be in violation of the standard.

Master MORE, we will endure,
your discipline that makes us pure.
Master MORE, intentions true,
as we are always one with you.

Master MORE, your Sacred Heart,
from this we will no more depart,
we are forever in your flow,
of Diamond Will that you bestow.

5. Master MORE, help me see that the overall effect is that it induces an inevitable fear in my being, the fear of violating the standard and the dire consequences that this has according to the standard. A standard always has the duality of the reward for following the standard and the punishment for violating it.

Master MORE, our vision raised,
the will of God is always praised.
Master MORE, creative will,
raising all life higher still.

Master MORE, your Sacred Heart,
from this we will no more depart,
we are forever in your flow,
of Diamond Will that you bestow.

6. Master MORE, help me see that the real way to evaluate the consequences of my creative efforts is: "Do I want more *of* this, or do I want more *than* this?"

> Master MORE, your peace is power,
> the demons of war it will devour.
> Master MORE, we serve all life,
> our flames consuming war and strife.

> **Master MORE, your Sacred Heart,**
> **from this we will no more depart,**
> **we are forever in your flow,**
> **of Diamond Will that you bestow.**

7. Master MORE, help me see that there is no need for fear because I can transcend any past choice I have made. I can transcend any past choice by making a better choice.

> Master MORE, we are so free,
> eternal bond from you we see.
> Master MORE, we find rebirth,
> in flow of your eternal mirth.

> **Master MORE, your Sacred Heart,**
> **from this we will no more depart,**
> **we are forever in your flow,**
> **of Diamond Will that you bestow.**

8. Master MORE, help me question my own standard. Help me step outside of my standard, look at it from the outside, and see that even though this standard offers certain advantages to my ego, I feel imprisoned by this standard. My Conscious You, the Spirit, feels imprisoned by this standard.

Master MORE, you balance all,
the seven rays upon our call.
Master MORE, forever MORE,
we are the Spirit's open door.

**Master MORE, your Sacred Heart,
from this we will no more depart,
we are forever in your flow,
of Diamond Will that you bestow.**

9. Master MORE, help me see that if I can leave that level of ego behind, I can rise to a new level of consciousness where I am free from my previous standard. I may still have some standard, but at least I am free from some limitation that is imprisoning me.

Master MORE, your Presence here,
filling up the inner sphere.
Life is now a sacred flow,
God Power we on all bestow.

**Master MORE, your Sacred Heart,
from this we will no more depart,
we are forever in your flow,
of Diamond Will that you bestow.**

Part 8

1. Master MORE, help me see that the standard of the dualistic consciousness, the serpentine mind, imposes this subtle lie that

I am confined by my past choices. The creation of a standard implies that some choices were wrong in an ultimate sense.

> Master Paul, venetian dream,
> your love for beauty's flowing stream.
> Master Paul, in love's own womb,
> your power shatters ego's tomb.

> **Master Paul, your love so true,**
> **and therefore we apply to you,**
> **to set all free in the great love,**
> **that you are shining from Above.**

2. Master MORE, help me see that the serpent says that some of my choices violated the standard, and thus what caused me to violate the standard was that I used my free will in a creative way.

> Master Paul, your counsel wise,
> our minds are raised to lofty skies.
> Master Paul, in wisdom's love,
> such beauty flowing from Above.

> **Master Paul, your love so true,**
> **and therefore we apply to you,**
> **to set all free in the great love,**
> **that you are shining from Above.**

3. Master MORE, help me see through the false promise that if I stop using my free will in a creative way, but instead confine my free will to the outer standard, then I will be guaranteed to go to heaven. Because God must accept me when I live up to the standard defined by the serpent here on earth.

Master Paul, love is an art,
it opens up the secret heart.
Master Paul, love's rushing flow,
our hearts awash in sacred glow.

Master Paul, your love so true,
and therefore we apply to you,
to set all free in the great love,
that you are shining from Above.

4. Master MORE, help me see that this is the underlying lie behind the false path. They say: You made a mistake by using your creativity. And therefore, the only way to avoid hell is to stop being creative and follow the rules that will get you to heaven. Yet this is a lie.

Master Paul, accelerate,
upon pure love we meditate.
Master Paul, intentions pure,
our self-transcendence will ensure.

Master Paul, your love so true,
and therefore we apply to you,
to set all free in the great love,
that you are shining from Above.

5. Master MORE, help me see that the entire purpose of life is for me to learn how to use my creative abilities to constantly transcend myself and become more. What the serpent is saying is that I cannot transcend myself, I cannot transcend my past choices.

Master Paul, your love will heal,
our inner light you do reveal.
Master Paul, all life console,
with you we're being truly whole.

Master Paul, your love so true,
and therefore we apply to you,
to set all free in the great love,
that you are shining from Above.

6. Master MORE, help me see that the serpent is saying that I can enter heaven by following rules instead of by transcending my sense of self. The serpent is saying that by following the outer rules, I can perfect my current sense of self. Yet this is a lie.

Master Paul, you serve the All,
by helping us transcend the fall.
Master Paul, in peace we rise,
as ego meets its sure demise.

Master Paul, your love so true,
and therefore we apply to you,
to set all free in the great love,
that you are shining from Above.

7. Master MORE, help me see that the only way to enter heaven is to transcend my current sense of self, by using my creative abilities to re-create my sense of self, to create a higher sense of self.

Master Paul, love all life free,
your love is for eternity.

Master Paul, you are the One,
to help us make the journey fun.

Master Paul, your love so true,
and therefore we apply to you,
to set all free in the great love,
that you are shining from Above.

8. Master MORE, help me see that I do this by learning from my past choices and then making better choices. I do not do this by refusing to make choices, by refusing to learn, by thinking I can follow an outer standard.

Master Paul, you balance all,
the seven rays upon our call.
Master Paul, you paint the sky,
with colors that delight the I.

Master Paul, your love so true,
and therefore we apply to you,
to set all free in the great love,
that you are shining from Above.

9. Master MORE, help me fundamentally change my outlook on life to where I realize that I will not grow through fear, but only through love. Therefore, my primary task is to free my creative abilities so that I can use them in love instead of using them in fear.

Master Paul, your Presence here,
filling up the inner sphere.
Life is now a sacred flow,
God Love we do on all bestow.

**Master Paul, your love so true,
and therefore we apply to you,
to set all free in the great love,
that you are shining from Above.**

Part 9

1. Master MORE, help me see that many people are using their creative abilities in fear because they are constantly reacting to the standard. They are seeking to avoid something or to compensate for what was done in the past.

> Master MORE, come to the fore,
> we will absorb your flame of MORE.
> Master MORE, our will so strong,
> our power centers cleared by song.

> **Master MORE, your Sacred Heart,
> from this we will no more depart,
> we are forever in your flow,
> of Diamond Will that you bestow.**

2. Master MORE, help me see that I do not need to compensate for my past choices. I need to learn from those choices and transcend the level of consciousness through which I made those choices.

> Master MORE, your wisdom flows,
> as our attunement ever grows.
> Master MORE, we have a tie,
> that helps us see through Serpent's lie.

**Master MORE, your Sacred Heart,
from this we will no more depart,
we are forever in your flow,
of Diamond Will that you bestow.**

3. Master MORE, help me see that there is nothing to compensate for in the sandbox of earth. I need to transcend the sense of self instead of continuing to co-create through that self. This is the requirement of a spiritual student.

Master MORE, your love so pink,
there is no purer love, we think.
Master MORE, you set us free,
from all conditionality.

**Master MORE, your Sacred Heart,
from this we will no more depart,
we are forever in your flow,
of Diamond Will that you bestow.**

4. Master MORE, help me use my ability to sense what lowers or raises the energies and apply it to how I look at life, my own standard. Help me realize that certain elements of my standard are based on fear.

Master MORE, we will endure,
your discipline that makes us pure.
Master MORE, intentions true,
as we are always one with you.

**Master MORE, your Sacred Heart,
from this we will no more depart,**

we are forever in your flow,
of Diamond Will that you bestow.

5. Master MORE, help me consider what it is I fear. Help me get in touch with those fears and feel how even thinking about this lowers my energies. Help me realize that whatever lowers my energies comes from fear, and whatever comes from fear kills my creativity.

Master MORE, our vision raised,
the will of God is always praised.
Master MORE, creative will,
raising all life higher still.

Master MORE, your Sacred Heart,
from this we will no more depart,
we are forever in your flow,
of Diamond Will that you bestow.

6. Master MORE, help me see that the will of God is not a straightjacket that requires me to give up my free will. The will of God is that I have free will! It is *free*. God gave me *free* will and it is God's will that I exercise it freely.

Master MORE, your peace is power,
the demons of war it will devour.
Master MORE, we serve all life,
our flames consuming war and strife.

Master MORE, your Sacred Heart,
from this we will no more depart,
we are forever in your flow,
of Diamond Will that you bestow.

7. Master MORE, help me see that exercising my will freely means that I freely look at the result of my past choice. And then I evaluate: Do I want more *of* this result or do I want something more *than* this result?

Master MORE, we are so free,
eternal bond from you we see.
Master MORE, we find rebirth,
in flow of your eternal mirth.

Master MORE, your Sacred Heart,
from this we will no more depart,
we are forever in your flow,
of Diamond Will that you bestow.

8. Master MORE, help me see that when I want more, I use my past choice to learn to re-create myself so that I can co-create the more. This is how I gradually raise my free will so that it becomes truly free.

Master MORE, you balance all,
the seven rays upon our call.
Master MORE, forever MORE,
we are the Spirit's open door.

Master MORE, your Sacred Heart,
from this we will no more depart,
we are forever in your flow,
of Diamond Will that you bestow.

9. Master MORE, help me see that no matter what I have chosen before, I can transcend that level of consciousness and choose something higher. I am not bound by my past choices.

I am not bound by rules. I am not bound by an outer standard on earth. The key to making progress on the spiritual path is to move away from fear and move into love.

> Master MORE, your Presence here,
> filling up the inner sphere.
> Life is now a sacred flow,
> God Power we on all bestow.

> **Master MORE, your Sacred Heart,**
> **from this we will no more depart,**
> **we are forever in your flow,**
> **of Diamond Will that you bestow.**

Sealing:

In the name of the Divine Mother, I fully accept that the power of these calls is used to set free the Ma-ter light, so it can outpicture the perfect vision of Christ for my own life, for all people and for the planet. In the name I AM THAT I AM, it is done! Amen.

11 | POWER AND ACCELERATION

Master MORE, I AM. Let me now take your instructions to the next level. What I have described so far is how I usually attempt to help people when their lifestreams first come to my retreat in Darjeeling. I have described how most new students must go through an initial period where I first seek to help them see the need to look beyond their expectations – their world view, their standard – for what a spiritual teacher should be like and what it is like to be a spiritual student and be in a spiritual retreat. For I cannot help people if they seek to force me to conform to their expectations, instead of being willing to help me take them beyond their present mental box.

I have described how I seek to reason with people because all people have the ability to reason one step beyond their current level of consciousness. I have described how I seek to make people feel loved and feel like I have no judgment of them whatsoever, but that I have only one goal, and that is to help them rise to higher levels of consciousness.

Healing in the Garden of Love

Yet I will also describe how many students need to go through a period where – after having realized the need to look beyond their standard, after having begun to reason – they need to go through a period of healing where they experience love. To this end I have extensive gardens around my retreat which, of course, are in the etheric realm where climate is not a consideration. For climate is created by me and those who help maintain the retreat.

We have created extensive gardens with beautiful flower arrangements, fragrant plants, fountains and streams and of course birds that sing constantly. I have earlier talked about the little blue bird of kindness but we have many different birds. We have a certain section of the garden where the main flower is the rose and where there are several birds that sing in a way that is designed to help students feel the vibrations of love.

Of course, the rose that you know on earth is the flower that has the fragrance that is closest to the vibration of love. When you smell a rose, you experience with your sense of smell the closest you can come with that sense to the vibration of love. There comes a point where the student has been at my retreat for some time, when it is literally time to smell the roses. Thus, many students go into the garden, they find a spot that they like, and then they just sit there and absorb the fragrance and the sound of the birds. Of course, I have helpers at my retreat who can read the vibration of people's auras and chakras and know exactly what they need to hear and smell and see and sense in order to receive the most healing.

Students can spend quite some time here, for you see, there really is no point in moving on until you have experienced true love whereby I mean a love that is beyond conditions. This is a love that is beyond what you usually experience as love on earth where you are so used to there always being conditions attached to people expressing love towards you. You have to earn it, you have to live up to some condition. But truly, ultimate healing comes from experiencing unconditional love.

In the beginning you may experience it from me, but the ultimate goal is that you experience it directly from your I AM Presence, which is the source of unconditional love for you. This love is, of course, the love of the Creator, the love that the Creator has for all self-aware extensions of itself. Thus, we cannot produce it. We can only be the open doors for it, but it is the ultimate healing agent.

Rejecting unconditional love

There are those who come to my retreat and have been so programmed by conditions on earth that they find it difficult to accept unconditional love. This presents somewhat of a challenge for me. For how can you truly help a person feel love, if that person has so many conditions attached to what love is—and how it should be expressed, and how the person has to live up to this or that standard before he or she can open the heart to actually experience love?

You may look at earth and see how you have been programmed to think that you have to live up to conditions before you can receive love, and many students transfer this to God and think that God is the one who has the most conditions. Because God's love is supposed to be special – more special that the love from human beings – so if you have to live up to certain conditions in order to receive love from human beings, then you must have to live up to even more and more strict conditions in order to receive this superior love of God.

This is how many students reason when they come to me. I can, of course, try to reason with them. But the question is: Can they come to the point where they can actually let go of their own conditions long enough to experience – and I mean not understand but truly experience – unconditional love? You see, nothing is more transforming than experiencing unconditional love. Until you experience at least a glimpse of it, you truly cannot move on to the next level of consciousness.

I have explained that at the 48th level you are faced with the need to look beyond your standard. But when you are somewhat willing to look beyond your standard, you can move to the 49th level. This does not mean that you have let go of all standards, for you usually cannot do that until you reach the 96th level and perhaps even beyond that level. Yet it does mean that you have experienced what it is like to look at yourself and life from a higher state of consciousness than the state defined by your current standard. And then you ascend to the 49th level.

At this level is where you need to learn to reason, so that you can actually consciously question an element of your standard and experience what it is like to let go of that element. Again, this does not mean that you let go of all of your standards, but you experience the process of letting go of some of it, and then you ascend to the 50th level.

The 50th level is where you now face the need to experience a love that is beyond your conditions. This does not mean that you can let go of all of your conditions, but it does mean that you have directly experienced a love that is beyond your current condition. And until you have that experience, you cannot move on to the 51st level. It simply cannot happen.

Your relationship with God

For some students this is a big challenge, for it requires you to rethink your view of God, your relationship with God. We have, of course, a very old tradition on earth – well, very old as measured with the normal standard of a human lifespan, but certainly not old when it comes to the total existence of intelligent life on earth – but we have a standard that portrays God as the angry, judgmental god in the sky. And there are indeed many people on earth today who are very much programmed by this standard, and the projection by the fallen beings that this is the only true image of God and that questioning this image is blasphemy.

Well, my beloved, the simple fact is that you cannot rise higher in consciousness than your image of God. You can come to my retreat with an image of an angry and judgmental God. You can make progress on the first couple of levels, but you will not go beyond the 50th level if you hold on to the image of an angry and judgmental God and insist on projecting that image upon me; wanting me to be the angry and judgmental teacher who comes down on you hard when you make a mistake.

You see, my beloved, many students come to my retreat with a state of consciousness where they are more afraid of making a mistake than they have a love for doing what is more. I have spoken about a standard. The essence of a standard is that it defines two polarities: one that is good, one that is evil, one that is right, one that is wrong. This is how most people have been programmed to evaluate every aspect of their lives and their consciousness, their feelings and their thoughts, who they think they are.

There must be a right and there must be a wrong—right? Wrong, my beloved! In the reality of God there is no right and wrong. These are dualistic concepts created out of the consciousness of separation, the consciousness of anti-christ. You will never know the real God if you insist on projecting that image upon God.

Master MORE is not an angry teacher

You will never know the real Master MORE if you insist on projecting that image upon me, as indeed many who call themselves ascended master students have done and continue to do. They want me to be the angry and judgmental teacher. Well, I am not that kind of a teacher. I never was. I have allowed students in past decades to project his image upon me, but I will no longer allow this. I will publicly denounce that image and denounce these students as not being willing to look at – or rather to experience – the reality of who I am.

I am not an angry and judgmental teacher. I am an unconditionally loving teacher, and I will support you unconditionally. But the way I support you and your growth is to help you transcend your conditions, for I am not the one holding you back. God is not the one holding you back; the devil is not the one holding you back. What is holding you back on your path is your own conditions, the ones you have defined or accepted. I grant you that the devil has defined many of the conditions that you have accepted, and therefore indirectly the devil is holding you back. But the devil has no power over your mind unless you give him power over your mind by accepting certain conditions.

You see, you will never know me if you project the image of an angry and judgmental God upon me and think that I am like that. You will never know me, my beloved. And that sometimes is a burden to my heart, quite frankly. For I, of course, know who I am. I know how much I have to give to students. And I see how they sit there and are stuck because they cannot let go of their conditions long enough to experience even a brief glimpse of unconditional love, the unconditional love I feel streaming through me from the Creator itself, from the I AM Presence directly to them.

I see how I become the open door for that love when they come to my retreat. And they sit there and they will not accept it because they insist on holding on to this or that condition that portrays them as not worthy—because I am the one who has defined the conditions that they cannot live up to. Actually, they are the ones who have the conditions, but they are projecting upon me that I am the one who has defined them. I am the one who is withholding love from them because I have defined such strict conditions that no one can live up to it. But I have defined no conditions. People come here with their own conditions.

There are sometimes when even a lengthy stay in the rose garden does not help a student. For he or she simply will not smell the roses and just experience the garden.

The First Ray is creative power

Students come with minds that have a track running – like a broken record over and over and over again – where they repeat these conditions. They are looking at my retreat thinking: "What conditions do I have to live up to? I cannot do something wrong here; I am in a spiritual retreat."

They are so concerned about not doing anything wrong that they dare not do anything at all. And why is that a problem?

It is a problem because I am the Chohan of the First Ray. And yes, in the past the First Ray has been portrayed as the ray of power and will, but it is because power and will are the essential ingredients of the creative drive.

You cannot create anything without having a certain outgoing power, and you cannot create anything without having the will to create. So do you see: I have no desire for you to look at power and will as fixed qualities, as some standard you must live up to. What have I said about a standard? It kills creativity. But do you think that I, Master MORE, the Chohan of the First Ray of Creative Drive wants to kill your creativity? For if you think so, I can assure you that if you are willing to reason about this, you can see that it is not so.

I am not the one who wants to kill your creativity. Your ego is, and the dark forces and the false teachers, but not I, Master MORE, for I only want you to be more. And you become more by being creative. And you become creative only by being willing to experiment. And you become willing to experiment only by looking at your own fear of being wrong and asking yourself: "Is there something I love more than the fear of being wrong? Is there some element of love in my being that is stronger than my fear of being wrong?"

I am not here talking about loving to be right according to an earthly standard, although this is in some cases a starting point. But ultimately, I am talking about the love for being more than any standard. For it is only by going beyond the standard that you are creative.

If staying in the rose garden cannot help a student, then I have another section of my retreat. Now, you may know that there is something called the akashic records. The akashic records can be seen as an energy field of very fine or high vibrations, far beyond the vibrations in the material realm. These vibrations are able to record any event, any action that takes place in the material universe, and they are therefore stored as images, much like video that can be replayed.

This can be especially helpful when a lifestream leaves physical embodiment and goes through a life review. For in most cases the lifestream will either have forgotten or distorted its view of a certain situation. Thus, we can go back and replay the actual situation, for what is recorded in the akashic records is simply the events that took place, not the feelings, not the inner experience that the people had during the event.

When a student sees this akashic record, it experiences the event in a completely neutral manner without the feelings involved. It can look at the event in a much more objective way – see it for what it is – which makes it easier for the student to move on, to process the event and heal from it. Of course, there are other levels of records where the feelings are recorded and where they also need to be erased before the student can truly move on.

Painting on your subconscious canvas

My point is that I have a section in my retreat where I have a room that has a 180 degree screen, and on that screen any image can be displayed. I also have a device that acts like a scanner, somewhat like the medical scanners you see on earth but more sophisticated. This device can scan the subconscious minds – the emotional, mental, and identity minds – of the student. The effect of this is that the large screen acts as a canvas upon which the student can paint any image it wants. However, here is how it works.

The student is sat down and is then scanned by the scanner. The scanner picks up all of the conditions that the student has in his or her subconscious minds. What it does then is it displays on the screen a white canvas that is like the canvas that a painter has. However, the size of the canvas – and mind you the screen is large and covers half of the room – the size of the canvas that is displayed as a white field on the screen depends on the conditions that the student has in his or her mind. The more conditions, the smaller the canvas.

Then, next to the student will be displayed a palette of painting tools, brushes and colors, and again this depends on the conditions. The more conditions, the fewer colors, the fewer brushes. Some students have only one brush, they only have black with which to paint on the small white canvas— that in some cases is so small there is hardly room to paint anything.

The student is given the task of painting something on the white canvas—anything. And this is for some students a very big challenge. Those who have the most conditions, will have the smallest canvas and the smallest selection of colors, but even so they cannot select a color—they cannot decide what to paint. They look at me with panic in their eyes and they want me to tell them what to paint on their life's canvas. They want some rule, some standard they can apply, so they can make sure they are doing the right thing and not doing something wrong.

But do you see, my beloved: There is no right or wrong here. For the purpose is not to paint a picture. The purpose is to give you an assessment of how many conditions you have that limit your creativity.

Thus, we will let a student alone in the room and come back later and see what that student has painted—if anything. Sometimes we come back later and the student has painted nothing. We then give the student more time. But again, there are students who are so trapped in their conditions that they dare not paint anything. Those we sometimes cannot help at this point but must send them back to the soup kitchen where they can take another round and go through receiving just that little bit more than they can take in at their present level.

But for students that eventually end up painting something, we seek to help them by asking them again: "When you painted your picture – when you looked at your picture – did it raise your energies or did it lower your energies? What was your reaction? What was your state of mind when you painted the picture and when you looked at it?"

We help them see that there is no exam here. This is not like one of these shows on TV where you have a panel of judges that have to make some silly comments about what others have created. We are not here to comment on your picture. We are here to help you see your state of mind and see how free – or in most cases unfree – you are to express yourself creatively.

Creativity through the chakras

After we have helped the student get in touch with his or her feelings, we ask the student to consider his or her creative potential. In other words, could you do more than what you have done now? And then in many cases the student will say: "Well, sure I could do more if I had a bigger canvas and more colors." And that is where we can help students see that we are not the ones limiting the size of the canvas or the number of colors: It is the student's own conditions. We can then point out – and we can even display on the screen – how the conditions limit the creative expression.

We can actually display an image on the screen of the student's aura and chakras. We can show how creative expression happens through the chakras. We can show how each chakra has a certain number of what has been called petals, to compare the chakra to a flower. But these petals are actually valves or portals that let through light. And in many cases students have closed almost all of these portals in the chakras, so that there is very little light coming through the chakras.

We can then show how a specific chakra has a specific portal that is blocked. We can show how this block is created by a certain condition that the student has accepted. Then, we can show how – if that condition is let go, is surrendered, is given up – then more light will stream through the chakra, and this will increase the student's color palette and the size of the canvas. And in this way we can sometimes – in fact most of the time – get students to take a look at specific conditions and gradually begin to give them up in order to expand the size of the canvas and the color palette that is available for painting.

Some students respond very well to this, and they eagerly throw themselves at the task of letting go of their conditions so they can expand the canvas. For we, of course, show them the potential size of the total canvas. We even show them, when they are ready for this – and with ready I mean that they can see this without being too discouraged – we show them what other students have painted. We show them students who have been able to use the full size of the canvas and the full color palette to paint incredibly beautiful pictures.

But then we also show them how those particular students started out with a very small canvas and a limited color palette, just like themselves. Thus, we show them the difference between their true creative potential and then the amount of that potential that is currently available to them, showing them of course that it is their own conditions and nothing else that limits their creative potential.

This can be a very effective exercise, and most students respond well to it. There are those who cannot let go of the angry, judgmental God and keep on denying that they are the ones who have defined their conditions. And again, in some cases such students must go back to the soup line. Some even go back to the School of Hard Knocks because they are not willing to take responsibility for themselves.

The decision to accelerate

You see, at the third level of my retreat – at the 50th level of consciousness – your task is love. Your task is to experience unconditional love. But experiencing love actually only sets a foundation for taking the next step. And the next step is to use the Fourth Ray, which has been seen as the ray of purity. But what is purity? It is when something of a lower vibration has been accelerated to a higher vibration.

How do you purify anything? By accelerating its vibration. So, there must come a point where you consciously acknowledge your love for something more—that you have a love for your own creative expression, for your own higher being, for your own creative potential. And you love that potential so much that you are willing to take a look at yourself and see that what limits your creative expression are the very conditions that you have accepted and allowed to exist in your consciousness.

Now, you make that decision: "Yes, I am willing to accelerate myself beyond those conditions. I am willing to accelerate my sense of self beyond the standard that I have come to accept, the standard that I now see as based on the fallen consciousness, the conscious of anti-christ. I will no longer be limited by that standard. I want to accelerate my sense of self beyond that standard, and I am accelerating myself beyond that standard."

But you see, you cannot make that decision until you have experienced at least a glimpse of unconditional love. Why is that so, my beloved? Because becoming more is a creative process, and a creative process cannot be forced. It cannot be based on fear; it must be based on love. You love something more, and therefore you are willing to accelerate yourself to a higher level in order to allow that more to flow through you.

You are beginning to see that your I AM Presence is the source of your creativity that your I AM Presence wants to express the fullness of its creativity as its gift to help raise the earth to a higher level. But your I AM Presence can express its creativity only though you. You have the potential – you, the Conscious You – have the potential to return to a state of pure awareness where you become the open door, the fully open door. And you see that because of your standard because of your conditions, you are not yet a fully open door. You only have a partial opening, sometimes a very small opening.

When you see this – and when you experience the love, the unconditional love that your I AM Presence has for you and wants to express through you – then you can make a decision that comes from the core of your being. It is not a decision made through the filter of the outer self and personality, for the outer self is based on separation and can only make decisions out of fear. My beloved, the First Ray is the ray of will, for true will is based on love—as opposed to the false will that is based on fear.

Now, here is a delicate consideration. There are students who come to my retreat and who are so afraid of making a wrong decision that they are not willing to make any decisions. They want me to tell them how to do everything. And again, such students I can only help by sending them to the soup kitchen. I cannot begin to actively work with a student until that student is at least willing to make decisions. But of course, in the beginning – especially those that have descended below the 48th level of consciousness – they can only make decisions based on fear.

Decisions based on fear

What do I mean when I say a decision based on fear? Well, it is a decision that is based on you reacting to something that you feel is forcing itself upon you. Just look at your own life and see how there may be conditions that you feel are limiting you. It may be other people, it may be your parents, it may be spouses, it may be teachers or authority figures of some kind, but you feel that they are setting parameters – they are putting demands upon you – and you are making a decision in order to avoid a negative reaction from these people.

This is a typical example of a decision based on fear. You are afraid of a negative reaction, and therefore you make a decision in order to avoid that reaction. Most of your decisions are avoidance decisions; you are seeking to avoid something bad happening. But even so, making these kinds of decisions is better than making no decisions because you are at least somewhat moving. And then I can at least start to work with you and maybe redirect you decisions by, as I said, making you aware of the standard, reasoning with you and getting you to the point where you realize you need to experience unconditional love. And therefore, you need to let go of your conditions for accepting love.

Once people have experienced a glimpse of unconditional love, they can begin to understand through reasoning that there is a level of decisions where you are not making decisions out of fear, you are not seeking to avoid something bad. You are making positive decisions, decisions based on a love for something more and a desire to experience something positive, something good.

For of course, when you are trapped in fear, you think that any decision can only lead to something bad. And you are so focused on the potential for something negative that you do not see the equally obvious truth that a decision could also lead to something good. It could also lead to progress, but making no decision can never lead anywhere.

The reality of the will of God

This is the higher will. The will of God is entirely positive. Think about this, my beloved. Do you truly believe that God has fear? Well, if you believe in the image of an angry and judgmental god, then you are indirectly believing that god has fear. For if a god is angry where does anger come from? It comes from fear. If a god is judgmental where does the need to judge come from? It comes from fear. You see, the common image of the angry and judgmental God in the sky is actually a fear-based image. And beyond that it portrays God as a fear-based God.

Of course, the devil's wet-dream, so to speak, is that God would be afraid of the devil and the power of the devil. There are indeed people on earth who believe this: that the devil has some power that God is afraid of. But of course the true God, the true God of unconditional love, is not afraid of anything. There is no fear in him.

God's will is not based on fear; God's decisions are not based on fear. And God's will is that you have free will, and God's will is that you exercise that free will as you see fit. But

God's highest will and vision is that you exercise your free will based on love and that all decisions you make help you become more, help creation – the matter sphere – become more, and ultimately helps your Creator become more. This is the process of life where everything becomes more.

This process has temporarily been reversed on planet earth, and planet earth is indeed a schoolroom for many lifestreams who are trapped in this fear-based consciousness. It is, so to speak, a half-way house between hell and heaven. It is not a high planet, as I might have mentioned a time or two before.

My point is, again that there comes a time when you must summon the will to accelerate yourself beyond your standard, the standard that limits your creativity. But this will, this decision, cannot be based on the outer mind that is steeped in fear. It must be based on love because otherwise it will not accelerate your sense of self.

This means that you can actually come to a point where you have started the upward path, but you still think that the goal of the path is to perfect the outer self and make the outer self live up to some kind of standard. Now, you think that if you just perfect that outer self according to that standard, then I must accept you – that outer self – and that God must accept that outer self. That is what Jesus explained in his parable about the wedding feast: You think you can enter the wedding feast without wearing a wedding garment. The wedding garment is a garment woven in love; it is not a garment made out of fear.

You may have the image of one of the old knights that had a steel helmet and chain mail covering his body. Well, this is not the wedding garment, for it is a fear-based contraption aimed at protecting you from the blows that you fear will come. Only when you let go of this fear and weave the seamless garment, the wedding garment, will you begin to transcend fear. And only then can you enter the wedding feast.

A celebration at Darjeeling

Of course, at this point you are not able to enter the wedding feast, for the seamless garment – the wedding garment – must be woven by using the threads from all of the seven rays. But you are nevertheless – once you begin to experience a glimpse of unconditional love – you are truly beginning to weave your wedding garment. And you will continue to perfect it, so to speak, as you rise to the 96th level.

There comes a point where the only way to progress is to make a decision to accelerate your sense of self – not beyond any standard, but certainly beyond the standard you have at this point – and that decision must be based on love. When you do make that decision, it gives such a joy to my heart that I can scarcely describe it. For it is a cause for celebration at my retreat when a student has experienced unconditional love and has made the decision to accelerate itself based on love.

This is truly what we work for; this is one of the great rewards. Not that it means we are done with the student, but it means that it is critical step on the path. And it is such a cause for rejoicing that we always throw a party for that student. Much like what you already see on earth in some Christian traditions where they have a confirmation ceremony for a teenage boy or girl, and thereafter a party where they are bestowed with gifts and speeches and so on and so forth. We have something similar – not exactly the same – but something similar where a students' progress is indeed celebrated—with some pomp and circumstance, I might say.

And I long for you to go through that ceremony. I love to see you go through that ceremony and come to that point where even in your waking awareness you have some sense of unconditional love that comes from above.

12 | INVOKING POWER AND ACCELERATION

In the name I AM THAT I AM, Jesus Christ, I call to my I AM Presence to flow through the I Will Be Presence that I AM and give this invocation with full power. I call to beloved Elohim Hercules and Amazonia and Astrea and Purity, Archangel Michael and Faith and Archangel Gabriel and Hope, Master MORE and Serapis Bey to help me accelerate my sense of self to a higher level. Help me see and surrender all patterns that block my oneness with Master MORE and my oneness with my I AM Presence, including ...

[Make personal calls]

Part 1

1. Master MORE, help me see that you have no judgment of me whatsoever, you have only one goal, and that is to help me rise to higher levels of consciousness.

O Hercules Blue, we're one with your will,
all space in our beings with Blue Flame you fill,
a beacon that radiates light to the earth,
bringing about our planet's rebirth.

O Hercules Blue, all life you defend,
giving us power to always transcend,
in you the expansion of self has no end,
as we in God's infinite spirals ascend.

2. Master MORE, help me go to your retreat at night and spend time in your gardens, so I can be healed by feeling the vibration of love.

O Hercules Blue, your wisdom so great,
within us a sense of knowing create,
a new frame of reference we suddenly gain,
for going beyond duality's pain.

O Hercules Blue, all life you defend,
giving us power to always transcend,
in you the expansion of self has no end,
as we in God's infinite spirals ascend.

3. Master MORE, help me experience true love, a love that is beyond conditions, beyond what I usually experience as love on earth.

O Hercules Blue, we lovingly raise,
our voices in giving God infinite praise,
in feeling your flame, so clearly we see,
transcending the self is the true alchemy.

**O Hercules Blue, all life you defend,
giving us power to always transcend,
in you the expansion of self has no end,
as we in God's infinite spirals ascend.**

4. Master MORE, help me see that ultimate healing comes from experiencing unconditional love.

O Hercules Blue, all life now you heal,
enveloping all in your Blue-flame Seal,
we're grateful for playing a personal part,
In God's infinitely intricate work of art.

**O Hercules Blue, all life you defend,
giving us power to always transcend,
in you the expansion of self has no end,
as we in God's infinite spirals ascend.**

5. Master MORE, help me experience love directly from my I AM Presence, which is the source of unconditional love for me.

O Hercules Blue, your Temple of Light,
revealed to us all through our inner sight,
your power allows us to forge on until,
we pierce every veil and climb every hill.

**O Hercules Blue, all life you defend,
giving us power to always transcend,
in you the expansion of self has no end,
as we in God's infinite spirals ascend.**

6. Master MORE, help me experience the love of the Creator, the love that the Creator has for all self-aware extensions of itself. Help me be the open door for it, as the ultimate healing agent.

> O Hercules Blue, I pledge now my life,
> in helping this planet transcend human strife,
> duality's lies are pierced by your light,
> restoring the fullness of our inner sight.

> **O Hercules Blue, all life you defend,**
> **giving us power to always transcend,**
> **in you the expansion of self has no end,**
> **as we in God's infinite spirals ascend.**

7. Master MORE, help me see if I have been so programmed by conditions on earth that I find it difficult to accept unconditional love.

> O Hercules Blue, we set all life free,
> from the subtlest lies of duality,
> the prince of this world no more has a bond,
> for with you we go completely beyond.

> **O Hercules Blue, all life you defend,**
> **giving us power to always transcend,**
> **in you the expansion of self has no end,**
> **as we in God's infinite spirals ascend.**

8. Master MORE, help me see my conditions relating to what love is, how it should be expressed and how I have to live up to this or that standard before I can open my heart to actually experience love.

O Hercules Blue, in oneness with thee,
we open our hearts to your reality,
your electric-blue fire within us reveal,
our innermost longing for all that is real.

**O Hercules Blue, all life you defend,
giving us power to always transcend,
in you the expansion of self has no end,
as we in God's infinite spirals ascend.**

9. Master MORE, help me see how I have been programmed to think that I have to live up to conditions before I can receive love, and how I have transferred this to God and think that God is the one who has the most conditions.

O Hercules Blue, you fill every space,
with infinite Power and infinite Grace,
you embody the key to creativity,
the will to transcend into Infinity.

**O Hercules Blue, all life you defend,
giving us power to always transcend,
in you the expansion of self has no end,
as we in God's infinite spirals ascend.**

Part 2

1. Master MORE, help me see if I think that since I have to live up to certain conditions in order to receive love from human beings, then I must have to live up to even stricter conditions in order to receive this superior love of God.

Beloved Astrea, your heart is so true,
your Circle and Sword of white and blue,
cut all life free from dramas unwise,
on wings of Purity our planet will rise.

**Beloved Astrea, in oneness with you,
your circle and sword of electric blue,
with Purity's Light cutting right through,
raising the earth into all that is true.**

2. Master MORE, help me let go of my own conditions long
enough to truly experience unconditional love.

Beloved Astrea, in God Purity,
accelerate all of our life energy,
we're rising beyond every impurity,
as Purity's Light forever we see.

**Beloved Astrea, in oneness with you,
your circle and sword of electric blue,
with Purity's Light cutting right through,
raising the earth into all that is true.**

3. Master MORE, help me rethink my view of God, my relationship with God. Help me transcend the standard that portrays God as the angry, judgmental god in the sky.

Beloved Astrea, from Purity's Ray,
send forth deliverance to all life today,
acceleration to Purity, we are now free
from all that is less than love's Purity.

Beloved Astrea, in oneness with you,
your circle and sword of electric blue,
with Purity's Light cutting right through,
raising the earth into all that is true.

4. Master MORE, help me see that I cannot rise higher in consciousness than my image of God.

Beloved Astrea, accelerate us all,
as for your deliverance we fervently call,
set all life free from vision impure
beyond fear and doubt, we're rising for sure.

Beloved Astrea, in oneness with you,
your circle and sword of electric blue,
with Purity's Light cutting right through,
raising the earth into all that is true.

5. Master MORE, help me so I do not take the image of an angry and judgmental God and project it upon you; wanting you to be the angry and judgmental teacher who comes down on me hard when I make a mistake.

Beloved Astrea, we're willing to see,
all of the lies that keep us unfree,
we surrender all lies causing the fall,
forever affirming the oneness of All.

Beloved Astrea, in oneness with you,
your circle and sword of electric blue,
with Purity's Light cutting right through,
raising the earth into all that is true.

6. Master MORE, help me see if I am more afraid of making a mistake than I have a love for doing what is more.

> Beloved Astrea, accelerate life
> beyond all duality's struggle and strife,
> consume all division between God and man,
> accelerate fulfillment of God's perfect plan.
>
> **Beloved Astrea, in oneness with you,**
> **your circle and sword of electric blue,**
> **with Purity's Light cutting right through,**
> **raising the earth into all that is true.**

7. Master MORE, help me see that the essence of a standard is that it defines two polarities: one that is good, one that is evil. Help me see how this has programmed me to evaluate every aspect of my life and my consciousness, my feelings and my thoughts, who I think I am.

> Beloved Astrea, we lovingly call,
> break down separation's invisible wall,
> raising our minds into true unity
> with the Masters of love in Infinity.
>
> **Beloved Astrea, in oneness with you,**
> **your circle and sword of electric blue,**
> **with Purity's Light cutting right through,**
> **raising the earth into all that is true.**

8. Master MORE, help me see that in the reality of God there is no right and wrong. These are dualistic concepts created out of the consciousness of separation, the consciousness of

anti-christ. I will never know the real God if I insist on projecting that image upon God.

> Beloved Astrea, help all of us find,
> the secret that we create with the mind,
> and thus what in ignorance we decreate,
> in knowledge we easily can recreate.

> **Beloved Astrea, in oneness with you,**
> **your circle and sword of electric blue,**
> **with Purity's Light cutting right through,**
> **raising the earth into all that is true.**

9. Master MORE, help me see that I will never know the real
Master MORE if I insist on projecting that image upon you.

> Beloved Astrea, we all do aspire,
> to learning to use your purity's fire,
> to raise every form in infamy sown,
> as Saint Germain makes this planet his own.

> **Beloved Astrea, in oneness with you,**
> **your circle and sword of electric blue,**
> **with Purity's Light cutting right through,**
> **raising the earth into all that is true.**

Part 3

1. Master MORE, help me see that you are not an angry and
judgmental teacher. You are an unconditionally loving teacher,
and you will support me unconditionally.

Michael Archangel, in your flame so blue,
there is no more night, there is only you.
In oneness with you, we're filled with your light,
what glorious wonder, revealed to our sight.

Michael Archangel, your Knowing so strong,
Michael Archangel, oh sweep us along.
Michael Archangel, we're singing your song,
Michael Archangel, with you we belong.

2. Master MORE, help me see that the way you support me and my growth is to help me transcend my conditions, for you are not the one holding me back. God is not the one holding me back; the devil is not the one holding me back.

Michael Archangel, protection you give,
within your blue shield, we ever shall live.
Sealed from all creatures, roaming the night,
we remain in your sphere, of electric blue light.

Michael Archangel, your Knowing so strong,
Michael Archangel, oh sweep us along.
Michael Archangel, we're singing your song,
Michael Archangel, with you we belong.

3. Master MORE, help me see that what is holding me back on my path is my own conditions, the ones I have defined or accepted.

Michael Archangel, what power you bring,
as millions of angels, praises will sing.
Consuming the demons, of doubt and of fear,
we know that your Presence, will always be near.

Michael Archangel, your Knowing so strong,
Michael Archangel, oh sweep us along.
Michael Archangel, we're singing your song,
Michael Archangel, with you we belong.

4. Master MORE, help me see that the devil has defined many of the conditions that I have accepted, and therefore indirectly the devil is holding me back. But the devil has no power over my mind unless I give him power by accepting certain conditions.

Michael Archangel, God's will is your love,
you bring to us all, God's light from Above.
God's will is to see, all life taking flight,
transcendence of self, our most sacred right.

Michael Archangel, your Knowing so strong,
Michael Archangel, oh sweep us along.
Michael Archangel, we're singing your song,
Michael Archangel, with you we belong.

5. Master MORE, help me see that I will never know you if I project the image of an angry and judgmental God upon you and think that you are like that.

Michael Archangel, you are the best friend,
from all worldly dangers you do us defend,
the devil no match for your power of light,
and therefore our souls can freely take flight.

Michael Archangel, your Knowing so strong,
Michael Archangel, oh sweep us along.

**Michael Archangel, we're singing your song,
Michael Archangel, with you we belong.**

6. Master MORE, I want to know you as you truly are. Help me let go of my conditions long enough to experience even a brief glimpse of the unconditional love you feel streaming through you from the Creator itself, from the I AM Presence directly to me.

Michael Archangel, as children we play,
we're bringing the earth into a new day,
we raise it from all of the patterns so old,
our planet's life story is by us retold.

**Michael Archangel, your Knowing so strong,
Michael Archangel, oh sweep us along.
Michael Archangel, we're singing your song,
Michael Archangel, with you we belong.**

7. Master MORE, help me see how you become the open door for that love when I come to your retreat. I will accept your love by letting go of any condition that portrays me as not worthy.

Michael Archangel, God's power you show,
that you are invincible, this we do know,
you are undivided and thus can withstand,
anything coming from serpentine band.

**Michael Archangel, your Knowing so strong,
Michael Archangel, oh sweep us along.
Michael Archangel, we're singing your song,
Michael Archangel, with you we belong.**

8. Master MORE, help me see that you are not the one who has defined the conditions that I cannot live up to. Help me see what conditions I am projecting upon you, thinking that you are the one who has defined them.

> Michael Archangel, come raise now the earth,
> giving her thus a complete rebirth,
> collective the mind that we do now raise,
> for this we do give our infinite praise.
>
> **Michael Archangel, your Knowing so strong,**
> **Michael Archangel, oh sweep us along.**
> **Michael Archangel, we're singing your song,**
> **Michael Archangel, with you we belong.**

9. Master MORE, help me see that you are not withholding love from me because you have defined no conditions. So if I am not experiencing your love, it can only be because of my own conditions.

> Michael Archangel, the earth is now new,
> covered in Blue-flame as the morning dew,
> our planet now sparkles throughout all of space,
> as we are receiving your infinite Grace.
>
> **Michael Archangel, your Knowing so strong,**
> **Michael Archangel, oh sweep us along.**
> **Michael Archangel, we're singing your song,**
> **Michael Archangel, with you we belong.**

Part 4

1. Master MORE, help me see if there is a track in my mind saying: "What conditions do I have to live up to? I cannot do something wrong here; I am in a spiritual retreat."

Gabriel Archangel, your light we revere,
immersed in your Presence, nothing we fear.
Disciples of Christ, we do leave behind,
the ego's desire for responding in kind.

Gabriel Archangel, of this we are sure,
Gabriel Archangel, Christ light is the cure.
Gabriel Archangel, intentions so pure,
Gabriel Archangel, in you we're secure.

2. Master MORE, help me see that you are the Chohan of the First Ray and although the First Ray has been portrayed as the ray of power and will, it is because power and will are the essential ingredients of the creative drive.

Gabriel Archangel, we fear not the light,
in purifications' fire, we delight.
With your hand in ours, each challenge we face,
we follow the spiral to infinite grace.

Gabriel Archangel, of this we are sure,
Gabriel Archangel, Christ light is the cure.
Gabriel Archangel, intentions so pure,
Gabriel Archangel, in you we're secure.

3. Master MORE, help me see that I cannot create anything without having a certain outgoing power, and I cannot create anything without having the will to create.

Gabriel Archangel, your fire burning white,
ascending with you, out of the night.
The ego has nowhere to run and to hide,
in ascension's bright spiral, with you we abide.

Gabriel Archangel, of this we are sure,
Gabriel Archangel, Christ light is the cure.
Gabriel Archangel, intentions so pure,
Gabriel Archangel, in you we're secure.

4. Master MORE, help me see that power and will are not fixed qualities, some standard I must live up to. Help me see that you, Master MORE, the Chohan of the First Ray of Creative Drive, does not want to kill my creativity.

Gabriel Archangel, your trumpet we hear,
announcing the birth of Christ drawing near.
In lightness of being, we now are reborn,
rising with Christ on bright Easter morn.

Gabriel Archangel, of this we are sure,
Gabriel Archangel, Christ light is the cure.
Gabriel Archangel, intentions so pure,
Gabriel Archangel, in you we're secure.

5. Master MORE, help me see that you are not the one who wants to kill my creativity. My ego is, and the dark forces and the false teachers, but not you, Master MORE, for you only want me to be more. And I become more by being creative.

Gabriel Archangel, the earth is now free,
embracing a nondual reality,
the judgment of Christ upon forces so dark,
who deny that all have a spiritual spark.

Gabriel Archangel, of this we are sure,
Gabriel Archangel, Christ light is the cure.
Gabriel Archangel, intentions so pure,
Gabriel Archangel, in you we're secure.

6. Master MORE, help me see that I become creative only by
being willing to experiment. And I become willing to experiment only by looking at my own fear of being wrong and asking myself: "Is there something I love more than the fear of
being wrong? Is there some element of love in my being that is
stronger than my fear of being wrong?"

Gabriel Archangel, with angels so white,
raising our planet out of the dark night,
as we now intone the Word of the Lord,
the beings who fell are bound by your sword.

Gabriel Archangel, of this we are sure,
Gabriel Archangel, Christ light is the cure.
Gabriel Archangel, intentions so pure,
Gabriel Archangel, in you we're secure.

7. Master MORE, help me connect to my love for being more
than any standard. For it is only by going beyond the standard
that I am creative.

Gabriel Archangel, we call now to you,
the astral plane your light burning through,

entities, demons, discarnates are bound,
as you and we intone Sacred Sound.

Gabriel Archangel, of this we are sure,
Gabriel Archangel, Christ light is the cure.
Gabriel Archangel, intentions so pure,
Gabriel Archangel, in you we're secure.

8. Master MORE, help me see the conditions I have and how they limit my creative expression. Help me see which of my chakras are blocked and limit my creative potential.

Gabriel Archangel, what glorious day,
your radiant angels have come here to stay,
your purifications fire burning white,
intentions so pure, our hearts taking flight.

Gabriel Archangel, of this we are sure,
Gabriel Archangel, Christ light is the cure.
Gabriel Archangel, intentions so pure,
Gabriel Archangel, in you we're secure.

9. Master MORE, help me see how a specific chakra has a specific portal that is blocked. Help me see how this block is created by a certain condition that I have accepted.

Gabriel Archangel, our planet so pure,
in our bright new future we do feel secure,
with your band of light encircling the earth,
Saint Germain's Golden Age is now given birth.

Gabriel Archangel, of this we are sure,
Gabriel Archangel, Christ light is the cure.

**Gabriel Archangel, intentions so pure,
Gabriel Archangel, in you we're secure.**

Part 5

1. Master MORE, help me see let go of that condition so more light will stream through the chakra and unlock my creative potential.

> Master MORE, come to the fore,
> we will absorb your flame of MORE.
> Master MORE, our will so strong,
> our power centers cleared by song.

> **Master MORE, your Sacred Heart,
> from this we will no more depart,
> we are forever in your flow,
> of Diamond Will that you bestow.**

2. Master MORE, help me see that experiencing love only sets a foundation for taking the next step. And the next step is to use the Fourth Ray of purity, which is when something of a lower vibration has been accelerated to a higher vibration.

> Master MORE, your wisdom flows,
> as our attunement ever grows.
> Master MORE, we have a tie,
> that helps us see through Serpent's lie.

> **Master MORE, your Sacred Heart,
> from this we will no more depart,**

we are forever in your flow,
of Diamond Will that you bestow.

3. Master MORE, help me consciously acknowledge my love
for something more—that I have a love for my own creative
expression, for my own higher being, for my own creative
potential.

Master MORE, your love so pink,
there is no purer love, we think.
Master MORE, you set us free,
from all conditionality.

Master MORE, your Sacred Heart,
from this we will no more depart,
we are forever in your flow,
of Diamond Will that you bestow.

4. Master MORE, I love that potential so much that I am willing to take a look at myself and see that what limits my creative
expression are the very conditions that I have accepted and
allowed to exist in my consciousness.

Master MORE, we will endure,
your discipline that makes us pure.
Master MORE, intentions true,
as we are always one with you.

Master MORE, your Sacred Heart,
from this we will no more depart,
we are forever in your flow,
of Diamond Will that you bestow.

5. Master MORE, I hereby make the decision: "Yes, I am willing to accelerate myself beyond those conditions. I am willing to accelerate my sense of self beyond the standard that I have come to accept, the standard that I now see as based on the fallen consciousness, the conscious of anti-christ. I will no longer be limited by that standard. I want to accelerate my sense of self beyond that standard, and *I am* accelerating myself beyond that standard."

Master MORE, our vision raised,
the will of God is always praised.
Master MORE, creative will,
raising all life higher still.

**Master MORE, your Sacred Heart,
from this we will no more depart,
we are forever in your flow,
of Diamond Will that you bestow.**

6. Master MORE, help me see that becoming more is a creative process, and a creative process cannot be forced. It cannot be based on fear; it must be based on love. I love something more, and therefore I am willing to accelerate myself to a higher level in order to allow that more to flow through me.

Master MORE, your peace is power,
the demons of war it will devour.
Master MORE, we serve all life,
our flames consuming war and strife.

**Master MORE, your Sacred Heart,
from this we will no more depart,**

we are forever in your flow,
of Diamond Will that you bestow.

7. Master MORE, help me see that my I AM Presence is the source of my creativity, and my I AM Presence wants to express the fullness of its creativity as its gift to help raise the earth to a higher level.

Master MORE, we are so free,
eternal bond from you we see.
Master MORE, we find rebirth,
in flow of your eternal mirth.

Master MORE, your Sacred Heart,
from this we will no more depart,
we are forever in your flow,
of Diamond Will that you bestow.

8. Master MORE, help me see that my I AM Presence can express its creativity only though me. I have the potential – I, the Conscious You – have the potential to return to a state of pure awareness where I become the open door, the fully open door.

Master MORE, you balance all,
the seven rays upon our call.
Master MORE, forever MORE,
we are the Spirit's open door.

Master MORE, your Sacred Heart,
from this we will no more depart,
we are forever in your flow,
of Diamond Will that you bestow.

9. Master MORE, help me see that because of my standard because of my conditions, I am not yet a fully open door. I only have a partial opening, sometimes a very small opening.

Master MORE, your Presence here,
filling up the inner sphere.
Life is now a sacred flow,
God Power we on all bestow.

Master MORE, your Sacred Heart,
from this we will no more depart,
we are forever in your flow,
of Diamond Will that you bestow.

Part 6

1. Master MORE, help me experience the unconditional love that my I AM Presence has for me and wants to express through me, so I can make a decision that comes from the core of my being and is based on love, not fear.

Serapis Bey, what power lies,
behind your purifying eyes.
Serapis Bey, it is a treat,
to enter your sublime retreat.

Serapis Bey, we call to you,
to help us dual lies see through,
come purify our inner sight,
we see the earth in your great light.

2. Master MORE, help me see that a decision based on fear is a decision that is based on me reacting to something I feel is forcing itself upon me, and I am making a decision in order to avoid a negative reaction from other people.

> Serapis Bey, what wisdom found,
> your words are always most profound.
> Serapis Bey, we tell you true,
> our minds have room for naught but you.

> **Serapis Bey, we call to you,**
> **to help us dual lies see through,**
> **come purify our inner sight,**
> **we see the earth in your great light.**

3. Master MORE, help me see that when I am afraid of a negative reaction, I make a decision in order to avoid that reaction. Most of my decisions are avoidance decisions; I am seeking to avoid something bad happening.

> Serapis Bey, what love beyond,
> our hearts do leap, as we respond.
> Serapis Bey, your life a poem,
> that calls us to our starry home.

> **Serapis Bey, we call to you,**
> **to help us dual lies see through,**
> **come purify our inner sight,**
> **we see the earth in your great light.**

4. Master MORE, help me see that there is a level of decisions where I am not making decisions out of fear, I am not seeking to avoid something bad. I am making positive decisions based

on a love for something more and a desire to experience something positive.

> Serapis Bey, your guidance sure,
> our base is clear and white and pure.
> Serapis Bey, no longer trapped,
> by soul in which the self was wrapped.

> **Serapis Bey, we call to you,**
> **to help us dual lies see through,**
> **come purify our inner sight,**
> **we see the earth in your great light.**

5. Master MORE, help me see that I have been conditioned to believe that God has fear. If a god is angry, the anger comes from fear. If a god is judgmental, the need to judge comes from fear.

> Serapis Bey, what healing balm,
> in mind that is forever calm.
> Serapis Bey, our thoughts are pure,
> your discipline we shall endure.

> **Serapis Bey, we call to you,**
> **to help us dual lies see through,**
> **come purify our inner sight,**
> **we see the earth in your great light.**

6. Master MORE, help me see that the common image of the angry and judgmental God in the sky is a fear-based image that portrays God as a fear-based God.

Serapis Bey, what secret test,
for egos who want to be best.
Serapis Bey, expose the "me,"
that takes away our harmony.

Serapis Bey, we call to you,
to help us dual lies see through,
come purify our inner sight,
we see the earth in your great light.

7. Master MORE, help me see that God's will is not based on fear; God's decisions are not based on fear. And God's will is that I have free will, and God's will is that I exercise that free will as I see fit.

Serapis Bey, what moving sight,
the self ascends to sacred height.
Serapis Bey, forever free,
in sacred synchronicity.

Serapis Bey, we call to you,
to help us dual lies see through,
come purify our inner sight,
we see the earth in your great light.

8. Master MORE, help me see that God's highest will and vision is that I exercise my free will based on love and that all decisions I make help me become more, help the matter sphere become more, and ultimately helps my Creator become more. This is the process of life where everything becomes more.

Serapis Bey, you balance all,
the seven rays upon our call.
Serapis Bey, in space and time,
the pyramid of self, we climb.

Serapis Bey, we call to you,
to help us dual lies see through,
come purify our inner sight,
we see the earth in your great light.

9. Master MORE, I hereby summon the will to accelerate myself beyond my standard, the standard that limits my creativity. This decision is not based on the outer mind that is steeped in fear. It is based on love that does accelerate my sense of self, for I AM MORE.

Serapis Bey, your Presence here,
filling up the inner sphere.
Life is now a sacred flow,
God Purity we do bestow.

Serapis Bey, we call to you,
to help us dual lies see through,
come purify our inner sight,
we see the earth in your great light.

Sealing:

In the name of the Divine Mother, I fully accept that the power of these calls is used to set free the Ma-ter light, so it can outpicture the perfect vision of Christ for my own life, for all people and for the planet. In the name I AM THAT I AM, it is done! Amen.

13 | POWER AND HEALING

Master MORE I AM. And let me build on the teaching I have given you about the party that we give to those who have come to the point of making that decision to be willing to accelerate themselves. I have compared it to the confirmation party that is often thrown for teenagers when they confirm their Christian faith.

I am aware, of course that many teenagers on earth see this as a cultural ceremony, a formality that gives them access to the party and the presents. But nevertheless, the deeper meaning behind it is that you actually come to a point of maturity where you can consciously confirm your Christian faith.

I am, of course, not asking you to confirm anything out of faith. What does faith have to do with what I teach, for I teach through experience. And when you experience, what is the need for believing in something that you have not experienced? Believing that the experience is possible is helpful in terms of opening your mind and heart to having the experience, but ultimately the goal is for you to have the experience.

A period of intense growth

When you do make this commitment, you can go into a phase where you now use the power you have discovered to greatly accelerate your sense of self. You can accelerate yourself beyond your previous sense of self. Many students now go into a period in my retreat that is paralleled by what they experience in their waking consciousness. For often, when people have gone through this ceremony in my retreat, they may not remember the ceremony with their conscious minds, but they do realize that the spiritual path is a tremendous opportunity for accelerating themselves.

Especially those who are aware of our teachings often now throw themselves at studying these teachings more earnestly and practicing the techniques of our decrees and invocations with greater fervor than before. This often launches them into a period of very intense growth where they shake off many of the old conditions where they shake off much of the baggage they have been carrying with them, often for lifetimes. This is a tremendous growth process, a tremendous acceleration.

Going to the retreats of other Chohans

This process is helped along by the fact that after you go through this ceremony of truly affirming your willingness to accelerate, you are no longer confined, so to speak, to my retreat only. Until you have made this commitment, you can only attend the retreat of the First Ray, for this is, so to speak, the testing ground to test your willingness to accelerate. I seek, as I have described in the first several steps, to get you to the point where you can make that decision. But until you have made that decision, you cannot go anywhere else; you cannot really go to the retreats of the other Chohans. But once you do make that decision, you can go to the retreat where you need to go in order to come over a certain threshold, a certain hump, on your path.

Some students might go to the retreat of Lord Lanto where they learn to expand their reasoning abilities because they need to reason about certain things in order to accelerate themselves beyond some of their past baggage. Other students go to the retreat of Paul the Venetian where they work even more on experiencing and absorbing love, working on their ability to accept that they are worthy of love. Other students, of course, at this point go to the retreat of Serapis Bey where they then receive tremendous help in using the power of acceleration, the Flame of Acceleration, the Flame of Purity, to accelerate themselves beyond much from the past.

You cannot ascend by following rules

Serapis, however, will also give these students a very clear sense that at this point on their personal path, there is a limit to what the Flame of Purity and Acceleration can do for them. For even though Serapis is the primary teacher of ascension and of the ascension spiral – the ascension coil – he makes it clear that at this point the students are not ready to enter the ascension spiral. And the reason for this is very simple: You cannot ascend by following rules.

We of the ascended masters can give you a teaching, an outer teaching on earth. It is a valid teaching, but this does not mean that you can ascend by studying that outer teaching. Some students have taken a valid outer teaching and used it to create various rules for themselves. And some students actually believe with their conscious minds that they will ascend if they keep following the rules and practicing the decrees and doing this and not doing that. But it is not so.

They believe this in their outer minds because at the inner levels of the their beings, they have not made the commitment to accelerate themselves and therefore have not been able to attend the retreat of Serapis. And they have not been able to learn the lesson that you cannot ascend by following rules. For what is the ascension? It is a creative process. You can ascend only by unlocking the fullness of your creative powers, first through the seven rays and then beyond that through the secret rays and your Christhood.

Only by creatively expressing what your I AM Presence wants to express through you, can you come to the point where the Presence has expressed the fullness of the gift it wants to give through you here on earth. And then you are ready to ascend. For you see, the I AM Presence did not send you here so that you would make karma, balance that karma, and leave. The Presence sent you here for a positive purpose, a positive goal, of bringing a gift, being the open door for bringing its gift to earth.

Until the Presence is satisfied that it has given its gift fully, you – the Conscious You, the embodied lifestream – cannot ascend, for you have not fulfilled your purpose of becoming the completely open door. Your canvas is too narrow and your palette of colors has been limited by the conditions that you have accepted as part of your outer being—and that you think must limit, or control or direct your creative expression.

Your need for healing

After you have been with Serapis Bey and learned this lesson, you come back to my retreat. And I now start working on the fifth step, which is, of course, using the ray of healing. And then I give you the understanding that you need healing. I help you see that even though you have used the Flame of Purity to accelerate yourself tremendously beyond your previous level, there is a limit to how much you can actually accelerate yourself through the Flame of Purity. Because you still have certain wounds in your subconscious minds, in the emotional, mental, and identity levels of the mind.

These are, so to speak, like anchors that are hanging behind your boat. And when you push down on the lever that increases the speed of the engine, you feel how there is something that resists the boat going forward. For how can you expect the boat to go forward at full speed, if you have several anchors hanging behind the boat? It is now time to take a little break from acceleration and instead take an honest look in the mirror and say: "Where do I need healing?"

But before we actually look at the specifics of how you need healing and what you need to have healed, we first need to deal with the question of why you need healing. This is a question that many students have not really considered with their conscious minds. In fact, many students will have some resistance to considering this with their conscious minds. This is in part due to the standard created by the false teachers because that standard makes many people believe that by following certain rules – certain teachings – by adopting a certain attitude, well, they are sure to qualify for their ascension or however they define the ultimate goal of their spiritual efforts.

I can tell you there are many, many people who are in spiritual and religious movements and who believe that by following the prescripts of their religion or their guru, they will automatically make it to the spiritual realm. This, of course, is not the case, for again everything is a creative process. In order to express your creativity in its fullness, you need to look at the conditions, and the wounds and the limitations that prevent the expression of your creative powers from the I AM Presence.

Why have you been wounded?

What are the wounds that need to be healed and why do you need to look at them? I earlier talked about how you enter the rose garden and receive healing from experiencing unconditional love. But again, even unconditional love cannot heal all of your wounds and the reason for this is simple. You cannot heal a wound if you are not consciously aware of what caused the wound. What caused the wound was that a certain outer event you experienced triggered a certain inner experience. And based on that inner experience, you made a decision.

It is that decision that has set up a condition in your being that limits your creative expression. The condition was made by you. You may not have been fully, consciously aware of what the decision entailed and what the consequences were. But in order to be free from that decision, you have to become consciously aware of the decision and its consequences. Then, you have to consciously replace the previous decision with a new decision, based on the higher level of awareness you have today. This is where students need to understand why they have been wounded here on earth.

Now, you will understand that when a student comes to my retreat that lifestream has experienced what it is like to be at my retreat and therefore has no problem accepting this teaching. But I am giving you this teaching in a book that you can read with your conscious mind, even if you have no conscious memory of going to my retreat. Therefore, I will ask you to be honest with yourself and ask yourself this question: Are you practicing the decrees and invocations we have given you? Have you made a habit of making daily calls to Archangel Michael for protection? If you have not, I am asking you to simply not read or listen to the rest of this discourse. For it is likely to be more than you can handle at your conscious level of awareness, and the reason of this is simple. When you practice the decrees and invocations for spiritual protection, you will, after some time, build a momentum. This momentum, combined with the instructions you receive at my retreat, will give you a sense that Archangel Michael is capable of protecting you from anything here on earth, any force whatsoever on earth.

When you know that you can be protected from a certain force, then you will be able to consciously look at that force and recognize that it exists, recognize that it has influenced you in the past and that you need to accelerate yourself beyond that influence. But you can do so only by consciously looking at the force and looking at what it is in your psychology that makes you vulnerable to this force.

No need for fear

Do you see this simple dynamic? I have no intention here whatsoever of scaring you with anything. Fear has no place in my teaching method. Sometimes I allow students to have fear for a while, if they are so attached to it that I cannot deal with them in any other way. For of course, I cannot demand that people are free of fear before they come to my door. But that does not mean that I use fear to scare people.

It is not my intention to induce fear here. And that is why I want you to be honest and recognize that only when you have built up a momentum of invoking spiritual protection, will you be ready to consciously encounter the instructions I will now give you. I trust that if you are reading this or listening to these words, you have some momentum of invoking spiritual protection. So then, the reality is this: It is impossible to embody on earth without being wounded. It is simply impossible. The Maha Chohan himself described how all of us who have taken embodiment have submitted to what he explained is the death consciousness. The death consciousness is extremely powerful on earth, and you cannot embody here without being wounded by it and without to some degree submitting to it.

What does it mean to submit to the death consciousness? Well, if you look at any of the students in the spiritual or New Age movements, you will see that some of them have come to believe that they do not need to look at anything dark, such as dark forces, or an evil force or the devil. For if they only focus on the positive, then they can still make it to their goal. They actually – many of them – believe that it is dangerous to put your attention on dark forces because you give them energy that reinforces them.

Of course, you have the popular saying that "What you resist persists." But you see, what you resist persists because when you resist something you do give it energy. But you can actually look at something without resisting it. In other words, you can look at dark forces without going into the reaction of thinking that you have to fight them. And when you invoke spiritual protection from Archangel Michael, you are not fighting the dark forces. You are sealing yourself from the energies they direct at you. But that is not resisting them, for it is not giving energy to them. So as long as you are not reacting with fear or with anger, then you are not resisting the dark forces and you are not giving them energy.

Acknowledging the existence of dark forces

Why is it important to acknowledge that dark forces exist? Well because, as the Maha Chohan has explained, the death consciousness is hanging over this planet like a dark cloud. The only way to really manifest a higher spiritual consciousness here on earth is to free yourself from the influence of this consciousness, and you cannot do this without being conscious of it. You cannot grow towards self-mastery, my beloved, without mastering the self, which means attaining mastery that takes you beyond all of the forces and conditions that seek to limit the self.

There comes a point on your spiritual path where you simply cannot progress unless you recognize that there are dark forces. These dark forces have caused you to become so wounded that you cannot accelerate yourself further, until you look at some of those wounds and look at the decisions that you made because you were attacked by dark forces.

If you will not acknowledge the existence of dark forces and look at how they have influenced you, then you are submitting and continuing to submit to the dark forces and to the death consciousness. I can assure you that many, many people in spiritual and New Age movements sit around feeling very comfortable, feeling that they are very spiritual because they are so positive and so good. But in reality they have submitted to the death consciousness.

They have, so to speak, made a pact with the devil – not consciously, of course, but at subconscious levels – and it says this: "If I don't accelerate myself beyond a certain point, then you won't attack me." When you make such a deal, then the devil will leave you alone. Because he has no problem with you sitting there in your spiritual movement feeling holier than thou, feeling absolutely convinced that you are a good and spiritual person. As long as you are not accelerating yourself towards Christhood, then the devil will leave you alone so you can feel ever so comfortable. But you see, you are not growing beyond a certain point.

Fear from past lives

The question is simple: "Why are there so many people in New Age and spiritual movements who will not acknowledge the existence of dark forces, who will not look at them and who will not do something to free themselves from their influence?" Well, it is partly because of a certain laziness – spiritual laziness – where they really do not want to accelerate themselves beyond a certain point. But it is also, as the deeper, underlying reason because of fear.

They have experienced, often in past lives that when you come to a certain point on the path – where you have actually started to rise beyond the level of the mass consciousness – you will be attacked by dark forces. They carry with them the inner memory of having been attacked by dark forces in the past. Therefore, they have a sense that it is dangerous to accelerate yourself beyond a certain level because then you will become a target for these very vicious, very personal, very direct attacks.

Because they have not been willing to confront this fear, they have gone into making this pact with the dark forces, saying: "If I don't accelerate myself, you will leave me alone in this lifetime." For some it may be necessary to spend some time like this. I am not disputing this; I am not condemning anyone. I am simple saying that I cannot help anyone go beyond a certain level of consciousness, a certain level of the spiritual path, unless you are willing to acknowledge one thing: "I have been wounded and I need to look at why I was wounded because that is the only way I can heal the wounds."

The worst nightmare of dark forces

What I will give you now is food for your conscious mind, which if you have followed the process of giving the invocations and decrees as you studied my previous discourses, you can then use to tie into your inner knowing. Then, what I will say here does not cause you fear, it does not cause you doubt, you do not need to argue with it or reject it. You tune in to your heart, and you feel that there is reality here and it is time for you to look at it.

The simple reality on planet earth is this: Currently the dark forces believe they are in control of this planet. Now, in the deeper reality they are not in control, for this planet is not an isolated unit; it is part of the entire material universe. And as we have explained, the entire material universe is in an upward spiral because there are numerous other planets where the inhabitants of those planets have put their planets into an upward spiral. And this has, as the Maha Chohan explained, created the force of the Holy Spirit that pulls all of the material universe upwards, including, of course, planet earth.

Planet earth is behind the general upward movement of the universe, and this is what makes the dark forces believe in the illusion that they are in control of this planet. And they do have a large degree of control because they have managed to cause so many people to submit to the death consciousness.

Now, what is it that can break this control? Well, it is that individual human beings accelerate their consciousness beyond a certain level that they begin to attain and they dare to express Christhood. The main lesson you can learn from the life of Jesus was that he was a primary example, an archetype, of a person who has accelerated his consciousness beyond the norm, beyond the mass consciousness, and manifested a high degree of Christhood—and he has dared to express it.

You saw, of course, what happened to Jesus. He was viciously persecuted and he was eventually killed in a very vicious way. The reason for this is that if even one individual attains and expresses Christhood, then this will lessen the control that the dark forces have over this planet.

But now imagine that 10,000 people expressed the kind of Christhood that Jesus expressed and that millions more expressed a lesser degree of Christhood. Then, you can see that this would be the worst nightmare of the dark forces. And as Jesus has said himself, there are presently 10,000 people in embodiment who have the potential to manifest a high degree of Christhood in this lifetime. There are millions more who have the potential to manifest some degree of Christhood in this lifetime. Many of these people have already started to express their Christhood, but many more have not because they are stuck at this level where they dare not fully accelerate themselves into expressing their Christhood. Because they are, from past lives, afraid of what will happen when they do so.

They have an inner knowing that the attacks will come the moment you start expressing your Christhood, and they know that these attacks are relentless and vicious. Nevertheless, if you have come to this point on your personal path, then you are ready to acknowledge that even though the attacks may come, the attacks can only hurt you because of your own conditions, the wounds and conditions you have accepted because in the past you made a certain decision. Therefore, if you are willing to resolve those wounds, resolve those decisions, you will become transparent to the attacks, and whatever they direct at you will simply pass right through you.

The limited powers of dark forces

Let me give you a sense of co-measurement here. Do you understand that the dark forces have cut themselves off from the spiritual realm? This means that they can only work with the energies at a certain level of the material realm. Everything you do is done with energy. Your creative ability, your power, is determined not only by how much energy you can access, but also the level of vibration of energy that you can access.

We have explained that there are four levels of the material universe. Well, you know that as a human being on earth your physical body can only work within a certain range of capabilities. And this is because your physical body can only make use of energies within a certain spectrum of frequencies. Now, in the emotional realm there is a higher level of frequencies. But nevertheless, the lower levels of energies in the emotional realm have no power whatsoever to influence the mental realm. And again, in the mental realm there is a limit to the frequencies that are found there, and these frequencies cannot influence the identity realm. Of course, nothing in the four levels of the material universe can influence your I AM Presence. That is why your I AM Presence has not been hurt by anything you have done or encountered or experienced on earth.

You now see something very simple. When you stop identifying yourself with the physical body (and if you are a spiritual student, as you surely are, you have stopped identifying yourself fully with the body), well then you cannot be ultimately hurt by anything that happens to the body. Of course, you will be affected by it but your lifestream – your lower being – will not be ultimately hurt by anything that happens to the body. When you accelerate your sense of self to the point where you do not identify yourself with the emotions, then you cannot be ultimately hurt by any of the energies that come at you in the emotional realm. When you no longer identify yourself with your thoughts, you cannot be hurt by the energies that can be directed at you in the mental realm. And when you no longer identify yourself as a human being that is limited or separate, then you cannot be hurt by those forces who reside at the lower levels of the etheric or identity realm.

You see, it is a matter of where you focus your sense of identity. Many people on earth are completely focused on and identified with the physical body. Therefore, if their body is killed or if their body gets ill, they are deeply wounded by this in their soul. And they carry that wound with them from lifetime to lifetime, often coming into embodiment with a great fear of being killed or a great fear of disease.

Then there are, of course, people who are completely identified with their emotions, and they live their whole lives seeking to avoid negative emotions, seeking to avoid being insulted and so forth. Others are very identified with their intellects and they live their whole lives as academics or intellectuals who are completely identified with their thoughts and who always seek to avoid being proven wrong in some intellectual arguments—or seek to prove others wrong in order to prove their superiority.

A correct sense of identity

Your task as a spiritual student is, of course, to raise your sense of identity so you let go of identification with the body. You let go of identification with the emotions. You let go of identification with thoughts, and you eventually let go of any lower or separate sense of identity. You come to identify yourself correctly as the pure awareness of the Conscious You that is an extension of your I AM Presence, and therefore cannot be hurt or even affected by the lower energies found in the material realm.

Your Conscious You is not made of the energies of the material realm. When you consciously acknowledge this, you cannot be hurt by anything that is directed at you in the material realm. Of course, the dark forces can only exist in the material realm. They can only use the energies of the material realm to direct at you, and therefore – when you come to the point where you are not identified with the material – then you become transparent. You fulfill the requirement described by Jesus, when he said: "The prince of this world cometh and has nothing in me." Thus, whatever they direct at you – whatever attacks they launch at you – will pass right through you.

Now, I am explaining this to you in order to give you the goal that this is what you are seeking to work towards. Of course, I recognize you are not there yet, and that is why you need to invoke spiritual protection. You still have certain wounds and certain identifications that make you vulnerable to the attacks of the dark forces. That is why you invoke spiritual protection: To create a shield of high-frequency energy around your energy field, so that the attacks coming at you cannot enter as easily. They can only enter where you have a specific attachment that forms an open door in the shield around your energy field. And it is these attachments that you need to deal with at this particular level, the ones that make you the most vulnerable to the attacks of the dark forces.

Why you were wounded in the past

Let me now explain to you how you got wounded in the first place. If you go back to your first descent into planet earth, you will see, as we have said that most of you did not actually descend to earth when this planet was still in its pristine, ideal conditions. Most of you, who are in embodiment today, have descended after this planet had fallen to a lower level. This means that when you first descended to earth, there were already fallen beings in embodiment on earth.

They, of course, had it as their goal to drag any lifestream that came here into a downward spiral. For this is how they eventually hope to prove the Creator wrong, by proving that free will does not work because it causes souls to go into a downward spiral and they eventually become lost. This is their entire plan, as we have explained before *[Healing Mother Earth]*.

The point I am making is that most of you descended to earth for the first time when there were already fallen beings here. When you came here you came to express a positive gift aimed at raising this planet. But the fallen ones in embodiment wanted none of that gift, for they, of course, as I have explained, saw this expression of your Christhood as a threat to them.

As soon as you embodied here and started to express your creative powers, they attacked you viciously in order to cause you to come the point where you decided to shut off your creative powers. They exposed you to such a vicious ridicule or physical attack that you decided to somehow limit or shut off your creative powers because you wanted to avoid this negative reaction.

Now my beloved, it is very understandable that you made this decision. I myself made that decision after I had first started embodying here on earth. So did every other ascended master that has ever embodied here. We were all so blown away, as they say, by the viciousness of the dark forces that we went into a state of shock, a state of trauma. At this point, it may be beyond your capacity to get in touch with your very deepest feeling, your deepest reaction to life on this planet. But if you could go into it, I can assure you that the very deepest feeling you have about life on earth is this sense of shock, this sense of being traumatized by the viciousness of the rejection of your creative abilities. This is the very deepest wound you have.

I am giving you this because it is important for you to have this in mind. I realize that at this point you are not ready to work on that wound, for this comes much later. In fact, it even comes beyond the 96th level. But it is important for you to know that basically the very first wound you received on earth was the vicious rejection of your creative abilities. And basically, every wound you have received since then is simply a variation of this original wound. In a sense, all of your succeeding wounds were reactions to that original rejection of your creativity.

The wound you must heal right now

When you understand this consciously, you can see that, first of all, the goal is to get back to a point where you are the open door and you can express your creativity. But you can also see the need to deal with some of these wounds. Again, you don't need to deal with the deepest wound at this point. But you do need to realize that you cannot accelerate yourself beyond your current level, until you have looked at one specific wound that is holding you back right now that is holding you back from taking the next step.

This is the anchor that is hanging after your boat and that you need to look at right now. My beloved, there is no shortcut here. You cannot simply cut the anchor line. You need to actually jump in the water and swim under the water, following the anchor line until you see the anchor. Then, when you see the anchor, you realize that it is based on a certain decision—and it is like pulling a pin that holds the anchor. And when you pull it, the anchor is released. But in order to pull the pin, you must see the decision and re-do, remake that decision.

This, of course, is what I will help you do at my retreat when you come to this level. Again, I will take you into the room with the screen where you can do a scan of your aura. You can come to see what is the wound you are dealing with right now, what is the one decision you made – often a decision you actually have reinforced in this lifetime – that is right now holding back your creative expression.

You can actually gain some feel for this by looking at your life in this lifetime. Perhaps you can already remember, otherwise you can come to remember, having been exposed to some form of ridicule or the putting down of your creative abilities and deciding not to express those abilities? I am not saying this was necessarily some vicious attack. It could have been well-meaning people who simply thought that they knew how creativity should be expressed according to some standard. But nevertheless, you were exposed to some kind of standard that caused you to shut down your creativity abilities, your creative expression.

I need you to be willing to look at this. And of course, as you study this discourse and continue to study the other discourses, as you continue to practice the decrees and ask to be taken to my retreat during the night, I will gradually help you. This is not something I can expose in a book, for it is individual to each one. I will help you get in touch with what it is for you personally. What was the decision you made in this lifetime to hold back your creative powers, to not express yourself creatively? Even though at some point you might have had a dream of being creative but you thought: "Oh, I cannot possible do that, or I cannot make a living by being creative, so I have to go into another field where I can make a better living."

My beloved, I am not saying you should give up your job and become an artist. But I am not saying you should not give up your job and become an artist. Frankly, it is not a matter of giving up your job and doing something on the outer. It is primarily a matter of getting in touch with the decision that psychologically limited your creative expression. For you do not need to be an artist in order to express yourself creatively. You can have a seemingly mundane job but still bring forth some creative expression through it. However, when you do begin to unlock your creativity, you find that you move on from mundane jobs to a job where there is more room for creative expression.

Getting in touch with your dreams

Nevertheless, my point here is this: If you are willing to look at this, if you are willing to look at your life, if you are willing to ask for my help and my direction, then I will help you. Your I AM Presence will help you, and my beloved brother, Hilarion, will help you, as you attend his retreat where you can come to a conscious recognition of what is your dream of being creative. You can come to a conscious awareness about how some event in your life really caused you to deny that dream, to see it as unrealistic and to decide to shut down your creative expression. Then, you can come to the point where you say: "I really did not need to make that decision, but I certainly do not need to uphold it anymore. And thus, I decide that I will set free my creative expression. I will be willing to express myself." Creative expression, as I said, is not just a matter of painting pictures or writing books or writing poems or this and that. There are many ways to be creative. Bringing forth new ideas that improve some aspect of life or society, this is creativity. Any way of doing things better, of improving life, is creativity.

It is important for you at this point on your path to get in touch with your built-in creativity, your love for some form of creative expression. I am not saying, again that you need to change careers and make this a living. But at least dare to dream. Dare to express it in some way. Dare to be creative. It may be in small ways at first, but dare to be creative. And then be willing to look at what standard you have accepted in your mind that you think you need to apply to your creativity. For this is the standard of the fallen beings.

As I have said, there is no standard that can be applied to creative expression, for creative expression brings something new. And how can something new be confined to and pre-defined by a standard? Is this not obvious when you use your reasoning abilities?

How could life ever improve on earth unless there was something new, some new idea that came in? If there was no room for something new, you would have a static society, as you have indeed seen, for example, in the feudal society in medieval Europe. For more than several hundred years, there was hardly any improvement in living conditions. There was very little room for creativity, for everything was locked down by a standard imposed by the fallen beings through the outer instrument of the Catholic Church and a noble class and the kings. They wanted to maintain their privileged positions in society regardless of the suffering this put upon the general population.

Your creative potential

Well then, be willing to be part of the spiritual, creative elite who will not let the power elite stop their creative expression. This is your calling. This is your potential in this lifetime. If it had not been your potential, you would not have found this teaching. You would not be reading or listening to these words.

I am Master MORE. I am the Chohan of the First Ray of creative expression. I am telling you: "You have a potential to be part of the elite that will bring this planet forward in a giant leap into the Golden Age of Saint Germain." This is why you chose to come into embodiment at this time. This is why you have been willing to endure being in embodiment many times on this planet over the past 2,000 years: to make sure that Jesus received the fulfillment of setting the pattern, the archetypal pattern for the Piscean age, of people manifesting their Christhood. You are here to make sure that as the Piscean age moves into the Aquarian Age, there will be thousands of people who manifest and express their Christhood on this planet.

This is the deeper purpose behind giving these books. It is to help these people unlock their creative abilities, so they can express their creative abilities in taking this planet up into the Golden Age matrix held in the mind of Saint Germain— held in the mind of all of us. For we are all one in the efforts to raise this earth into the Golden Age. You are all one with us in those efforts, and I am simply here to help you unlock the conscious awareness that you are part of this endeavor. For by becoming consciously aware of it, you can accelerate your creative expression. You can accelerate the healing of the wounds that hold back that creative expression.

Oh my beloved, it is a joy for me to see when students at my retreat begin to unlock their creative power and begin to dare to express those creative powers—not just at my retreat but even more so in their waking awareness. There is such rejoicing when we see students dare to step beyond the mold in which they were brought up, and they dare to do something different and dare to express something which is more.

Seeking Mother Mary's help

I only wish I could help each one of you come to that point. But sometimes I must acknowledge that even my abilities to help you are limited. And that is, of course, when I do what every good general does: I call in reinforcements. There are indeed students at my retreat who have a hard time overcoming a particular wound to their creativity. And then I call in my beloved sister, Mother Mary, who is the representative of the Divine Mother for earth.

She has an ability to take a student in her arms and hold that student, as you might have seen the pictures of her holding the infant Jesus. But of course, the pictures and statues you see on earth are nothing compared to the real, translucent beauty of Mother Mary. But nevertheless, you might be able to imagine yourself surrendering yourself fully to the embrace of the Divine Mother, surrendering yourself fully into feeling the unconditional love that the Mother of God has for you, when she holds you in her arms.

You can feel the healing radiance penetrating your energy field, immediately targeting the wound that you are dealing with, radiating her healing energies into that wound, so that you can suddenly look at it without that intense, emotional pain that you otherwise feel. You can look at it with her immaculate vision and you can see that it really is just a wound. It is just a decision.

You made the decision, but you did not become the decision. The decision created a spirit, as the Maha Chohan has explained, but you did not become that spirit. And therefore, you do not have to forever look at the decision through the perception filter of the spirit. For this, of course, is what causes you pain. This is what causes you to think you can never undo that decision because the spirit can never undo that decision. The spirit can only look at the decision with pain, for the spirit was created out of the pain of that original, traumatic experience of having your creativity rejected.

Mother Mary will help you step outside of the pain – outside of the spirit – and see a very simple reality. Your creativity was not rejected by God. It was not even truly rejected by the fallen beings, for they could not see your creativity. They could not see it for what it was. They only sensed that your creative expression disturbed their sense of being in control, and therefore they reacted the only way that the fallen beings can react.

My beloved, have you ever had the experience as a child of being confronted by an angry dog? Perhaps a dog that is chained or barking behind a fence, but it is barking and snarling at you. And you might have tried to talk to it in a gentle voice, but it keeps barking and snarling at you. Some dogs you can calm down by talking to them, but others you cannot. And that is when you come to the point of realizing that an angry dog will always do what a mad dog does: bark and snarl at you no matter what you say.

What do you then do? You have to simply walk away. But you are not feeling that this angry dog is rejecting your creative expression, for you realize that the mad dog is simply a mad dog. And likewise for the fallen beings. They can only react like a mad dog. Whenever they sense anyone expressing anything creative, they feel threatened and they do what they have always done: They seek to hammer it down. But there is nothing personal about it. They don't even see the uniqueness of your being and your creative expression. For they only see the images created in their own minds and they have nothing to do with the reality of your creative expression.

Disconnecting creativity from results

When you sit in the arms of Mother Mary and see this, then you might be able to see that the decision you made was based on you thinking that because you are now in physical embodiment, you have to accept the standard projected at you by the fallen beings. In other words, you thought that you had to see your creative expression through the filter of their rejection, instead of seeing your creative expression through the pure awareness that you are.

Do you see why you came to believe this? It was actually because you came into embodiment with an intent to change things on earth. You came here with the desire to bring a positive gift, to make a difference, to raise this planet up to a higher state. It is very understandable that you came here with this intent—for why else would you have volunteered to descend into a dense environment like this?

Indeed, as I have said, you are here to help bring the planet into a Golden Age. But what you have to realize is one simple consideration: Bringing the planet closer to the Golden Age does not depend on the reaction to your creative efforts that you get from the fallen beings and the death consciousness. You are not here to change specific other lifestreams. Have I not earlier talked about the need to overcome the desire to change other people's minds? You are not here to change the minds of the fallen beings. The success of your creative expression does not in any way depend on the reaction or the acceptance or non-acceptance from people in the fallen state of consciousness—for they will always reject.

The success of your creative expression depends on only one thing: the expression being expressed. When you have expressed your creativity, you have the success for the expression itself is a success in itself. It is not the reaction from other people that matters at all. And this is what you see, when you sit in the loving arms of Mother Mary. This is the immaculate vision, the immaculate concept.

How to raise the earth

For you see, what will inevitably raise the earth? Well, if you have a dark room and you want to increase the light in the room, how do you do this? You do it by bringing more light. And every time you bring more light, you decrease the darkness. It can be no other way, for darkness is the absence of light. You see, every time you express your creative powers, you are helping increase the light on this planet and this brings it closer to the Golden Age.

But what do you also see in a dark room when you increase the light? Well, first there is a period where everything appears grey. But as the light increases even more, there will be greater contrast between the areas where the sun's rays shine directly on the floor and the areas that are now in deep shadows. There will be a greater contrast between light and dark.

This is what you see on planet earth today. This is why you have been so viciously attacked by the fallen beings, by those who are still trapped in the fallen mindset. This is why you might be attacked when you begin to express your Christhood in a public way. But I am not asking you to express your Christhood in a public way yet. I am simply asking you to express it for yourself, so that you can start the process of unlocking your creative abilities.

When you come to that point of having your major wound healed, you will be able to see that your expression should not be evaluated based on the rejection of those in the fallen mindset. For you have the right to express your creative abilities, despite the fact that there are those who will vehemently reject it and who will viciously attack you. But you can continue to be who you are, for you have permission from the Mother of God – who is the ultimate authority for earth – to express your divine creativity. You have the permission of the Creator itself – who is the ultimate authority for the world of form – to be who you are and to be the open door for the expression from your I AM Presence.

My beloved, when you have the permission from God and the Mother of God, why would you need permission from the fallen beings who have cut themselves off from God and who have rejected and persecuted the Mother of God and her offspring? Why would you need their permission? And if you don't need their permission, why would you let their rejection stop you from giving the gift of your creative expression to this planet, the gift that you came here to give, the gift that it is your highest potential to give?

When you begin to lock in to this in your conscious mind, you can begin to heal from the wounds. You can begin to accept your true role that you are here to express your creativity. You are here to go through the process of the Path of the Seven Veils whereby you gradually become a more and more open door for the expression of that which is more, the MORE that I AM.

14 | INVOKING POWER AND HEALING

In the name I AM THAT I AM, Jesus Christ, I call to my I AM Presence to flow through the I Will Be Presence that I AM and give this invocation with full power. I call to beloved Elohim Hercules and Amazonia and Cyclopea and Virginia, Archangel Michael and Faith and Archangel Raphael and Mother Mary, Master MORE and Hilarion to help me heal the traumas that block my creative expression. Help me see and surrender all patterns that block my oneness with Master MORE and my oneness with my I AM Presence, including ...

[Make personal calls]

Part 1

1. Master MORE, help me accelerate my sense of self and see the spiritual path as a tremendous opportunity for accelerating myself.

> O Hercules Blue, we're one with your will,
> all space in our beings with Blue Flame you fill,
> a beacon that radiates light to the earth,
> bringing about our planet's rebirth.
>
> **O Hercules Blue, all life you defend,**
> **giving us power to always transcend,**
> **in you the expansion of self has no end,**
> **as we in God's infinite spirals ascend.**

2. Master MORE, help me see if I have used an ascended master teaching to create rules for myself, thinking I will ascend if I keep following the rules and practicing the decrees.

> O Hercules Blue, your wisdom so great,
> within us a sense of knowing create,
> a new frame of reference we suddenly gain,
> for going beyond duality's pain.
>
> **O Hercules Blue, all life you defend,**
> **giving us power to always transcend,**
> **in you the expansion of self has no end,**
> **as we in God's infinite spirals ascend.**

3. Master MORE, help me see if I have not made the commitment to accelerate myself, and therefore I have not been

able to attend the retreat of Serapis and learn the lesson that I cannot ascend by following rules.

O Hercules Blue, we lovingly raise,
our voices in giving God infinite praise,
in feeling your flame, so clearly we see,
transcending the self is the true alchemy.

O Hercules Blue, all life you defend,
giving us power to always transcend,
in you the expansion of self has no end,
as we in God's infinite spirals ascend.

4. Master MORE, help me see that the ascension is a creative process. I can ascend only by unlocking the fullness of my creative powers, first through the seven rays and then beyond that through the secret rays and my Christhood.

O Hercules Blue, all life now you heal,
enveloping all in your Blue-flame Seal,
we're grateful for playing a personal part,
In God's infinitely intricate work of art.

O Hercules Blue, all life you defend,
giving us power to always transcend,
in you the expansion of self has no end,
as we in God's infinite spirals ascend.

5. Master MORE, help me see that only by creatively expressing what my I AM Presence wants to express through me, can I come to the point where the Presence has expressed the fullness of the gift it wants to give through me here on earth. And then I am ready to ascend.

O Hercules Blue, your Temple of Light,
revealed to us all through our inner sight,
your power allows us to forge on until,
we pierce every veil and climb every hill.

**O Hercules Blue, all life you defend,
giving us power to always transcend,
in you the expansion of self has no end,
as we in God's infinite spirals ascend.**

6. Master MORE, help me see that my I AM Presence did not send me here so that I would make karma, balance that karma and leave. My Presence sent me here for a positive purpose of being the open door for bringing its gift to earth.

O Hercules Blue, I pledge now my life,
in helping this planet transcend human strife,
duality's lies are pierced by your light,
restoring the fullness of our inner sight.

**O Hercules Blue, all life you defend,
giving us power to always transcend,
in you the expansion of self has no end,
as we in God's infinite spirals ascend.**

7. Master MORE, help me see that until the Presence is satisfied that it has given its gift fully, I – the Conscious You, the embodied lifestream – cannot ascend, for I have not fulfilled my purpose of becoming the completely open door.

O Hercules Blue, we set all life free,
from the subtlest lies of duality,

the prince of this world no more has a bond,
for with you we go completely beyond.

O Hercules Blue, all life you defend,
giving us power to always transcend,
in you the expansion of self has no end,
as we in God's infinite spirals ascend.

8. Master MORE, help me see how my creativity has been limited by the conditions I have accepted as part of my outer being—and that I think must limit, control or direct my creative expression.

O Hercules Blue, in oneness with thee,
we open our hearts to your reality,
your electric-blue fire within us reveal,
our innermost longing for all that is real.

O Hercules Blue, all life you defend,
giving us power to always transcend,
in you the expansion of self has no end,
as we in God's infinite spirals ascend.

9. Master MORE, help me see that even though I have used the Flame of Purity to accelerate myself tremendously beyond my previous level, there is a limit to how much I can accelerate myself through the Flame of Purity.

O Hercules Blue, you fill every space,
with infinite Power and infinite Grace,
you embody the key to creativity,
the will to transcend into Infinity.

O Hercules Blue, all life you defend,
giving us power to always transcend,
in you the expansion of self has no end,
as we in God's infinite spirals ascend.

Part 2

1. Master MORE, help me see that I still have wounds in my subconscious minds, in the emotional, mental, and identity levels of the mind, and they are like anchors that are hanging behind my boat.

> Cyclopea so dear, the truth you reveal,
> the truth that duality's ailments will heal,
> your Emerald Light is like a great balm,
> our emotional bodies are perfectly calm.

> **Cyclopea so dear, in Emerald Sphere,**
> **in raising perception we shall persevere,**
> **as deep in our hearts your truth we revere,**
> **to immaculate vision the earth does adhere.**

2. Master MORE, help me take an honest look in the mirror and see where I need healing.

> Cyclopea so dear, with you we unwind,
> all negative spirals clouding the mind,
> we know pure awareness is truly our core,
> the key to becoming the wide-open door.

Cyclopea so dear, in Emerald Sphere,
in raising perception we shall persevere,
as deep in our hearts your truth we revere,
to immaculate vision the earth does adhere.

3. Master MORE, help me see that everything is a creative process. In order to express my creativity in its fullness, I need to look at the conditions, the wounds and the limitations that prevent the expression of my creative powers from my I AM Presence.

Cyclopea so dear, clear our inner sight,
empowered, we pierce the soul's fearful night,
we now see our life through your single eye,
beyond all disease we're ready to fly.

Cyclopea so dear, in Emerald Sphere,
in raising perception we shall persevere,
as deep in our hearts your truth we revere,
to immaculate vision the earth does adhere.

4. Master MORE, help me see what are the wounds that need to be healed and why I need to look at them. Help me see that I cannot heal a wound if I am not consciously aware of what caused the wound.

Cyclopea so dear, life can only reflect,
the images that the mind does project,
the key to our healing is clearing the mind,
from the images the ego is hiding behind.

Cyclopea so dear, in Emerald Sphere,
in raising perception we shall persevere,

as deep in our hearts your truth we revere,
to immaculate vision the earth does adhere.

5. Master MORE, help me see that what caused the wound was that a certain outer event triggered a certain inner experience. And based on that inner experience, I made a decision.

Cyclopea so dear, we want to aim high,
to your healing flame we ever draw nigh,
through veils of duality we now take flight,
bathed in your penetrating Emerald Light.

Cyclopea so dear, in Emerald Sphere,
in raising perception we shall persevere,
as deep in our hearts your truth we revere,
to immaculate vision the earth does adhere.

6. Master MORE, help me see that it is this decision that has set up a condition in my being that limits my creative expression.

Cyclopea so dear, your Emerald Flame,
exposes every subtle, dualistic power game,
including the game of wanting to say,
that truth is defined in only one way.

Cyclopea so dear, in Emerald Sphere,
in raising perception we shall persevere,
as deep in our hearts your truth we revere,
to immaculate vision the earth does adhere.

7. Master MORE, help me see that the condition was made by me, but I may not have been fully, consciously aware of what the decision entailed and what the consequences were.

Cyclopea so dear, we're feeling the flow,
as your Living Truth upon us you bestow,
from all dual vision we are now set free,
planet earth in immaculate matrix will be.

Cyclopea so dear, in Emerald Sphere,
in raising perception we shall persevere,
as deep in our hearts your truth we revere,
to immaculate vision the earth does adhere.

8. Master MORE, help me see that in order to be free from
that decision, I have to become consciously aware of the decision and its consequences. Then, I have to consciously replace
the previous decision with a new decision, based on the higher
level of awareness I have today.

Cyclopea so dear, the truth is now clear,
we see higher purpose for which we are here
we know truth transcends all systems below,
immersed in your light, we continue to grow.

Cyclopea so dear, in Emerald Sphere,
in raising perception we shall persevere,
as deep in our hearts your truth we revere,
to immaculate vision the earth does adhere.

9. Master MORE, I am making a commitment to making daily
calls to Archangel Michael for protection, so that I build a
momentum and develop the sense that Archangel Michael is
capable of protecting me from any force whatsoever on earth.

Cyclopea so dear, we're feeling your joy,
as creative vision we now do employ,

in lifting earth out of serpentine cage,
to manifest Saint Germain's Golden Age.

**Cyclopea so dear, in Emerald Sphere,
in raising perception we shall persevere,
as deep in our hearts your truth we revere,
to immaculate vision the earth does adhere.**

Part 3

1. Master MORE, help me see that when I know that I can be protected from a certain force, then I will be able to consciously look at that force and recognize that it exists, recognize that it has influenced me in the past and that I need to accelerate myself beyond that influence.

Michael Archangel, in your flame so blue,
there is no more night, there is only you.
In oneness with you, we're filled with your light,
what glorious wonder, revealed to our sight.

**Michael Archangel, your Knowing so strong,
Michael Archangel, oh sweep us along.
Michael Archangel, we're singing your song,
Michael Archangel, with you we belong.**

2. Master MORE, help me see that I can become free only by consciously looking at the force and looking at what it is in my psychology that makes me vulnerable to this force.

Michael Archangel, protection you give,
within your blue shield, we ever shall live.
Sealed from all creatures, roaming the night,
we remain in your sphere, of electric blue light.

Michael Archangel, your Knowing so strong,
Michael Archangel, oh sweep us along.
Michael Archangel, we're singing your song,
Michael Archangel, with you we belong.

3. Master MORE, help me see that it is not your intention to induce fear. I will be honest and recognize that only when I have built up a momentum of invoking spiritual protection, will I be ready to consciously encounter your next instructions.

Michael Archangel, what power you bring,
as millions of angels, praises will sing.
Consuming the demons, of doubt and of fear,
we know that your Presence, will always be near.

Michael Archangel, your Knowing so strong,
Michael Archangel, oh sweep us along.
Michael Archangel, we're singing your song,
Michael Archangel, with you we belong.

4. Master MORE, help me see that it is impossible to embody on earth without being wounded. The death consciousness is extremely powerful on earth, and I cannot embody here without being wounded by it and without to some degree submitting to it.

Michael Archangel, God's will is your love,
you bring to us all, God's light from Above.

God's will is to see, all life taking flight,
transcendence of self, our most sacred right.

Michael Archangel, your Knowing so strong,
Michael Archangel, oh sweep us along.
Michael Archangel, we're singing your song,
Michael Archangel, with you we belong.

5. Master MORE, help me see that what I resist persists because when I resist something, I give it energy. But I can look at something without resisting it. I can look at dark forces without thinking that I have to fight them.

Michael Archangel, you are the best friend,
from all worldly dangers you do us defend,
the devil no match for your power of light,
and therefore our souls can freely take flight.

Michael Archangel, your Knowing so strong,
Michael Archangel, oh sweep us along.
Michael Archangel, we're singing your song,
Michael Archangel, with you we belong.

6. Master MORE, help me see that when I invoke spiritual protection from Archangel Michael, I am not fighting the dark forces. I am sealing myself from the energies they direct at me. This is not resisting them, for it is not giving energy to them.

Michael Archangel, as children we play,
we're bringing the earth into a new day,
we raise it from all of the patterns so old,
our planet's life story is by us retold.

Michael Archangel, your Knowing so strong,
Michael Archangel, oh sweep us along.
Michael Archangel, we're singing your song,
Michael Archangel, with you we belong.

7. Master MORE, help me see that it is important to acknowledge that dark forces exist because the death consciousness is hanging over this planet like a dark cloud.

Michael Archangel, God's power you show,
that you are invincible, this we do know,
you are undivided and thus can withstand,
anything coming from serpentine band.

Michael Archangel, your Knowing so strong,
Michael Archangel, oh sweep us along.
Michael Archangel, we're singing your song,
Michael Archangel, with you we belong.

8. Master MORE, help me see that the only way to manifest a higher spiritual consciousness on earth is to free myself from the influence of this consciousness, and I cannot do this without being conscious of it.

Michael Archangel, come raise now the earth,
giving her thus a complete rebirth,
collective the mind that we do now raise,
for this we do give our infinite praise.

Michael Archangel, your Knowing so strong,
Michael Archangel, oh sweep us along.
Michael Archangel, we're singing your song,
Michael Archangel, with you we belong.

9. Master MORE, help me see that I cannot grow towards self-mastery without mastering the self, which means attaining mastery that takes me beyond all of the forces and conditions that seek to limit the self.

Michael Archangel, the earth is now new,
covered in Blue-flame as the morning dew,
our planet now sparkles throughout all of space,
as we are receiving your infinite Grace.

Michael Archangel, your Knowing so strong,
Michael Archangel, oh sweep us along.
Michael Archangel, we're singing your song,
Michael Archangel, with you we belong.

Part 4

1. Master MORE, help me see that there comes a point on my spiritual path where I cannot progress unless I recognize that dark forces have caused me to become so wounded that I cannot accelerate myself further, until I look at some of those wounds and look at the decisions that I made because I was attacked by dark forces.

Raphael Archangel, your light so intense,
raise us beyond all human pretense.
Mother Mary and you have a vision so bold,
to see that our highest potential unfold.

Raphael Archangel, for vision we pray,
Raphael Archangel, show us the way,

Raphael Archangel, your emerald ray,
Raphael Archangel, our lives a new day.

2. Master MORE, help me see that if I do not acknowledge the existence of dark forces and look at how they have influenced me, then I am submitting and continuing to submit to the dark forces and to the death consciousness.

Raphael Archangel, in emerald sphere,
to immaculate vision we always adhere.
Mother Mary enfolds us in her Sacred Heart,
from Mother's true love, we're never apart.

Raphael Archangel, for vision we pray,
Raphael Archangel, show us the way,
Raphael Archangel, your emerald ray,
Raphael Archangel, our lives a new day.

3. Master MORE, help me see if I have made a pact with the devil, saying at subconscious levels: "If I don't accelerate myself beyond a certain point, then you won't attack me."

Raphael Archangel, all ailments you heal,
each cell in our bodies in light now you seal.
Mother Mary's immaculate concept we see,
perfection of health our new reality.

Raphael Archangel, for vision we pray,
Raphael Archangel, show us the way,
Raphael Archangel, your emerald ray,
Raphael Archangel, our lives a new day.

4. Master MORE, help me see that when I start to rise beyond the level of the mass consciousness, I will be attacked by dark forces.

> Raphael Archangel, your light is so real,
> the vision of Christ in us you reveal.
> Mother Mary now helps us to truly transcend,
> in emerald light with you we ascend.

> **Raphael Archangel, for vision we pray,**
> **Raphael Archangel, show us the way,**
> **Raphael Archangel, your emerald ray,**
> **Raphael Archangel, our lives a new day.**

5. Master MORE, help me see if I have been attacked in past lives and carry with me an inner memory that it is dangerous to accelerate myself beyond a certain level because then I will become a target for these very vicious, very personal, very direct attacks.

> Raphael Archangel, diseases are done,
> as you help us see that all life is One,
> we no longer do your true love reject,
> immaculate vision on all we project.

> **Raphael Archangel, for vision we pray,**
> **Raphael Archangel, show us the way,**
> **Raphael Archangel, your emerald ray,**
> **Raphael Archangel, our lives a new day.**

6. Master MORE, help me confront this fear and acknowledge: "I have been wounded and I need to look at why I was wounded because that is the only way I can heal the wounds."

Raphael Archangel, we're healing the earth,
in immaculate vision we give her rebirth,
a new era has on this day begun,
your emerald light now shines like a sun.

Raphael Archangel, for vision we pray,
Raphael Archangel, show us the way,
Raphael Archangel, your emerald ray,
Raphael Archangel, our lives a new day.

7. Master MORE, help me see that the dark forces believe they are in control of this planet. And they do have a large degree of control because they have managed to cause so many people to submit to the death consciousness.

Raphael Archangel, the fall is behind,
as all of earth's people the Christ path do find,
we call now to you all people to heal,
as four lower bodies in love you do seal.

Raphael Archangel, for vision we pray,
Raphael Archangel, show us the way,
Raphael Archangel, your emerald ray,
Raphael Archangel, our lives a new day.

8. Master MORE, help me see that what can break this control is that individual human beings accelerate their consciousness beyond a certain level, so that they begin to express Christhood.

Raphael Archangel, as you bring the light,
the forces of darkness swiftly take flight,
their day is now done as we claim the earth,
spreading to all an innocent mirth.

Raphael Archangel, for vision we pray,
Raphael Archangel, show us the way,
Raphael Archangel, your emerald ray,
Raphael Archangel, our lives a new day.

9. Master MORE, help me see that Jesus was a primary example, an archetype, of a person who has accelerated his consciousness beyond the norm, beyond the mass consciousness, and manifested a high degree of Christhood—and he dared to express it.

Raphael Archangel, our vision set free,
as we can now see God's reality,
as Saint Germain's vision is manifest here,
the earth is now sealed in immaculate sphere.

Raphael Archangel, for vision we pray,
Raphael Archangel, show us the way,
Raphael Archangel, your emerald ray,
Raphael Archangel, our lives a new day.

Part 5

1. Master MORE, help me see that if even one individual attains and expresses Christhood, this will lessen the control that the dark forces have over this planet. If 10,000 people expressed the kind of Christhood that Jesus expressed, it would be the worst nightmare of the dark forces.

Master MORE, come to the fore,
we will absorb your flame of MORE.

Master MORE, our will so strong,
our power centers cleared by song.

**Master MORE, your Sacred Heart,
from this we will no more depart,
we are forever in your flow,
of Diamond Will that you bestow.**

2. Master MORE, help me see if I am one of the 10,000 people in embodiment who have the potential to manifest a high degree of Christhood in this lifetime. Or if I am one of millions who have the potential to manifest some degree of Christhood in this lifetime.

Master MORE, your wisdom flows,
as our attunement ever grows.
Master MORE, we have a tie,
that helps us see through Serpent's lie.

**Master MORE, your Sacred Heart,
from this we will no more depart,
we are forever in your flow,
of Diamond Will that you bestow.**

3. Master MORE, help me see if I have delayed expressing my Christhood because I am, from past lives, afraid of what will happen when I do so.

Master MORE, your love so pink,
there is no purer love, we think.
Master MORE, you set us free,
from all conditionality.

**Master MORE, your Sacred Heart,
from this we will no more depart,
we are forever in your flow,
of Diamond Will that you bestow.**

4. Master MORE, help me acknowledge that even though the attacks may come, the attacks can only hurt me because of my own conditions, the wounds and conditions I have accepted because in the past I made a certain decision.

Master MORE, we will endure,
your discipline that makes us pure.
Master MORE, intentions true,
as we are always one with you.

**Master MORE, your Sacred Heart,
from this we will no more depart,
we are forever in your flow,
of Diamond Will that you bestow.**

5. Master MORE, help me see that if I am willing to resolve those wounds, resolve those decisions, I will become transparent to the attacks, and whatever they direct at me will simply pass right through me.

Master MORE, our vision raised,
the will of God is always praised.
Master MORE, creative will,
raising all life higher still.

**Master MORE, your Sacred Heart,
from this we will no more depart,**

we are forever in your flow,
of Diamond Will that you bestow.

6. Master MORE, help me see that nothing in the four levels
of the material universe can influence my I AM Presence. That
is why my I AM Presence has not been hurt by anything I have
done or experienced on earth.

Master MORE, your peace is power,
the demons of war it will devour.
Master MORE, we serve all life,
our flames consuming war and strife.

Master MORE, your Sacred Heart,
from this we will no more depart,
we are forever in your flow,
of Diamond Will that you bestow.

7. Master MORE, help me see that when I stop identifying
myself with the physical body, I cannot be ultimately hurt by
anything that happens to the body.

Master MORE, we are so free,
eternal bond from you we see.
Master MORE, we find rebirth,
in flow of your eternal mirth.

Master MORE, your Sacred Heart,
from this we will no more depart,
we are forever in your flow,
of Diamond Will that you bestow.

8. Master MORE, help me see that when I accelerate my sense of self to the point where I do not identity myself with the emotions, then I cannot be ultimately hurt by any of the energies that come at me in the emotional realm.

Master MORE, you balance all,
the seven rays upon our call.
Master MORE, forever MORE,
we are the Spirit's open door.

**Master MORE, your Sacred Heart,
from this we will no more depart,
we are forever in your flow,
of Diamond Will that you bestow.**

9. Master MORE, help me see that when I no longer identify myself with my thoughts, I cannot be hurt by the energies that can be directed at me in the mental realm.

Master MORE, your Presence here,
filling up the inner sphere.
Life is now a sacred flow,
God Power we on all bestow.

**Master MORE, your Sacred Heart,
from this we will no more depart,
we are forever in your flow,
of Diamond Will that you bestow.**

Part 6

1. Master MORE, help me see that when I no longer identify myself as a human being that is limited or separate, then I cannot be hurt by those forces who reside at the lower levels of the identity realm.

> Hilarion, on emerald shore,
> we're free from all that's gone before.
> Hilarion, we let all go,
> that keeps us out of sacred flow.

> **Hilarion, with light so green,**
> **we see behind the matter screen,**
> **immaculate our inner sight,**
> **we see the earth is taking flight.**

2. Master MORE, help me see that it is a matter of where I focus my sense of identity. My task as a spiritual student is to raise my sense of identity, so I let go of identification with the body, the emotions, the thoughts, and any lower or separate sense of identity.

> Hilarion, the secret key,
> is wisdom's own reality.
> Hilarion, all life is healed,
> the ego's face no more concealed.

> **Hilarion, with light so green,**
> **we see behind the matter screen,**
> **immaculate our inner sight,**
> **we see the earth is taking flight.**

3. Master MORE, help me come to identify myself correctly as the pure awareness of the Conscious You that is an extension of my I AM Presence, and therefore cannot be hurt or even affected by the lower energies found in the material realm.

Hilarion, your love for life,
helps us surrender inner strife.
Hilarion, your loving words,
thrill our hearts like song of birds.

**Hilarion, with light so green,
we see behind the matter screen,
immaculate our inner sight,
we see the earth is taking flight.**

4. Master MORE, help me see that my Conscious You is not made of the energies of the material realm. When I consciously acknowledge this, I cannot be hurt by anything that is directed at me in the material realm.

Hilarion, invoke the light,
your sacred formulas recite.
Hilarion, your secret tone,
philosopher's most sacred stone.

**Hilarion, with light so green,
we see behind the matter screen,
immaculate our inner sight,
we see the earth is taking flight.**

5. Master MORE, help me see that dark forces can only exist in the material realm and they must use the energies of the

material realm to direct at me. When I am not identified with the material, I become transparent.

> Hilarion, with love you greet,
> us in your temple over Crete.
> Hilarion, your emerald light,
> the third eye sees with Christic sight.

> **Hilarion, with light so green,**
> **we see behind the matter screen,**
> **immaculate our inner sight,**
> **we see the earth is taking flight.**

6. Master MORE, help me see if I have a specific attachment that forms an open door in the shield around my energy field. Help me deal with my attachments at this particular level, the ones that make me the most vulnerable to the attacks of the dark forces.

> Hilarion, you give us fruit,
> of truth that is so absolute.
> Hilarion, all stress decrease,
> as our ambitions we release.

> **Hilarion, with light so green,**
> **we see behind the matter screen,**
> **immaculate our inner sight,**
> **we see the earth is taking flight.**

7. Master MORE, help me see that when I embodied on earth and started to express my creative powers, the dark forces attacked me viciously in order to cause me to decide to shut off my creative powers. They exposed me to such a vicious attack

that I decided to limit my creative powers because I wanted to avoid this negative reaction.

> Hilarion, our chakras clear,
> as we let go of subtlest fear.
> Hilarion, we are sincere,
> as freedom's truth we do revere.

> **Hilarion, with light so green,**
> **we see behind the matter screen,**
> **immaculate our inner sight,**
> **we see the earth is taking flight.**

8. Master MORE, help me see that the very deepest feeling I have about life on earth is this sense of shock, this sense of being traumatized by the viciousness of the rejection of my creative abilities. This is the very deepest wound I have.

> Hilarion, you balance all,
> the seven rays upon our call.
> Hilarion, you keep us true,
> as we remain all one with you.

> **Hilarion, with light so green,**
> **we see behind the matter screen,**
> **immaculate our inner sight,**
> **we see the earth is taking flight.**

9. Master MORE, help me see that every wound I have received since then is simply a variation of this original wound. All of my succeeding wounds were reactions to that original rejection of my creativity.

Hilarion, your Presence here,
filling up the inner sphere.
Life is now a sacred flow,
God Vision we on all bestow.

Hilarion, with light so green,
we see behind the matter screen,
immaculate our inner sight,
we see the earth is taking flight.

Part 7

1. Master MORE, help me see that I cannot accelerate myself beyond my current level, until I have looked at one specific wound that is holding me back right now that is holding me back from taking the next step.

Master MORE, come to the fore,
we will absorb your flame of MORE.
Master MORE, our will so strong,
our power centers cleared by song.

Master MORE, your Sacred Heart,
from this we will no more depart,
we are forever in your flow,
of Diamond Will that you bestow.

2. Master MORE, help me see that the wound is based on a certain decision, and I must see the decision and remake that decision.

Master MORE, your wisdom flows,
as our attunement ever grows.
Master MORE, we have a tie,
that helps us see through Serpent's lie.

Master MORE, your Sacred Heart,
from this we will no more depart,
we are forever in your flow,
of Diamond Will that you bestow.

3. Master MORE, help me see what is the one decision I made, the decision I have reinforced in this lifetime that is right now holding back my creative expression.

Master MORE, your love so pink,
there is no purer love, we think.
Master MORE, you set us free,
from all conditionality.

Master MORE, your Sacred Heart,
from this we will no more depart,
we are forever in your flow,
of Diamond Will that you bestow.

4. Master MORE, help me remember having been exposed to some form of ridicule or the putting down of my creative abilities and deciding not to express those abilities. Help me see how I was exposed to a standard that caused me to shut down my creativity abilities.

Master MORE, we will endure,
your discipline that makes us pure.

Master MORE, intentions true,
as we are always one with you.

**Master MORE, your Sacred Heart,
from this we will no more depart,
we are forever in your flow,
of Diamond Will that you bestow.**

5. Master MORE, help me see my dream of being creative and how I thought: "Oh, I cannot possible do that, or I cannot make a living by being creative, so I have to go into another field where I can make a better living."

Master MORE, our vision raised,
the will of God is always praised.
Master MORE, creative will,
raising all life higher still.

**Master MORE, your Sacred Heart,
from this we will no more depart,
we are forever in your flow,
of Diamond Will that you bestow.**

6. Master MORE, help me get in touch with the decision that psychologically limited my creative expression. I do not need to be an artist in order to express myself creatively. I can bring forth some creative expression in any area of life.

Master MORE, your peace is power,
the demons of war it will devour.
Master MORE, we serve all life,
our flames consuming war and strife.

**Master MORE, your Sacred Heart,
from this we will no more depart,
we are forever in your flow,
of Diamond Will that you bestow.**

7. Master MORE, help me say: "I really did not need to make that decision, but I certainly do not need to uphold it anymore. And thus, I decide that I will set free my creative expression. I am willing to express myself."

Master MORE, we are so free,
eternal bond from you we see.
Master MORE, we find rebirth,
in flow of your eternal mirth.

**Master MORE, your Sacred Heart,
from this we will no more depart,
we are forever in your flow,
of Diamond Will that you bestow.**

8. Master MORE, help me get in touch with my built-in creativity, my love for some form of creative expression. I will dare to dream, dare to express it in some way, dare to be creative.

Master MORE, you balance all,
the seven rays upon our call.
Master MORE, forever MORE,
we are the Spirit's open door.

**Master MORE, your Sacred Heart,
from this we will no more depart,
we are forever in your flow,
of Diamond Will that you bestow.**

9. Master MORE, help me see that there is no standard that can be applied to creative expression, for creative expression brings something new. And how can something new be confined to and pre-defined by a standard?

> Master MORE, your Presence here,
> filling up the inner sphere.
> Life is now a sacred flow,
> God Power we on all bestow.

> **Master MORE, your Sacred Heart,**
> **from this we will no more depart,**
> **we are forever in your flow,**
> **of Diamond Will that you bestow.**

Part 8

1. Master MORE, I am willing to be part of the spiritual, creative elite who will not let the power elite stop my creative expression. This is my calling. This is my potential in this lifetime. If it had not been my potential, I would not have found this teaching.

> O Blessed Mary's Song of Life,
> consuming every form of strife.
> As I attune to sound so fair,
> each cell is healthy, I declare.

> **O Mother Mary, generate,**
> **the song that does accelerate,**

**my mind into a peaceful state,
God's perfect love I radiate.**

2. Master MORE, help me accept that I have a potential to be part of the elite that will bring this planet forward in a giant leap into the Golden Age of Saint Germain. This is why I chose to come into embodiment at this time.

As life's own song I ever hear,
it does consume all sense of fear.
In tune with Mother's symphony,
from all diseases I AM free.

**O Mother Mary, generate,
the song that does accelerate,
my mind into a peaceful state,
God's perfect love I radiate.**

3. Master MORE, help me see that this is why I have been willing to endure being in embodiment many times on this planet over the past 2,000 years: to make sure that Jesus received the fulfillment of setting the pattern for the Piscean age, of people manifesting their Christhood.

In Mother's love I do transcend,
and all my struggles hereby end.
For when with Mother's eye I see,
no imperfection touches me.

**O Mother Mary, generate,
the song that does accelerate,
my mind into a peaceful state,
God's perfect love I radiate.**

4. Master MORE, help me see that I am here to make sure that the Piscean age moves into the Aquarian Age where thousands of people will manifest and express their Christhood on this planet.

I see that healing must begin
by finding Living Christ within.
For as I see with single eye,
each cell the light does amplify.

O Mother Mary, generate,
the song that does accelerate,
my mind into a peaceful state,
God's perfect love I radiate.

5. Master MORE, help me unlock my creative abilities so I can express them in taking this planet into the Golden Age matrix held in the mind of Saint Germain. For we are all one in the efforts to raise this earth into the Golden Age.

In Mother's music I am free,
from memories of a lesser me.
My vision in a perfect state,
that all my cells regenerate.

O Mother Mary, generate,
the song that does accelerate,
my mind into a peaceful state,
God's perfect love I radiate.

6. Master MORE, I am one with you in those efforts, and I want to unlock the conscious awareness that I am part of this endeavor. I want to accelerate my creative expression,

accelerate the healing of the wounds that hold back that creative expression.

> O Mother's Love, sweet melody,
> from imperfections I AM free.
> O Mother Mary, sound of sounds,
> within my heart your love abounds.

> **O Mother Mary, generate,**
> **the song that does accelerate,**
> **my mind into a peaceful state,**
> **God's perfect love I radiate.**

7. Mother Mary, I surrender myself fully to the embrace of the Divine Mother, surrender myself fully into feeling the unconditional love that the Mother of God has for me, when you hold me in your arms.

> Through Mother's beauty so sublime,
> transcending bounds of space and time.
> All cells beyond the mortal tomb,
> as they are whole in Mother's womb.

> **O Mother Mary, generate,**
> **the song that does accelerate,**
> **my mind into a peaceful state,**
> **God's perfect love I radiate.**

8. Mother Mary, I feel the healing radiance penetrating my energy field, immediately targeting the wound that I am dealing with, radiating your healing energies into that wound, so that I can look at it without that intense, emotional pain that

I otherwise feel. I can look at it with your immaculate vision and I can see that it really is just a wound. It is just a decision.

> In resonance with life's own song,
> in life's harmonics I belong.
> The blueprint of my perfect state
> does every cell reconsecrate.

> **O Mother Mary, generate,**
> **the song that does accelerate,**
> **my mind into a peaceful state,**
> **God's perfect love I radiate.**

9. Mother Mary, I made the decision, but I did not *become* the decision. The decision created a spirit, but I did not *become* that spirit. Therefore, I do not have to forever look at the decision through the perception filter of the spirit.

> The tuning fork in every cell
> is now attuned to Mother's bell.
> From curse of death I AM now free,
> I claim my immortality.

> **O Mother Mary, generate,**
> **the song that does accelerate,**
> **my mind into a peaceful state,**
> **God's perfect love I radiate.**

Part 9

1. Mother Mary, help me step outside of the pain – outside of the spirit – and see that my creativity was not rejected by God. It was not even rejected by the fallen beings, for they could not see my creativity. They only sensed that my creative expression disturbed their sense of being in control, and therefore they reacted the only way they can react.

> O Blessed Mary's Song of Life,
> consuming every form of strife.
> As I attune to sound so fair,
> each cell is healthy, I declare.

> **O Mother Mary, generate,**
> **the song that does accelerate,**
> **my mind into a peaceful state,**
> **God's perfect love I radiate.**

2. Mother Mary, help me see that the decision I made was based on me thinking that because I am now in physical embodiment, I have to accept the standard projected at me by the fallen beings. I thought that I had to see my creative expression through the filter of their rejection, instead of seeing my creative expression through the pure awareness that I am.

> As life's own song I ever hear,
> it does consume all sense of fear.
> In tune with Mother's symphony,
> from all diseases I AM free.

O Mother Mary, generate,
the song that does accelerate,
my mind into a peaceful state,
God's perfect love I radiate.

3. Mother Mary, help me see that I came to believe this because I came into embodiment with an intent to change things on earth. I came here with the desire to bring a positive gift, to make a difference, to raise this planet up to a higher state.

In Mother's love I do transcend,
and all my struggles hereby end.
For when with Mother's eye I see,
no imperfection touches me.

O Mother Mary, generate,
the song that does accelerate,
my mind into a peaceful state,
God's perfect love I radiate.

4. Mother Mary, help me see that bringing the planet closer to the Golden Age does not depend on the reaction to my creative efforts that I get from the fallen beings and the death consciousness. I am not here to change specific other lifestreams.

I see that healing must begin
by finding Living Christ within.
For as I see with single eye,
each cell the light does amplify.

O Mother Mary, generate,
the song that does accelerate,

**my mind into a peaceful state,
God's perfect love I radiate.**

5. Mother Mary, help me see that the success of my creative expression depends on only one thing: the expression being expressed. When I have expressed my creativity, I have the success, for the expression itself is a success in itself.

In Mother's music I am free,
from memories of a lesser me.
My vision in a perfect state,
that all my cells regenerate.

**O Mother Mary, generate,
the song that does accelerate,
my mind into a peaceful state,
God's perfect love I radiate.**

6. Mother Mary, help me see that it is not the reaction from other people that matters at all. Help me see the immaculate vision, the immaculate concept that every time I express my creative powers, I am helping increase the light on this planet and this brings it closer to the Golden Age.

O Mother's Love, sweet melody,
from imperfections I AM free.
O Mother Mary, sound of sounds,
within my heart your love abounds.

**O Mother Mary, generate,
the song that does accelerate,
my mind into a peaceful state,
God's perfect love I radiate.**

7. Mother Mary, help me have my major wound healed so I can see that my expression should not be evaluated based on the rejection of those in the fallen mindset. For I have the right to express my creative abilities, despite the fact that there are those who will vehemently reject it and who will viciously attack me.

Through Mother's beauty so sublime,
transcending bounds of space and time.
All cells beyond the mortal tomb,
as they are whole in Mother's womb.

O Mother Mary, generate,
the song that does accelerate,
my mind into a peaceful state,
God's perfect love I radiate.

8. Mother Mary, help me see that I can continue to be who I am, for I have permission from the Mother of God – who is the ultimate authority for earth – to express my divine creativity. I have the permission of the Creator itself – who is the ultimate authority for the world of form – to be who I am and to be the open door for the expression from my I AM Presence.

In resonance with life's own song,
in life's harmonics I belong.
The blueprint of my perfect state
does every cell reconsecrate.

O Mother Mary, generate,
the song that does accelerate,
my mind into a peaceful state,
God's perfect love I radiate.

9. Mother Mary because I have the permission from God and the Mother of God, I do not need permission from the fallen beings. Since I don't need their permission, I will not let their rejection stop me from giving the gift of my creative expression to this planet, the gift that I came here to give, the gift that it is my highest potential to give.

> The tuning fork in every cell
> is now attuned to Mother's bell.
> From curse of death I AM now free,
> I claim my immortality.
>
> **O Mother Mary, generate,**
> **the song that does accelerate,**
> **my mind into a peaceful state,**
> **God's perfect love I radiate.**

Sealing:

In the name of the Divine Mother, I fully accept that the power of these calls is used to set free the Ma-ter light, so it can outpicture the perfect vision of Christ for my own life, for all people and for the planet. In the name I AM THAT I AM, it is done! Amen.

15 | POWER AND PEACE

Master MORE, I AM. I come to give you the next installment in this series of discourses, helping you grasp – not only understand intellectually – but actually experience the vibration and qualities of the First Ray.

Of course, one of the basic qualities of the First Ray is power. But when I say power, many students immediately have associations to the way they have seen power used on earth. So let me give you some comments on what it truly means to be powerful. For when you look at earth, especially when you look at history, you will see that there have been certain powerful people who have been able to exercise great physical power over others. Thus, you might set up a standard, which says that people who had this kind of dictatorial power were very powerful. Yet according to a non-dualistic definition, these people were not powerful at all.

My beloved, if you want a comparison to this, you might go and look at an anthill. You might know that an anthill has a very hierarchical structure. But there is one ant who is at the top of the food chain, or the power chain, so to speak. Some of the other ants are soldiers, but most of them are just workers who have no real will of their own or mind of their own. You might then see that this one ant has great power in the anthill. But you, as a human, could take a shovel and within a few minutes you could completely shatter the anthill to the point where it was almost beyond the ability to be reassembled to its former state.

What is real power?

When you step up to the perspective of an ascended master, you see that even the most so-called powerful people on earth were no more than the top ant in the anthill, and their power is as nothing compared to the power of the Elohim, or even the power seen on certain other planets where you do not have the lower manifestations that you have on earth. There are other planets in the material universe where there are people who have developed the powers of their minds to the point where if they appeared on earth they could, by simply waiving their hand, wipe out even the most powerful army ever assembled on earth. Thus you see, what you call powerful is not truly powerful. It is only powerful within a certain context, for as you should know – by Einstein's famous theory of relativity – everything is relative—at least in the material universe.

Is it really power that you have power over others in the anthill on earth? Nay. As I am fond of saying, if the guru be an ant, heed him. So learn from this that the power you have in the material universe is as nothing compared to the creative power of God.

My point for giving you this instruction is, of course, to help you see that the purpose of the Path of the Seven Veils is to help you unlock your real powers, the creative powers that come from your I AM Presence, and that your Presence is longing to have stream through you as soon as you become an open door for the Presence.

The purpose of the Path of the Seven Veils is not to raise you up to where you become powerful as judged by a human standard, but where you actually become the open door for the power of God. But you see, the power of God wants to express itself on earth, but it will not express itself according to human expectations and standards. That is why – as long as you hold on to such expectations and standards – your mind will be the closed door. You are subconsciously imposing conditions on how the creative power of God can be expressed through you, and this will effectively close the valves in your chakras and prevent the power of God from streaming through. For of course, the power of God, while all-powerful, will not violate the power of free will.

The dream of having special powers

Let me address a topic that I often have to deal with at my retreat, and that is that many spiritual students have a dream of having special powers. This is not necessarily physical powers, but it is certain spiritual or psychic powers. So many dream of being able to show some miraculous feat that would convince anyone about the reality of the spiritual realm or the spiritual path, or the value of a certain teaching, or a certain guru, or even the existence of ascended masters. Many ascended master students dream of a day when we of the ascended masters will appear in some physical, undeniable manifestation, so that everyone will be convinced that we exist—and therefore see that these students, who were among the early people to recognize us, were right all along.

My beloved, most of such dreams and expectations simply come from the ego, and they are what psychologists call "delusions of grandeur" where you dream of suddenly being changed, much as you see in the fairy tales that are called "from rags to riches." You are suddenly changed by some miraculous event, and now you are recognized as being someone special, as being someone superior.

My beloved, this is not how we work with our students. We have no desire to raise our students up to some superior status according to the standards on earth for what is power or what is special ability. We desire our students to be the open doors for true power. But true power does not work the way you expect based on the standards on earth. So I would now like to take you on a little journey where we go and look at the root cause of these dreams, these delusions of grandeur.

Quite frankly, most spiritual and religious people on earth have these delusions of grandeur, as do for that matter many non-spiritual and non-religious people. Look, for example, at the Soviet Union and how many people were caught up in the communist dream of world domination and superiority. Look at Nazism and how many people were caught up in the dream of the superiority of the Aryan race and the German people ruling the world. And look at how many New Age and spiritual people dream of their guru being recognized as the one and only who saved the earth. Or look at how many religious people dream that their religion or their particular sect or church will be recognized as the one. So many Christians think that Jesus will return and validate their particular church as the only true church of Christ. Ah yes, delusions of grandeur, my beloved.

Now, for those who are my students and who have gone through the first several levels of my retreat, then they come to the sixth level where we have both the First Ray and the Sixth Ray in combination. Now, they need to look at these delusions of grandeur, they need to look at where they come from—and where do they come from?

Feeling powerless

Well, I have earlier talked about the fact that when you first come to earth, you are viciously and deliberately rejected by the fallen beings. They do everything they can to put down your creative abilities, to get you to shut off these creative abilities. And what is the net effect of this? Well, when you shut off your creative abilities and submit to the standard, or even the physical power, of the fallen beings, then what do you feel? You feel powerless. You feel that you as an individual cannot withstand the power structures created by the fallen beings.

How could one human being have withstood the power structure of the Soviet Union or Nazi Germany or many of the empires of the past? You see here, almost as a twin to the sense of being rejected, comes the feeling of being powerless. And then, as you go through many embodiments of feeling powerless, you build this desire for some miraculous power from outside yourself to come in and set things right. And this, then, is the root cause of these delusions of grandeur.

This is, of course, what the fallen ones are very clever at tying into, by creating the entire illusion of the external savior. You see this most obviously in Christianity, but Jesus came to give an example of what all have the potential to accomplish when they allow the power of God to stream through them like he did. This is why he said that those who believe on him – or rather that those who dare to demonstrate the level of consciousness that he demonstrated – will do the works that he did. But how many have dared to do so? Nay because they have been tricked and forced by the fallen beings into seeing

Jesus as an exception rather than as an example. And now they are waiting for Jesus to come back and set things right, while not realizing that because of the Law of Free Will, Jesus is sitting up in heaven waiting for them to take up his example and let the power of God stream through them.

The second coming of Christ is not that Jesus comes back to earth in some undeniable manifestation, but that thousands and tens of thousands and millions of people begin to express their individual Christhood. This is the second coming of Christ. It is the second coming of Christ in you, as we have explained in several of our books.

What can you do then to overcome this sense of being powerless? Well, it may seem paradoxical, but there is really only one way to overcome this sense of being powerless, and that is to use a combination of the First and the Sixth Ray to be completely at peace with being powerless. For you see, in the past you have not been at peace with this. You felt that your creative abilities were rejected. You felt that you being powerless in the face of the fallen beings and their obvious abuses of power was not right, was no just. And what was the effect of this? Well, it was that you came to believe in another lie put out there by the false teachers on earth. This is the lie that we expose in much greater detail in our book *[Healing Mother earth]*. Yet what I wish to give you here is just a brief summary.

Nothing has gone wrong

The essence of this lie is that the fallen beings have projected out the illusion that something has gone wrong with God's overall plan for the universe. There is a flaw in God's design. That flaw is that God gave you and all other self-aware beings free will because free will gives you the opportunity to go into the duality consciousness and thereby potentially be lost. They project out that this was a mistake made by God.

In reality, as we have explained, the only way that you could grow in self-awareness is to have completely free will. The only way you can become a God, which is the goal of life, is for you to have free will and for you to exercise it—and to realize that your free will is always free because you can always undo a choice that you made in the past. You can never make a choice that can take away your power to change that choice.

Yet the fallen ones project out there that something has gone wrong, and then they project a dualistic view that what has gone wrong is that there is now an evil force that has the potential to overthrow the power of God in the universe. And this is, as we explained in *Healing Mother Earth,* reinforced by the fact that there are two divisions among the fallen beings: One that uses deception, and is therefore rarely recognized by most people, and one that uses obvious physical power and the abuse of power.

You are now caught between the rock and the hard spot of those who are abusing physical power and those that are the serpentine teachers, the false teachers, who come in with the illusion that something has gone wrong—but that you are here to help set things right. You are here to do what God cannot do for himself, and therefore you must engage in this epic battle of good against evil. And therefore you must seek to get whatever power you can, or you must support the power of certain fallen beings in their quest to set things right.

My beloved, many people in the former Soviet Union were not particularly religious, but they actually came to believe in this "religious" belief that is at the very core of Marxism. Namely the dictatorship of the proletariat, the communist-socialist utopia that is at its core based on the idea that you, who are the powerless masses, must help set things right in the universe by supporting the Communist revolution.

Of course, the Communist revolution was guided by a small elite, and they never intended to give up their power to the proletariat. They always wanted to be a privileged elite, as you indeed saw them be in the Soviet Union where they had power to kill as many people as threatened their position. And thereby, actually, through the killing of those people they could use the energies – the life energies spilled in the torture and the killing – to reinforce their own power—and the demons behind them who gave them their outer power.

The epic struggle

My point here is simply this: There are many variants of this epic battle, this epic struggle. You find them in most religions. You find them in many New Age teachings. You even find them in some of the previous teachings we have given within the last century where we had to give teachings designed to help people rise from a certain level of consciousness to the next level up. And therefore, we could not directly challenge the epic mindset, for people would not have been able to handle it at that level of consciousness.

Yet, when you have gone through the first five levels of my retreat, you are ready to use your reasoning abilities to take a look at the epic battle and the epic mindset behind it. Of course, this will happen under the guidance of myself but also under the guidance of Nada where you will either go to her retreat over Saudi Arabia or she will come to my retreat. And we will guide the students who are ready to take a look at this epic mindset. What you first of all need to come to is the understanding, as I started out talking about, of the difference between true power and spiritual power. Now, you may look at Jesus, for example, and you will see that he had, certainly, clearly super-human – as human is currently defined – powers. Clearly, if he had these powers, he could have avoided being arrested. He could have, at any time, broken out of prison or called angels to come and rescue him, like he even said while hanging on the cross that he could command the Father to send him angels to set him free.

Why did he not use these powers? Why did he allow himself to be persecuted and crucified? Because the power of God is not expressing itself in a vacuum. And as I have said before, the power of God does not even have the goal to manifest certain conditions on earth. The power of God respects a simple fact: Planet earth is a schoolroom.

The ultimate law on earth is the Law of Free Will. The power of God will not come into earth and change everything in human society according to even the vision for the Golden Age. The power of God will not force the Golden Age upon humankind, for humankind must co-create the Golden Age by using their co-creative powers. The purpose is not to manifest the Golden Age with a certain outer, physical design. The purpose is to help people on earth raise their consciousness. That is the greater purpose.

You see it in Jesus and many others, who have attained spiritual mastery, how they will bow to the Law of Free Will and do whatever is needed – whatever is appropriate in the situation – in order to help people raise their consciousness, not to some ultimate degree in one giant leap but from one level to the next.

We have said before that Jesus could only give teachings 2,000 years ago that were appropriate for the level of consciousness that most people had at the time. He did not come to give forth an ultimate teaching, and he did not give forth an ultimate teaching. Neither did the Buddha 2,500 years ago. Neither are we today trying to set forth an ultimate teaching. We are always setting forth a teaching that will help people who are ready for it rise from one level to the next, but hopefully also set them on a path that they can continue where they have the momentum and knowledge to carry them all the way through to the 144th level.

Letting free will outplay itself

When you come to this point of receiving these Sixth Ray instructions on the First Ray, you must first come to the point where you learn to see the grander vision of how free will must be allowed to outplay itself. It may be that you, as a spiritual student, can see that certain things on earth are clearly not living up to their highest potential. They are causing much suffering, they are causing much injustice. There is great abuse of power. But you see, this does not mean that it is right for you, as a spiritual student, to engage in some epic struggle against those whom you label as the cause of the injustice.

If you want a visible illustration of this, as I am giving this dictation, there has, in the last couple of years, been uprisings in certain Arab countries. It has been called the Arab Spring. Yet as you can see in both Egypt, Tunisia, Libya and now Syria, overthrowing a dictator does not necessarily guarantee democracy, progress and peace. And the reason is simple. What can bring democracy and peace is only a raising of the collective consciousness where they begin to transcend the epic mindset.

I am not saying that the epic mindset cannot exist in a democratic nation, as is certainly proven by the United States in great abundance. But what I am saying is that you need to start rising out of the epic mindset before a democracy can be manifest in a nation, at least at a functioning level. And this obviously has not happened in the Arab nations. The equation is relatively simple: When you violently overthrow a dictator, it is demonstrated that the people have not started rising out of the epic mindset. And that is why this act of violence will set the stage for further conflict between different groups of people within that nation.

Do you not see this even in the United States? The United States has a Constitution that is in many ways sponsored by the ascended masters and based on true, non-dualistic ideas. Nevertheless, the American nation was born in a bloody revolution, in a violent fight against the British Empire, and this set the stage for the Civil War, which almost tore the American nation apart. It was only because certain leaders and many among the people were willing to rise beyond a certain level of the epic mindset that the Union was preserved and that the American nation survived as one nation under God.

An in-depth study of history

What Nada and I do is we take students and we use our ability to project the Akashic records upon a screen, and we show them various periods of history where we go into an in-depth study, not only of the events that took place but also of the deeper causes. We are able to show how the fallen angels and the false teachers worked in many of these situations. How the two polarities of those who use obvious physical force and those who use deception played into a situation and set up situations where it really did not matter which outer faction won because in any event the people were suppressed by a power elite of the fallen beings. So it was really, in many cases, just a dualistic fight between two factions of fallen beings and, in any event, the fallen beings ended up being in control, as you can clearly see in the French Revolution, the Bolshevik Revolution, and many other examples.

When students see this, they can begin to realize, first of all that they do not desire to have the kind of physical power where they could go in and instantly change the situation. They realize that if they were to go into a situation like that and exercise spiritual power, their spiritual powers would actually support – and thereby empower – a faction of fallen beings. This would, of course, be a grave misuse and misqualification of their spiritual powers, and of course no student who has come to this point in my retreat desires to use spiritual power in this way, to support the fallen beings who are working against God's purpose.

The students can then realize that it would actually be very dangerous for them if they had great spiritual power but still had the same vision that they have right now. Because if they did have the power, their lack of vision – their limited vision – would cause them to abuse that power, and thereby actually give a tremendous amount of spiritual energy to the fallen beings—which would allow them to tighten the stranglehold they have on the people on earth.

When students see this, they come to realize that what they truly need to work on is a higher vision. And then Nada is very adept at explaining to students and showing them how the key to having a higher vision, the key to stepping up to giving, actually, true Christ-like service, is to first attain inner peace. And this is attained by looking at the Law of Free Will and how the Law of Free Will outplays itself and must be allowed to outplay itself.

For you may look at earth at any time in history, even today – and you may go to certain areas of the earth today – and you can see that the general population is very much oppressed by a small elite. They are kept at a level of poverty, they have no justice in the courts, they are exposed to a military dictatorship that can do anything they want to the people and get away with it, or other abuses of power. You may have a desire to set the people free from this. You may have a desire to wipe out the power elite who is oppressing the people.

The essential lesson on the spiritual path

But when you look deeper, you see that this can only happen because the people themselves have not been willing to step up in consciousness. They have not been willing to look at their sense of being powerless and begin to recognize one simple fact: Being powerless in a physical sense has nothing whatsoever to do with your spiritual powers, for your spiritual powers come from within. You do not need the permission of an earthly authority in order to go within, find the kingdom that Jesus said is within you, and begin to be the open door for the expressions of the powers from that kingdom.

No authority here on earth can stop you from doing this. This is the *the* essential lesson to learn on the spiritual path. And this goes as well for the people you see being oppressed as for you, yourself. You do not need the permission of any authority on earth in order to open your mind and allow the powers from your I AM Presence to stream through you. This is the lesson that Nada and I seek to help you fully grasp and begin to internalize.

Then, you can see that even if people are oppressed by the most evil dictator, it is still because of one simple thing: The Law of Free Will mandates that if people will not learn from within, they must learn from without. If they will not learn by being given guidance from the ascended masters, they must learn from the School of Hard Knocks. And in the School of Hard Knocks it is sometimes so that the question of when people will turn around is simply a question of how hard do the knocks have to become before people have had enough and are willing to look at themselves and say: "Is there something that I can do to change this situation? Is there something that I can change in myself, instead of thinking that it is always outside of me that the change must happen?"

The outplaying of free will

Why are you a spiritual student? Why are you attending my retreat? Why are you reading this or listening to this teaching? Because you have long ago made the decision that you are willing to look at something in yourself. And that is why Nada and I can then build on this willingness and help you see that you need to come to the point where you look at planet earth, you look at everything that is happening, you look at everything that has been happening in history and you see that it is all the outplaying of free will.

Nothing can be done to people that is not a reflection of their state of consciousness. And when the people of a certain nation raise their state of consciousness above a certain level, then the dictatorial government of that nation must give way to a higher form of government.

Instead of one power elite giving way to another power elite – that is even more tyrannical than the first one – there will be a shift, so that a higher form of government will manifest. Not necessarily an ideal form of government in the beginning, but a higher form of government. And then, as the people raise their consciousness even more, well, a higher form of government can come in, and the spiral will continue towards the Golden Age ideal. When you see this, you can look at the earth and you can say to yourself: "I see how ingenious is God's design for the outplaying of free will." And then, you can look at the illusion of the epic mindset, the illusion that something is fundamentally flawed in God's design, and you can say: "I no longer believe in you. I see the unreality behind you." And then, you can be at peace with the way things are.

Then, you can go even deeper, for now you can take a look at your sense of feeling so rejected when the fallen beings put down your creative efforts when you first came into embodiment. You can then realize that this was in many ways an unavoidable situation, given the fact that the fallen beings have such control on planet earth and given the fact that you were in a relatively immature state of consciousness at the time.

We need not here go into the deeper aspects of why you descended and why many of you descended before you were actually ready to deal with the fallen beings, for that has been described in greater detail in Maitreya's book *[Master Keys to Spiritual Freedom]*. But my point here is this: When you come to see reality, you see that it was simply an inevitable consequence. It was, so to speak, the cost of doing business that you felt so rejected when you first came to earth.

Then you can go a little bit deeper, and you can see that you actually came here with the desire to change things according to a specific vision that you have. And then you can begin, especially under the guidance of Nada, to question that vision. For she has such a momentum on the Sixth Ray of service that she is an expert at helping you see the difference between true service and false service, between service that springs from complete inner peace and service that springs from a lack of peace, namely the sense that something is wrong and must be corrected.

Do not limit your I AM Presence

Have I not earlier in these discourses talked about the standard of the fallen beings and how you cannot apply a standard to creativity? Can you not see, then that when you come with the epic mindset, when you want to change something according to a pre-conceived vision, you cannot be an open door for the creative powers of your I AM Presence. Because you are superimposing a vision upon what your I AM Presence could or should express through you, and that vision will be based on the limited perspective you have by being in embodiment.

That is when you can realize that it is absolutely inevitable that when you come into embodiment on a dense planet like earth, you will start out with a limited perspective. And that is why you could say that it is simply inevitable that the process of learning to express your co-creative abilities on a planet like this is actually a two-fold process. On the one hand you must learn about the creative energies and characteristics of the seven rays and you must learn how to express them, but on the other hand the way to actually learn to express the seven rays in their creative form is to overcome the false concepts created by the perversions of the seven rays by the fallen beings on earth.

In a sense, on a planet like earth you are, as we have said before, not facing the ideal scenario. You are facing a scenario where you will start out with a limited vision and you must then purify that vision through several steps and layers, until you become that fully open door at the 96th level of consciousness. Where you have given up certain aspects of the fallen consciousness, and the standard for creativity that they have imposed through the epic mindset and the underlying belief that there is a flaw in God's design. You cannot give true service until you are completely at peace. And of course we do not – Nada and I – expect that you can be completely at peace at the sixth level of my retreat. But we do expect that we can set a foundation where you at least begin to grasp the importance of overcoming the epic mindset and being at peace and giving service from a state of peace rather than a state of fear, a state of anger, a state of hatred, a state of agitation.

A critical turning point on the path

My beloved, we have seen people find ascended master teachings and throw themselves into giving decrees with a feeling of hatred against the fallen angels or some particular manifestation of fallen angels on earth—as they see it. And thereby, their decrees can actually to some degree misqualify light. This, of course, is not something we seek to see continue, for it makes karma for the students and, in a sense, it makes karma for us, although we can limit that karma by limiting the power streaming through the decrees that people give with an impure mindset.

You will see, of course that this is a rather important level of my retreat instruction. For those students who cannot or who will not begin to question the epic mindset simply cannot rise beyond this level in my retreat. Some students actually come to such a point that they go back into the School of Hard Knocks because they have to once again experience what it is like to fight someone else based on the epic mindset. They have not had enough of that experience to truly recognize their desire to grow beyond this epic struggle.

Perhaps you are beginning to realize a simple truth: You can, of course, leave the Path of the Seven Veils at any point up until the 96th level, but especially the first seven levels in my retreat are the most critical. This is where, at each level, students can actually decide to leave the path and go back into the School of Hard Knocks.

I have to say that the sixth level is where many students – well, not most students, but certainly a considerable number – actually decide – by not being willing to question the epic mindset – that they will go back into the School of Hard Knocks and again fight against some epic injustice. Then, hopefully, in one or several lifetimes they can come back to my retreat. But then, when they do come back, they often have considerable karma that they need to work through, before they can again open their minds to receiving our instruction.

Students trapped in power plays

There are students who come to my retreat and who have a long momentum on actually attaining powerful positions on earth. There are not many. Most students who are open to the spiritual path have many lifetimes ago decided not to engage in power plays on earth. And therefore, they have often accepted a position as being the downtrodden. Or perhaps they have been in spiritual orders and withdrawn from society. But there are certainly those who – as I did myself in several embodiments – have engaged in the life of power on earth. And therefore, almost inevitably, as I did myself, have become pulled into these power struggles.

These students, of course, present a different challenge because they now need to learn the same lesson, but they need to learn it without coming to the point of condemning themselves for having engaged in these power struggles and in many cases having abused power. I mentioned earlier that in my embodiment as Thomas More, I had abused power and actually had people executed for what I considered to be blasphemy. I can assure you that the most difficult challenge that I faced after that embodiment was to acknowledge that this was an abuse of power without feeling so down upon myself that it caused me to give up.

I could acknowledge this because, as you will see in that same embodiment, I also refused to use power against a king but allowed the king to persecute and execute me. Thereby, I showed that I had started the process of questioning the abuse of power. Yet it was still a great challenge for me to question this in myself. For it is, of course, always easier to see how others have abused power than to see how you yourself have abused power.

Again, Nada and I have devised special tools for working with students who in recent embodiments have been in powerful positions, so that we can help them see the universal lesson that it is not by exercising power in the epic struggle that you actually further the cause of the ascended masters in the raising of the collective consciousness and the brining in of the Golden Age.

This can be a very hard lesson to learn, but again, when students come to this point, we certainly have tools and the experience to help most students go through this. But there are a few that come and they not only have a momentum on having abused power, perhaps even in this lifetime, but they also have such pride that they are not willing to admit that they have been wrong. For of course you do see on earth that these two characteristics often go hand in hand where those who have the most power have fallen prey to another illusion, projected by the fallen beings that in order to maintain a position of power you have to always be right.

Overcoming this mindset is a special challenge, a special initiation, and this is one of the reasons why Jesus allowed himself to be persecuted and humiliated by the power elite.

This was not just to bring their judgment; it was actually so that Jesus could demonstrate – both to himself and his spiritual teachers – that he had let go of this pride. Thus, I can assure you that being willing to allow the fallen angels, the fallen beings in embodiment, to put you down and ridicule and humiliate you, and say all manner of things falsely against you for Christ's sake, is indeed part of the initiation.

If you see that you have experienced this kind of ridicule and persecution from people in this lifetime, be of good cheer. For when you can learn to look at this and be non-attached – and simply realize that this is the outplaying of the Law of Free Will – then you have made a major step forward on your personal path. You have been willing to let the Law of Free Will outplay itself whereby those who are ridiculing you have received an opportunity to see why they want to ridicule others and thereby begin to question their own state of consciousness. But you have also received an opportunity to demonstrate that you are willing to be ridiculed, for you are willing to step up to a higher state of consciousness where you do not take it seriously and you do not let other people's ridicule stop you from fulfilling your divine plan and expressing your creative energies.

This is an extremely important initiation, and therefore Nada and I will help you see that you can learn to meet this ridicule from the world with non-attachment. You can actually learn to de-personalize your life. But here I am starting to get ahead of myself, for this will be my next level of instruction. For how can you attain freedom, if you take everything that happens to you personally? It cannot be done. And that is where Saint Germain and I have devised certain methods for helping people rise to the next level. And thus, I shall return to give you this level of instruction.

16 | INVOKING POWER AND PEACE

In the name I AM THAT I AM, Jesus Christ, I call to my I AM Presence to flow through the I Will Be Presence that I AM and give this invocation with full power. I call to beloved Elohim Hercules and Amazonia and Peace and Aloha, Archangel Michael and Faith and Archangel Uriel and Aurora, Master MORE and Nada to help me overcome the wound that disturbs my inner peace. Help me see and surrender all patterns that block my oneness with Master MORE and my oneness with my I AM Presence, including ...

[Make personal calls]

Part 1

1. Master MORE, help me see that what we on earth call powerful is only powerful within a certain context, for everything is relative—at least in the material universe.

> O Hercules Blue, we're one with your will,
> all space in our beings with Blue Flame you fill,
> a beacon that radiates light to the earth,
> bringing about our planet's rebirth.

> **O Hercules Blue, all life you defend,**
> **giving us power to always transcend,**
> **in you the expansion of self has no end,**
> **as we in God's infinite spirals ascend.**

2. Master MORE, help me see that the purpose of the path is to help me unlock my real powers, the creative powers that come from my I AM Presence. My Presence is longing to have these powers stream through me as soon as I become an open door.

> O Hercules Blue, your wisdom so great,
> within us a sense of knowing create,
> a new frame of reference we suddenly gain,
> for going beyond duality's pain.

> **O Hercules Blue, all life you defend,**
> **giving us power to always transcend,**
> **in you the expansion of self has no end,**
> **as we in God's infinite spirals ascend.**

3. Master MORE, help me see that the purpose of the path is *not* to raise me up to where I become powerful as judged by a human standard, but where I become the open door for the power of God.

O Hercules Blue, we lovingly raise,
our voices in giving God infinite praise,
in feeling your flame, so clearly we see,
transcending the self is the true alchemy.

O Hercules Blue, all life you defend,
giving us power to always transcend,
in you the expansion of self has no end,
as we in God's infinite spirals ascend.

4. Master MORE, help me see that the power of God wants to express itself on earth, but it will not express itself according to human expectations and standards.

O Hercules Blue, all life now you heal,
enveloping all in your Blue-flame Seal,
we're grateful for playing a personal part,
In God's infinitely intricate work of art.

O Hercules Blue, all life you defend,
giving us power to always transcend,
in you the expansion of self has no end,
as we in God's infinite spirals ascend.

5. Master MORE, help me see that as long as I hold on to such expectations and standards, my mind will be a closed door.

O Hercules Blue, your Temple of Light,
revealed to us all through our inner sight,
your power allows us to forge on until,
we pierce every veil and climb every hill.

O Hercules Blue, all life you defend,
giving us power to always transcend,
in you the expansion of self has no end,
as we in God's infinite spirals ascend.

6. Master MORE, help me see if I am subconsciously imposing conditions on how the creative power of God can be expressed through me, and how this closes the valves in my chakras.

O Hercules Blue, I pledge now my life,
in helping this planet transcend human strife,
duality's lies are pierced by your light,
restoring the fullness of our inner sight.

O Hercules Blue, all life you defend,
giving us power to always transcend,
in you the expansion of self has no end,
as we in God's infinite spirals ascend.

7. Master MORE, help me see if I have a dream of having special powers, being able to show some miraculous feat that would convince anyone about the reality of the spiritual realm.

O Hercules Blue, we set all life free,
from the subtlest lies of duality,
the prince of this world no more has a bond,
for with you we go completely beyond.

O Hercules Blue, all life you defend,
giving us power to always transcend,
in you the expansion of self has no end,
as we in God's infinite spirals ascend.

8. Master MORE, help me see that most of such dreams and expectations come from the ego, and they are "delusions of grandeur" where I dream of suddenly being changed by some miraculous event, and now I am recognized as being someone special.

O Hercules Blue, in oneness with thee,
we open our hearts to your reality,
your electric-blue fire within us reveal,
our innermost longing for all that is real.

O Hercules Blue, all life you defend,
giving us power to always transcend,
in you the expansion of self has no end,
as we in God's infinite spirals ascend.

9. Master MORE, help me see that you have no desire to raise your students up to some superior status according to the standards on earth, for you desire your students to be the open doors for true power.

O Hercules Blue, you fill every space,
with infinite Power and infinite Grace,
you embody the key to creativity,
the will to transcend into Infinity.

O Hercules Blue, all life you defend,
giving us power to always transcend,

**in you the expansion of self has no end,
as we in God's infinite spirals ascend.**

Part 2

1. Master MORE, help me see how I was attacked by the fallen beings, shut off my creative abilities, submitted to the fallen beings and felt powerless. I felt that I could not withstand the power structures created by the fallen beings.

> O Elohim Peace, in Unity's Flame,
> there is no more room for duality's game,
> we know that all form is from the same source,
> empowering us to plot a new course.

> **O Elohim Peace, through your tranquility,
> we are free from the chaos of duality,
> in oneness with God a new identity,
> we are raising the earth into Infinity.**

2. Master MORE, help me see that as I go through many embodiments of feeling powerless, I build the desire for some miraculous power from outside myself to come in and set things right. This is the root cause of delusions of grandeur.

> O Elohim Peace, the bell now you ring,
> causing all atoms to vibrate and sing,
> we give up the sense of a separate "me,"
> we're crossing Samsara's turbulent sea.

**O Elohim Peace, through your tranquility,
we are free from the chaos of duality,
in oneness with God a new identity,
we are raising the earth into Infinity.**

3. Master MORE, help me see that the second coming of Christ is not that Jesus comes back to earth in some undeniable manifestation, but that tens of thousands of people begin to express their individual Christhood.

O Elohim Peace, you help us to know,
that Jesus has come your Flame to bestow,
upon all who are ready to give up the strife,
by following Christ into infinite life.

**O Elohim Peace, through your tranquility,
we are free from the chaos of duality,
in oneness with God a new identity,
we are raising the earth into Infinity.**

4. Master MORE, help me see that the way to overcome this sense of being powerless is to use a combination of the First and the Sixth Ray to be completely at peace with being powerless.

O Elohim Peace, through your eyes we see,
that only in oneness will we ever be free,
we now see that there is no separate thing,
to the ego-based self we no longer cling.

**O Elohim Peace, through your tranquility,
we are free from the chaos of duality,**

**in oneness with God a new identity,
we are raising the earth into Infinity.**

5. Master MORE, help me see that as a result of feeling powerless in the face of the fallen beings and their obvious abuses of power, I came to accept the lie of the fallen beings, namely that something has gone wrong with God's overall plan for the universe.

O Elohim Peace, you show us the way,
for clearing the mind from duality's fray,
you pierce the illusions of both time and space,
separation consumed by your Infinite Grace.

**O Elohim Peace, through your tranquility,
we are free from the chaos of duality,
in oneness with God a new identity,
we are raising the earth into Infinity.**

6. Master MORE, help me see how the fallen beings claim there is a flaw in God's design, namely that God gave us free will whereby we can go into the duality consciousness and potentially be lost.

O Elohim Peace, what beauty your name,
consuming within us duality's shame,
the earth is set free from burden of fear,
accepting your peace is now manifest here.

**O Elohim Peace, through your tranquility,
we are free from the chaos of duality,
in oneness with God a new identity,
we are raising the earth into Infinity.**

7. Master MORE, help me see that in reality, the only way we could grow in self-awareness is to have completely free will. The only way we can become a God, which is the goal of life, is for us to have free will and for us to exercise it.

O Elohim Peace, with Christ at our side,
no force of duality can evermore hide,
It was through the vibration of your Golden Flame,
that Christ the illusion of death overcame.

**O Elohim Peace, through your tranquility,
we are free from the chaos of duality,
in oneness with God a new identity,
we are raising the earth into Infinity.**

8. Master MORE, help me see that free will is always free because I can always undo a choice that I made in the past. I can never make a choice that can take away my power to change that choice.

O Elohim Peace, you bring now to earth,
the unstoppable flame of Cosmic Rebirth,
we give up the sense that something is "mine,"
allowing your Light through our beings to shine.

**O Elohim Peace, through your tranquility,
we are free from the chaos of duality,
in oneness with God a new identity,
we are raising the earth into Infinity.**

9. Master MORE, help me see that the fallen beings project that something has gone wrong, and then they project the dualistic

view that what has gone wrong is that there is now an evil force
that has the potential to overthrow the power of God.

O Elohim Peace, as peace now we feel,
all records of war you totally heal,
the earth is now free from forces of war,
restoring her purity known from before.

O Elohim Peace, through your tranquility,
we are free from the chaos of duality,
in oneness with God a new identity,
we are raising the earth into Infinity.

Part 3

1. Master MORE, help me see that there are two divisions
among the fallen beings: One that uses deception and one that
uses physical power and the abuse of power.

Michael Archangel, in your flame so blue,
there is no more night, there is only you.
In oneness with you, we're filled with your light,
what glorious wonder, revealed to our sight.

Michael Archangel, your Knowing so strong,
Michael Archangel, oh sweep us along.
Michael Archangel, we're singing your song,
Michael Archangel, with you we belong.

2. Master MORE, help me see that the serpentine teachers
spread the illusion that something has gone wrong—but that

we are here to help set things right. We are here to do what God cannot do for himself, and therefore we must engage in this epic battle of good against evil.

Michael Archangel, protection you give,
within your blue shield, we ever shall live.
Sealed from all creatures, roaming the night,
we remain in your sphere, of electric blue light.

Michael Archangel, your Knowing so strong,
Michael Archangel, oh sweep us along.
Michael Archangel, we're singing your song,
Michael Archangel, with you we belong.

3. Master MORE, help me see that the fallen beings project that we must seek to get whatever power we can, or we must support the power of certain fallen beings in their quest to set things right.

Michael Archangel, what power you bring,
as millions of angels, praises will sing.
Consuming the demons, of doubt and of fear,
we know that your Presence, will always be near.

Michael Archangel, your Knowing so strong,
Michael Archangel, oh sweep us along.
Michael Archangel, we're singing your song,
Michael Archangel, with you we belong.

4. Master MORE and Nada, help me use my reasoning abilities to take a look at the epic battle and the epic mindset behind it.

Michael Archangel, God's will is your love,
you bring to us all, God's light from Above.
God's will is to see, all life taking flight,
transcendence of self, our most sacred right.

Michael Archangel, your Knowing so strong,
Michael Archangel, oh sweep us along.
Michael Archangel, we're singing your song,
Michael Archangel, with you we belong.

5. Master MORE, help me see that the power of God does
not have the goal to manifest certain conditions on earth.
The power of God respects a simple fact: Planet earth is a
schoolroom.

Michael Archangel, you are the best friend,
from all worldly dangers you do us defend,
the devil no match for your power of light,
and therefore our souls can freely take flight.

Michael Archangel, your Knowing so strong,
Michael Archangel, oh sweep us along.
Michael Archangel, we're singing your song,
Michael Archangel, with you we belong.

6. Master MORE, help me see that the ultimate law on earth
is the Law of Free Will. The power of God will not change
everything in human society according to even the vision for
the Golden Age.

Michael Archangel, as children we play,
we're bringing the earth into a new day,

we raise it from all of the patterns so old,
our planet's life story is by us retold.

Michael Archangel, your Knowing so strong,
Michael Archangel, oh sweep us along.
Michael Archangel, we're singing your song,
Michael Archangel, with you we belong.

7. Master MORE, help me see that the power of God will not force the Golden Age upon humankind, for humankind must co-create the Golden Age by using our co-creative powers. The purpose is not to manifest the Golden Age with a certain outer, physical design. The purpose is to help people on earth raise their consciousness.

Michael Archangel, God's power you show,
that you are invincible, this we do know,
you are undivided and thus can withstand,
anything coming from serpentine band.

Michael Archangel, your Knowing so strong,
Michael Archangel, oh sweep us along.
Michael Archangel, we're singing your song,
Michael Archangel, with you we belong.

8. Master MORE, help me see the grander vision of how free will must be allowed to outplay itself. Certain things on earth are not living up to their highest potential, but this does not mean that it is right for me to engage in some epic struggle against those whom I label as the cause of the injustice.

Michael Archangel, come raise now the earth,
giving her thus a complete rebirth,

336 The Mystical Initiations of Power

collective the mind that we do now raise,
for this we do give our infinite praise.

Michael Archangel, your Knowing so strong,
Michael Archangel, oh sweep us along.
Michael Archangel, we're singing your song,
Michael Archangel, with you we belong.

9. Master MORE, help me see that I do not desire to have
the kind of physical power where I could go in and instantly
change a situation. I see that this would actually support a faction of fallen beings.

Michael Archangel, the earth is now new,
covered in Blue-flame as the morning dew,
our planet now sparkles throughout all of space,
as we are receiving your infinite Grace.

Michael Archangel, your Knowing so strong,
Michael Archangel, oh sweep us along.
Michael Archangel, we're singing your song,
Michael Archangel, with you we belong.

Part 4

1. Master MORE, help me see that I do not desire to use spiritual power in a way that supports the fallen beings who are
working against God's purpose.

Uriel Archangel, immense is the power,
of angels of peace, all war to devour.

The demons of war, no match for your light,
consuming them all, with radiance so bright.

Uriel Archangel, use your great sword,
Uriel Archangel, consume all discord,
Uriel Archangel, we're of one accord,
Uriel Archangel, we walk with the Lord.

2. Master MORE, help me see that it would be very dangerous for me if I had great spiritual power but still had the same
vision that I have right now.

Uriel Archangel, intense is the sound,
when millions of angels, their voices compound.
They build a crescendo, piercing the night,
life's glorious oneness revealed to our sight.

Uriel Archangel, use your great sword,
Uriel Archangel, consume all discord,
Uriel Archangel, we're of one accord,
Uriel Archangel, we walk with the Lord.

3. Master MORE, help me see that if I did have the power,
my limited vision would cause me to abuse that power, and
thereby actually give a tremendous amount of spiritual energy
to the fallen beings—which would allow them to tighten the
stranglehold they have on people.

Uriel Archangel, from out the Great Throne,
your millions of trumpets, sound the One Tone.
Consuming all discord with your harmony,
the sound of all sounds will set all life free.

Uriel Archangel, use your great sword,
Uriel Archangel, consume all discord,
Uriel Archangel, we're of one accord,
Uriel Archangel, we walk with the Lord.

4. Master MORE, help me see that what I truly need to work on is a higher vision. Nada, show me how the key to having a higher vision is to first attain inner peace. And this is attained by looking at the Law of Free Will and how it must be allowed to outplay itself.

Uriel Archangel, all war is now done,
for you bring a message, from heart of the One.
The hearts of all men, now singing in peace,
the spirals of love, forever increase.

Uriel Archangel, use your great sword,
Uriel Archangel, consume all discord,
Uriel Archangel, we're of one accord,
Uriel Archangel, we walk with the Lord.

5. Master MORE, help me see that being powerless in a physical sense has nothing to do with my spiritual powers, for my spiritual powers come from within.

Uriel Archangel, your infinite peace,
from all warring beings our planet release,
war is a prison from which we are free,
embracing the peace of true unity.

Uriel Archangel, use your great sword,
Uriel Archangel, consume all discord,

Uriel Archangel, we're of one accord,
Uriel Archangel, we walk with the Lord.

6. Master MORE, help me see that I do not need the permission of an earthly authority in order to go within, find the
kingdom that Jesus said is within me, and begin to be the open
door for the expressions of the powers from that kingdom.

Uriel Archangel, we send forth the call,
reveal now the oneness that unifies all,
help us the vision of peace now to see,
so we from all conflicts and struggles are free.

Uriel Archangel, use your great sword,
Uriel Archangel, consume all discord,
Uriel Archangel, we're of one accord,
Uriel Archangel, we walk with the Lord.

7. Master MORE, help me see that no authority on earth can
stop me from doing this. This is *the* essential lesson to learn on
the spiritual path.

Uriel Archangel, in service to life,
you give us release from struggle and strife,
forgetting the self is truly the key,
to living a life in true harmony.

Uriel Archangel, use your great sword,
Uriel Archangel, consume all discord,
Uriel Archangel, we're of one accord,
Uriel Archangel, we walk with the Lord.

8. Master MORE, help me see that I do not need the permission of any authority on earth in order to open my mind and allow the powers from my I AM Presence to stream through me. Nada, help me fully grasp and internalize this lesson.

Uriel Archangel, the earth now you raise,
out of duality's death-bringing haze,
we call now upon your great Flame of Peace,
commanding that all petty squabbles do cease.

Uriel Archangel, use your great sword,
Uriel Archangel, consume all discord,
Uriel Archangel, we're of one accord,
Uriel Archangel, we walk with the Lord.

9. Master MORE, help me see that even if people are oppressed by the most evil dictator, it is because the Law of Free Will mandates that if people will not learn through guidance from the ascended masters, they must learn from the School of Hard Knocks.

Uriel Archangel, as peace is the norm,
to your higher vision the earth does conform,
as people have found your peace from within,
a Golden Age is the prize that we win.

Uriel Archangel, use your great sword,
Uriel Archangel, consume all discord,
Uriel Archangel, we're of one accord,
Uriel Archangel, we walk with the Lord.

Part 5

1. Master MORE, help me see that I have long ago made the decision that I am willing to look at something in myself.

Master MORE, come to the fore,
we will absorb your flame of MORE.
Master MORE, our will so strong,
our power centers cleared by song.

Master MORE, your Sacred Heart,
from this we will no more depart,
we are forever in your flow,
of Diamond Will that you bestow.

2. Master MORE, help me look at planet earth, look at everything that is happening, look at everything that has been happening in history and see that it is all the outplaying of free will.

Master MORE, your wisdom flows,
as our attunement ever grows.
Master MORE, we have a tie,
that helps us see through Serpent's lie.

Master MORE, your Sacred Heart,
from this we will no more depart,
we are forever in your flow,
of Diamond Will that you bestow.

3. Master MORE, help me see that nothing can be done to people that is not a reflection of their state of consciousness.

Master MORE, your love so pink,
there is no purer love, we think.
Master MORE, you set us free,
from all conditionality.

**Master MORE, your Sacred Heart,
from this we will no more depart,
we are forever in your flow,
of Diamond Will that you bestow.**

4. Master MORE, help me look at the earth and say: "I see how ingenious is God's design for the outplaying of free will."

Master MORE, we will endure,
your discipline that makes us pure.
Master MORE, intentions true,
as we are always one with you.

**Master MORE, your Sacred Heart,
from this we will no more depart,
we are forever in your flow,
of Diamond Will that you bestow.**

5. Master MORE, help me look at the illusion of the epic mindset, the illusion that something is fundamentally flawed in God's design, and say: "I no longer believe in you. I see the unreality behind you." And then, I can be at peace with the way things are.

Master MORE, our vision raised,
the will of God is always praised.
Master MORE, creative will,
raising all life higher still.

Master MORE, your Sacred Heart,
from this we will no more depart,
we are forever in your flow,
of Diamond Will that you bestow.

6. Master MORE, help me look at my sense of feeling so rejected when the fallen beings put down my creative efforts. Help me realize that this was an unavoidable situation, given the fact that the fallen beings have such control on planet earth and given the fact that I was in a relatively immature state of consciousness.

Master MORE, your peace is power,
the demons of war it will devour.
Master MORE, we serve all life,
our flames consuming war and strife.

Master MORE, your Sacred Heart,
from this we will no more depart,
we are forever in your flow,
of Diamond Will that you bestow.

7. Master MORE, help me see that this was simply an inevitable consequence. It was, the cost of doing business that I felt so rejected when I first came to earth.

Master MORE, we are so free,
eternal bond from you we see.
Master MORE, we find rebirth,
in flow of your eternal mirth.

Master MORE, your Sacred Heart,
from this we will no more depart,

we are forever in your flow,
of Diamond Will that you bestow.

8. Master MORE, help me see that I came here with the desire to change things according to a specific vision that I have.

Master MORE, you balance all,
the seven rays upon our call.
Master MORE, forever MORE,
we are the Spirit's open door.

Master MORE, your Sacred Heart,
from this we will no more depart,
we are forever in your flow,
of Diamond Will that you bestow.

9. Master MORE and Nada, help me question that vision and see the difference between true service and false service, between service that springs from complete inner peace and service that springs from a lack of peace, namely the sense that something is wrong and must be corrected.

Master MORE, your Presence here,
filling up the inner sphere.
Life is now a sacred flow,
God Power we on all bestow.

Master MORE, your Sacred Heart,
from this we will no more depart,
we are forever in your flow,
of Diamond Will that you bestow.

Part 6

1. Master MORE, help me see that when I come with the epic mindset, when I want to change something according to a pre-conceived vision, I cannot be an open door for the creative powers of my I AM Presence.

Master Nada, beauty's power,
unfolding like a sacred flower.
Master Nada, so sublime,
a will that conquers even time.

Master Nada, peace you give,
forevermore in peace we live,
our planet has a peaceful morn,
the Golden Age is hereby born.

2. Master MORE, help me see how I am superimposing a vision upon what my I AM Presence could or should express through me, and that vision will be based on the limited perspective I have by being in embodiment.

Master Nada, you bestow,
upon us wisdom's rushing flow.
Master Nada, mind so strong
rising on your wings of song.

Master Nada, peace you give,
forevermore in peace we live,
our planet has a peaceful morn,
the Golden Age is hereby born.

3. Master MORE, help me see that it is absolutely inevitable that when I come into embodiment on a dense planet like earth, I will start out with a limited perspective.

Master Nada, precious scent,
your love is truly heaven-sent.
Master Nada, kind and soft
on wings of love we rise aloft.

**Master Nada, peace you give,
forevermore in peace we live,
our planet has a peaceful morn,
the Golden Age is hereby born.**

4. Master MORE, help me see that the process of learning to express my co-creative abilities is a two-fold process. I must learn about the creative energies of the seven rays, and I must learn to express the seven rays in their creative form by overcoming the false concepts created through the perversions of the seven rays.

Master Nada, mother light,
our hearts are rising like a kite.
Master Nada, from your view,
all life is pure as morning dew.

**Master Nada, peace you give,
forevermore in peace we live,
our planet has a peaceful morn,
the Golden Age is hereby born.**

5. Master MORE, help me see that I am facing a scenario where I will start out with a limited vision, and I must then

purify that vision until I become that fully open door at the 96th level of consciousness.

> Master Nada, truth you bring,
> as morning birds in love do sing.
> Master Nada, we now feel,
> your love that all four bodies heal.

> **Master Nada, peace you give,**
> **forevermore in peace we live,**
> **our planet has a peaceful morn,**
> **the Golden Age is hereby born.**

6. Master MORE, help me give up certain aspects of the fallen consciousness, and the standard for creativity that they have imposed through the epic mindset and the underlying belief that there is a flaw in God's design.

> Master Nada, serve in peace,
> as all emotions we release.
> Master Nada, life is fun,
> the solar plexus is a sun.

> **Master Nada, peace you give,**
> **forevermore in peace we live,**
> **our planet has a peaceful morn,**
> **the Golden Age is hereby born.**

7. Master MORE, help me grasp the importance of overcoming the epic mindset, being at peace and giving service from a state of peace rather than a state of fear, a state of anger, a state of hatred, a state of agitation.

Master Nada, love is free,
conditions we no longer see.
Master Nada, rise above,
all human forms of lesser love.

Master Nada, peace you give,
forevermore in peace we live,
our planet has a peaceful morn,
the Golden Age is hereby born.

8. Master MORE, help me see that while I can leave the path
at any point up until the 96th level, the first seven levels in your
retreat are the most critical. This is where I can decide to leave
the path and go back into the School of Hard Knocks.

Master Nada, balance all,
the seven rays upon our call.
Master Nada, rise and shine,
your radiant beauty most divine.

Master Nada, peace you give,
forevermore in peace we live,
our planet has a peaceful morn,
the Golden Age is hereby born.

9. Master MORE, help me see if I have a momentum on
attaining powerful positions on earth or if I have lifetimes ago
decided not to engage in power plays on earth.

Nada Dear, your Presence here,
filling up the inner sphere.
Life is now a sacred flow,
God Peace we do on all bestow.

Master Nada, peace you give,
forevermore in peace we live,
our planet has a peaceful morn,
the Golden Age is hereby born.

Part 7

1. Master MORE, help me see if I have become pulled into power struggles. Help me see this without condemning myself for having engaged in these struggles and having abused power.

Master MORE, come to the fore,
we will absorb your flame of MORE.
Master MORE, our will so strong,
our power centers cleared by song.

Master MORE, your Sacred Heart,
from this we will no more depart,
we are forever in your flow,
of Diamond Will that you bestow.

2. Master MORE, help me start the process of questioning the abuse of power in myself. For it is always easier to see how others have abused power than to see how I myself have abused power.

Master MORE, your wisdom flows,
as our attunement ever grows.
Master MORE, we have a tie,
that helps us see through Serpent's lie.

Master MORE, your Sacred Heart,
from this we will no more depart,
we are forever in your flow,
of Diamond Will that you bestow.

3. Master MORE, help me learn the universal lesson that it is not by exercising power in the epic struggle that I further the cause of the ascended masters and bring in the Golden Age.

Master MORE, your love so pink,
there is no purer love, we think.
Master MORE, you set us free,
from all conditionality.

Master MORE, your Sacred Heart,
from this we will no more depart,
we are forever in your flow,
of Diamond Will that you bestow.

4. Master MORE, help me see that the abuse of power often leads to pride. Those who have the most power have often fallen prey to another illusion, projected by the fallen beings that in order to maintain a position of power they have to always be right.

Master MORE, we will endure,
your discipline that makes us pure.
Master MORE, intentions true,
as we are always one with you.

Master MORE, your Sacred Heart,
from this we will no more depart,

we are forever in your flow,
of Diamond Will that you bestow.

5. Master MORE, help me see that being willing to allow the fallen beings to ridicule and humiliate me, saying all manner of things falsely against me for Christ's sake, is indeed part of the initiation.

Master MORE, our vision raised,
the will of God is always praised.
Master MORE, creative will,
raising all life higher still.

Master MORE, your Sacred Heart,
from this we will no more depart,
we are forever in your flow,
of Diamond Will that you bestow.

6. Master MORE, help me see that having experienced ridicule and persecution from people in this lifetime is an opportunity to look at this and be non-attached, simply realizing that this is the outplaying of the Law of Free Will.

Master MORE, your peace is power,
the demons of war it will devour.
Master MORE, we serve all life,
our flames consuming war and strife.

Master MORE, your Sacred Heart,
from this we will no more depart,
we are forever in your flow,
of Diamond Will that you bestow.

7. Master MORE, I am willing to let the Law of Free Will out-play itself whereby those who are ridiculing me have received an opportunity to see why they want to ridicule others and thereby begin to question their own state of consciousness.

Master MORE, we are so free,
eternal bond from you we see.
Master MORE, we find rebirth,
in flow of your eternal mirth.

**Master MORE, your Sacred Heart,
from this we will no more depart,
we are forever in your flow,
of Diamond Will that you bestow.**

8. Master MORE, help me see such situations as an opportunity to demonstrate that I am willing to be ridiculed. I am willing to step up to a higher state of consciousness where I do not take it seriously. I do not let other people's ridicule stop me from fulfilling my divine plan and expressing my creative energies.

Master MORE, you balance all,
the seven rays upon our call.
Master MORE, forever MORE,
we are the Spirit's open door.

**Master MORE, your Sacred Heart,
from this we will no more depart,
we are forever in your flow,
of Diamond Will that you bestow.**

9. Master MORE, help me learn to meet the ridicule from the world with non-attachment. Help me learn to de-personalize my life so I do not take everything that happens to me personally.

Master MORE, your Presence here,
filling up the inner sphere.
Life is now a sacred flow,
God Power we on all bestow.

Master MORE, your Sacred Heart,
from this we will no more depart,
we are forever in your flow,
of Diamond Will that you bestow.

Sealing:

In the name of the Divine Mother, I fully accept that the power of these calls is used to set free the Ma-ter light, so it can outpicture the perfect vision of Christ for my own life, for all people and for the planet. In the name I AM THAT I AM, it is done! Amen.

17 | POWER AND FREEDOM

Master MORE, I AM, and I am free. Will you be free with me? That is the question you might ask yourself. And you might find reason to step back and look at – even at this point where you have studied my previous discourses – you might consider the question: "Am I able to be free with Master MORE?"

Imagine that you and I had walked into the garden around my retreat at Darjeeling. We had found a secluded spot, we had sat down, and here we are just the two of us. We can talk about absolutely anything that you want to talk about. How free would you feel in that situation?

Would you be able to freely share with me what are your concerns in life, what are your concerns about your own growth, your own state of consciousness? Would you be able to freely ask any questions you have, or are there questions you would be afraid to ask because you are afraid of what the answer might be?

You see, what I have attempted to explain is that I run the retreat of the First Ray, and the First Ray is the first place where spiritual beings come when they are ready to seek a higher path under direct guidance from the ascended masters, from the Chohans. This means that you do not have to be at the 48th level of consciousness in order to come to my retreat. You have to have come to that turning point where you are sincerely wanting something more than repeating the same old patterns that you have been repeating for a long time.

How free are you?

When you have the desire to be more, you can, in your finer bodies, attend my retreat. I will then attempt to help you according to your present level of consciousness and your willingness to transcend that level of consciousness. You see, in a sense, we could say that what determines my ability to help you is how free you are in terms of stepping back from your present state of consciousness, your present perception filter, your way of looking at life. How willing are you to step back, freely look at where you are at in consciousness and recognize: "I no longer want to be here, I want to come up higher?"

Many of the students who come here have very little freedom in terms of being willing and able to question the way they look at life. They often feel very much locked in a pattern. There is only a certain way they can look at life. They are not willing or able to realize that the way they look at life right now is only one possible way to look at life and that there are many others—and that it is only by considering some of those other ways that they have a chance of ascending to a higher state of consciousness. For if you continue to look at life the way you look at life right now without questioning it, then you cannot rise, can you? It is that simple, is it not?

How free do you feel in terms of stepping back, looking at your present state of consciousness or in asking me: "Master MORE, show me where I am in consciousness. Show me what it is that is holding me back right now that prevents me from taking the next step to a higher level."

Your reactionary patterns

You might realize that what this very much comes down to is how personally you take everything that happens to you in life. Be willing to look at your life and see where there are situations where other people say or do something and you take it very personally. You feel that they are personally attacking you, ridiculing you, seeking to put you down, seeking to embarrass you, seeking to make you angry. And therefore, you go into a reactionary pattern that you can clearly see—if you are willing to take a look.

Then, be willing to ask yourself where these reactions come from. Where does this pattern of reaction come from? And then recognize that it comes from one simple place: It comes from the spirits that you have allowed to enter your lower being or that you have created within that lower being.

When you know that you are the Conscious You – when you know that you have experienced glimpses of pure awareness – you can see that this Consciousness You, which is simply pure awareness, cannot take anything on earth personally. Because it knows that it is not the body, it knows it is not the lower mind, it knows it is not the spirits. Why then would *you* take anything personally? You see, the Conscious You does not take anything personally. You take things personally only when you look at a situation through the filter of a certain spirit.

Now, as Saint Germain has mentioned before *[Flowing With the River of Life]*, his main retreat is called the Cave of Symbols. He has the ability there to help you see the symbol that is holding you back that is limiting you. But this teaching was given before the teaching given by the Maha Chohan on the creation of spirits. So you now see that what is actually the first line of reaction is the spirit. But of course, the spirit was created out of a particular thought matrix, which is what Saint Germain called a symbol because it is nothing but a symbol. It is not real. It is only a thought matrix created in the mind. And it is created based on a limited, selective view of life.

Thus you see, when a given spirit is created, it is created based on this symbol, based on this particular view of life. And this was a view of life that you either accepted because of something that happened to you here on earth, or that you chose to create in order to deal with certain situations here on earth.

Dealing with being attacked

What have I told you earlier? This planet is a dark planet with many fallen beings in embodiment and many beings that are trapped in the fallen consciousness. They can only see themselves as separate beings, they can only see themselves as being in opposition to others, as being in competition with others, always seeking to feel superior by putting others down. When you display any kind of creativity, any kind of spirituality, they feel threatened and thus they want to put you down. And that is why, from the moment you embodied here and dared to express your creative drive, then you have been ridiculed, you have been put down, you have been attacked in various ways: physical, emotional, mental and even at the identity level.

What did you do, when you were a new lifestream that came here with the best of intentions and feeling like the innocent child that was suddenly viciously attacked by these adults, who had only one desire and that was to put you down, to shut you up and to destroy you—if they had to in order to keep you from expressing your creative drive.

Well, what you did was that you did not know how to deal with this, and therefore you created a spirit to deal with this situation. This spirit was created based on the limited sense of self that you had at the time, and therefore you were not able to look at the situation with the same clarity that your I AM Presence looked at the situation. You had forgotten that you are a Conscious You that is pure awareness and therefore does not have to react to anything on earth but can allow the Presence to react.

You had come to believe that you had to react to things on earth based on your present level of self-awareness. Thus, you reacted, but because you did not know quite how to react, and because you did not want to react to these attacks, and because you thought there was no constructive or purposeful way to react to these attacks, you created a spirit to react for you. And that spirit was created based on your level of consciousness, based on the way you looked at life through the self you had taken on at the time. Thus, it is by nature a limited spirit. It only has limited options for reacting to certain situations.

Once the spirit is created, it is locked by the matrix that created it, the matrix that defined it. It has not the self-awareness to transcend that matrix, so it can only continue to react to these situations in the same basic way based on the same pattern. Only, it can take this pattern more and more towards an extreme, so that if the pattern is to become angry, you can become more and more angry until you are almost constantly angry, constantly ready to lash out at anything that irritates you or comes your way.

Seeing the spirits that react for you

What happens when students come to my retreat and are stuck in these patterns, then I can – if they are willing to go through the firsts six steps that I have described in my previous discourses – I can take them to the retreat of Saint Germain at the Cave of Symbols. Where we can then show people visually, on a screen, how it is actually certain spirits that are reacting when they take things personally.

It is, of course, not always anger. It is many times other feelings. Many spiritual people have a deep sense of being embarrassed or ridiculed in many situations where they do not feel they are being accepted by others. What we can show our students is, first of all, how their reaction is not a creative reaction where they make a choice how to react. They are simply reacting automatically by, in certain situations, completely stepping back – essentially giving up their self-awareness – and allowing a spirit to take over their reactions.

We can show them how this spirit is reacting. We can show them what the spirit looks like, and it is often not a pretty sight. Then, we can see how this spirit is reacting, but then we can also show them what is coming at them to which they are reacting. We can show them that what is coming at them is not a creative reaction because anytime someone is attacking you or ridiculing you or putting you down, it is not a creative reaction from the other person.

The other persons have also allowed spirits to take over their minds, and thus it is this aggressive spirit that is attacking you. And you are now reacting to it, either with an aggressive spirit of your own, or with a passive spirit that submits to the attack and deals with it in various ways by taking it inwards. Where you either blame yourself, or feel stupid, or ridiculed, or embarrassed or feel angry at yourself for not defending yourself and not attacking back.

You see, once you are at the retreat of Saint Germain and you look at the screen, you can see how your reaction is a spirit, but the attack is also a spirit. So there is one spirit attacking you and there is another spirit reacting to the attack. When you have gone through the first six levels of my retreat, then you are often ready to see that it is completely meaningless to allow your life, your attention, to be eaten up by these spirits attacking each other or defending themselves from the attacks of other spirits. You can see how this is eating up your attention, it is eating up your life, and this can then give students the determination to say: "Stop! I will no longer allow my freedom to be taken away by these spirits."

Then, of course, you can take the next step which is to look at the spirit that you are dealing with right now – the spirit that is running your life – the spirit that is the main spirit that you are allowing to take over your reactions to life or specific situations in life. You can realize that the only way to really be free of this is that you must make the decision that you no longer want this spirit to control your reactions to this particular type of situation. Because you are actually willing to use your power and your will to make a creative decision about how to react to these situations.

Making creative decisions

What do I mean with a creative decision? I mean a creative decision where you are free to react in a way that you have not done before. You are free to react based on how you want to react, not letting a spirit take over your reactions. You are willing to make a decision where you say: "Yes, I see that I have created a spirit. I see that I have in the past reacted in certain ways so many times in this kind of situation. But why should I be bound in the now by the way I have reacted in the past? This is not free will. I am not exercising my willpower when I am allowing a spirit to take over my reactions because I do not want to choose. And thus, I take back my will power. I take back my power of will, and I am willing to choose. For I realize that the spirit that I created many lifetimes ago, was created based on the state of consciousness I had at the time, the sense of self I had at the time. But I have grown. I have expanded my sense of self. Therefore, I am able and willing to react in a more mature, a more conscious and a more aware way now than I did in the past."

Do you see? Freedom can be lost by not making decisions. But freedom cannot be won without making conscious, willful, deliberate decisions. You may think that freedom is something passive where nothing from the outside is obstructing you. But this is not freedom.

Freedom is an active force. It requires power to be free and power can be unleashed only through will. You cannot be free by being passive and hoping for a point where no one will attack you. For that point will not come on planet earth, at least not in the foreseeable future. There are still too many beings in the fallen consciousness in embodiment, and they *will* attack you. Their lives are taken over by spirits who are created by a certain matrix that is an aggressive, attacking matrix. They cannot live their lives any other way at the present.

When you see this, this is when you can start to depersonalize your life. Because you realize that these people who are attacking or ridiculing you are not actually ridiculing you personally. They are not even actually seeing you, for they are seeing you through the filter of the spirit that is dominating their consciousness. What that spirit sees is based on the matrix that defined that spirit. In fact, what that spirit sees is the matrix. It is not seeing the reality of who you are. It is not capable of seeing the reality of who you are. It is simply seeing the pattern that is created in the mind of the spirit when this spirit encounters you, your energy field, or even the spirit that is running your life.

You see, the spirit in the other person is not seeing you. The other person is not conscious, is not aware. Nobody can attack you, or ridicule you or put you down if they are fully aware of who they are as spiritual beings. For then they would also be aware that you are a spiritual being. And why would one spiritual being put down another? But one spirit would indeed put down another spirit or another spiritual being, but they are not seeing the spiritual being that you are. They are, as I said, only seeing a mirage created in their own minds by their perception filter encountering who you are.

Depersonalizing your life

When you know this – when you begin to realize this, when you begin to see it – you can say: "But if they are not actually attacking me personally, why am I taking it personally? I realize that if anybody else was in my situation, they would attack that person too if they were doing what I am doing. So it is not really about me. Why am I then feeling that I am personally attacked?"

You can then realize that you, the Conscious You – the pure awareness – you are not feeling personally attacked. It is the spirit through which you are looking at the situation that is feeling personally attacked. And in a sense you can say that the spirit is being personally attacked by the other spirit. Or you can say that your spirit was created to feel personally attacked and to deal with this kind of situation in a personal, specific way. But when you realize you are not the spirit, you can see that you do not need to feel what the spirit is feeling. So even though the spirit takes it personally, you do not need to take it personally.

What is the "I" that is reacting to this situation? Is it the same I that is asking this question? And when you realize that you have the ability to ask yourself which I is reacting to the situation, then you realize that there is an I that is the Conscious You and there is an I that is only the spirit—and that this I that thinks it is the spirit has no reality to it. The spirit has no reality to it.

Thus, you can see that you are not bound by the way this spirit reacts. You are not bound by the matrix. You can make a creative decision to look at the matrix, see how it is limiting you, and say: "I do not want to look at this situation through this matrix. I want to look at it in a more creative way. I want to be more free to look at this situation from a higher perspective and therefore react from the higher vision."

This is how you begin to attain freedom, the freedom of will, the freedom to express your power. For what is it that the spirits you have created are doing? They are limiting your power. They are in essence saying to you that you cannot react in a creative way to a certain situation, you have to react the way you have always reacted because you have to react through the spirit. Well, this is not expressing your creative power. The more spirits you have created, the more you will actually limit the amount of creative power that will stream through you from your I AM Presence. Your I AM Presence does this as a grace to you, so that you do not reinforce the spirits even more whereby they will completely take over your life.

Losing your innocence

Of course, the spirits that are attacking you likewise are not creative spirits. They were created by the fallen beings in the beginning in order to prevent you from expressing your creative powers. The fallen beings knew from experience that if they attack the holy innocents with enough viciousness and injustice, then a certain percentage – in fact a high percentage of these holy innocents – will at first feel so traumatized, so shocked, by this vicious attack that they will be deceived out of their innocence by thinking that they have to react to the attack from a similar level of consciousness as that from which the attack originated. Thus, they think that they have to create these spirits who can react to the attacking spirits from the same level of consciousness.

In a sense, there is a mechanism here that is subtle. When you are in innocence, there is no way you can turn back an attack at a low level of consciousness. You cannot turn back an attack at a low level without neutralizing it or blocking it by energies of a certain level also. For every action, there is a reaction. This is the law of an unascended sphere. And that is why it is easy to fall into the trap of thinking that when there is an action directed against you from a certain level of vibration, you have to counteract it with a reaction from the same level of vibration and the same level of consciousness. And this is what causes you to lose your holy innocence.

What am I then saying? Am I saying that in order to remain innocent, you have to allow the fallen beings to continually attack you? That is indeed what I am saying. For what does it matter that they direct an action against you, if you are transparent so that it passes right through you? Ultimate innocence is transparency where whatever they direct at you from the fallen consciousness passes right through you, for there is nothing within you of the same vibration that it can interact with.

That is why the deeper reality is that the dark forces, the fallen beings, could not force you to react to them. You have to choose to react at the same level. Now, they are very clever at fooling you into thinking that it is necessary, or even justified by a higher cause that you react at this level. Just as they could get, for example, the good Christians to go on a crusade, thinking it was justified that they killed men, women and children of the Muslim faith in order to free Jerusalem. When in reality the Crusades was just one big conflict, created by the fallen beings and the dark spirits to feed the spirits and to prevent people from manifesting their Christhood by dragging them into an unending conflict.

This is not freedom when you are dragged into this action-and-reaction sequence that can go on forever. When you come to the seventh level of my retreat, I attempt to help you see this. Some will not, and they must leave my retreat and go back to the School of Hard Knocks. Others get so scared that they have to go back to the soup line for a while and receive healing.

Some even see a glimpse of the spirits they have created themselves and it actually creates a scar. They have such a reaction to seeing this that it creates a new spirit. So they go back to the first level of my retreat and work their way back up, receiving healing on the way. Or they go to one of the other retreats of the Chohans where they can receive healing or love or whatever it is they need, before they are ready to come again to that seventh level where they now can look calmly at the spirit that is holding them back at this level and say: "You have

had your day. You are not going to control my life any longer.
You are not going to control my reaction to this particular type
of situation, and thus I am willing to make conscious decisions
about how to react here."

Changing your relationships

My beloved, there are many students who come to my retreat
who do not have a conscious awareness of what I am telling
you here. Part of the reason I am telling you is to help you
retain some conscious memory of the initiations, so you can
more easily implement them in your daily life. But yet I can
tell you that many students have already started implement-
ing these initiations without being consciously aware of where
they come from. And the effect of coming to my retreat, and
successfully going through the initiation at the seventh level, is
that a student will begin to deliberately change his or her reaction to specific situations.

This is often in a relationship with a specific other person,
whether it be a parent, or a spouse, or a good friend or a child.
It can also be people at work. It is people that you have found
it difficult to deal with – sometimes for years or even decades
– but now you suddenly find yourself realizing that you do
not want to continue the relationship based on this same old
pattern.

You suddenly find yourself realizing that the other person
is not likely to change. So if the dynamic of the relationship
is going to change, who is it that is going to change? Well, it
must be me because I am more conscious. I am more aware.
I am more willing to make decisions. And thus, you can
suddenly look at the relationship and you can say: "Well, if the
relationship is to change, which is what I want, then I am the

one who must do something to change the dynamic. And that means I must change my reaction and I must change the way I treat the other person."

My beloved, when you come to this point, you will find that when you deliberately and consciously choose to change the way you treat the other person, one of two things will happen: Either the other person will be surprised and will also begin to change or, if the other person does not change but continues to react in the same way as before, then you will in many cases find that you will simply move out of that relationship and move into another situation where you are not confronted with this kind of person.

Now, there are sometimes where you have specific reasons for remaining in a relationship. This can especially be the case with children or even spouses and of course parents. And then, you will find that if the other person does not change, you will still have changed so much that the other person's behavior does not bother you anymore because you do not take it personally. This means that you can continue to have a relationship with that person, but you will often find that you withdraw somewhat from that person and only have minimal contact. But when you do have contact, you are able to maintain your depersonalized reaction to the other person. You can simply let the other person ramble on as he or she has been doing for decades because you know that the person is stuck in a pattern.

If it is a parent or child, you love that person, you accept them for who they are, and then you accept that perhaps they will not be able to change for the remainder of that lifetime. And you realize that it is not really your job to force the other person to change, even if it is a close relationship to you. You can allow yourself to be who you are. You can allow the other person to be who he or she is because you accept the Law of Free Will.

You accept that you have exercised your free will by changing your reaction. You will continue to exercise your free will by not allowing yourself to be deceived by the serpentine mind into thinking that it is somehow your responsibility to change the other person. You can allow the other person to continue to repeat these old patterns because the person is not willing to exercise his or her free will. But you are still exercising your free will by continuing to react in an impersonal way to the other person.

You do not take this personally. You maintain your freedom. And sometimes it is necessary for your own growth that you maintain a depersonalized reaction to another person for a long time because it gradually anchors this depersonalized reaction in the four levels of your being. And it comes to a point where you have demonstrated to yourself that you are able to confront such a person, to deal with such a person, without snapping back into the old pattern that you might have repeated for lifetimes.

Depersonalization and dehumanization

Again, be nonattached to the outer situation and the outcome of that situation. This is one of the essential steps to freedom. One of the primary ways in which the serpents, and those in the serpentine mind, tempt you to enter this action-reaction pattern is by making you believe that there is a certain outcome – a certain physical outcome – that must be attained. They often do this with the epic mindset that there is some superior cause that demands the manifestation of a certain outcome.

My beloved, how did Adolph Hitler manage to deceive the majority of the German population into thinking it was essential that the Aryan race be purified? How did the architects of world Communism manage to deceive so many people into actually believing that it was justified to kill or torture other people in order to bring about the Communist Utopia?

Do you think that a human being who is in touch with his or her spirituality can kill or torture someone else? It cannot be done. It can only be done when the person allows a spirit to take over his or her reactions. But why do people do this? Because they become convinced that a certain outcome is absolutely necessary for some greater epic cause, and therefore it is necessary that they do what they cannot do as human beings. Thus, they depersonalize themselves by letting a spirit take over their reactions and their actions. Thus, they can depersonalize the act, so that they do not see that they are torturing or killing another human being. They think that it is somehow a sub-person, a non-person that is being killed or shoved into the gas chamber.

You see, what I am getting at here is that it is necessary to depersonalize your life. But depersonalizing your life can also be taken too far where you dehumanize yourself and others. You need to realize that both the personal reaction – where you take everything personally – and the dehumanized reaction – where you do not think other people are human – both of these reactions come from spirits.

When you begin to see this, then you can begin to truly free yourself from this action-reaction pattern. You can free yourself from the deception and from the reaction to the two kinds of fallen beings, those who attack you with obvious physical force and those who attack you through deception, so you do not even see that you are being attacked and being forced into a pattern.

It is not beyond your level of consciousness, when you are at the seventh level of my retreat, to reason about this. You have the ability to reason and see how power has been abused and how the key to getting human beings to abuse power is to actually get them into a situation where they are both taking things personally and at the same time depersonalizing what they do to others. The Germans, for example, during the Second World War were taking it personally what they believed the Jews were doing to Germany and to them. But they had also depersonalized the Jews, so that they thought they were not really killing human beings.

The dualistic extremes

Do you see this reaction? There are always two extremes, two polarities, in the duality consciousness. And that is why you need both in order to be trapped in this consciousness. You are fully trapped when you are personally reacting to certain things that other people supposedly do, but you are depersonalizing what you do to them. For you do not think that they should have a right to feel that what you do to them is a personal attack. For, after all, they are the bad people.

Thus, you do not realize that when you commit violence against them, it is just as wrong as what you think they are doing against you. If you realize this, this can be the higher reasoning that can snap people out of this reaction where they suddenly realize: "But I cannot consistently accuse them of using violence against me while at the same time using violence against them. This is hypocrisy."

This is where your reasoning ability can help you snap out of this reactionary pattern. But you cannot do this as long as you are looking at the situation through a spirit because you understand that the spirit cannot reason beyond its matrix. The spirit is depersonalized and many spirits were created based on a thought matrix that does dehumanize certain other people. They cannot break this matrix. They cannot think creatively.

Thus, as long as you are fully identified with the spirits and seeing the situation through the spirits, you cannot see that what you are doing is hypocrisy. You cannot see, for example that you claim to be a good Christian but killing Muslim women and children is completely against all of the commandments of Christ.

Now, you – when you are in touch with your own spiritually – can see this. But when you have dehumanized yourself by allowing spirits to run your life, then you cannot see this. For you are not actually any more a spiritual being. You have become a human being who reacts by feeling threatened by, other human beings.

It is only when you snap back into recognizing your own higher humanity – your spirituality – that you can begin to see what you are doing and reason that you cannot allow yourself to claim to be a good Christian, if you are violating the commandments of Christ. Or you can, for that matter, not allow yourself to be working for any good cause, if you are killing, or torturing, or putting down, or ridiculing or discriminating against other human beings. Because they are spiritual beings too, and a spiritual being cannot treat other spiritual beings in an inhumane way. It simply is not possible.

The catch-22 of guilt

This then, is what Saint Germain and I attempt to achieve when you are at the seventh level of my retreat. We are not attempting to help you be completely free of the action-reaction pattern, but we are attempting to take you to the point where you have consciously recognized a specific spirit that is causing you to react in a way that is inhumane towards others and also inhumane towards yourself. Then, we are attempting to help you experience what it is like to see this spirit, to see that it is not you, to see that it is unreal, and thereby deciding to completely let it go without going into the reaction of feeling guilty for having created that spirit in the first place.

This is often a big challenge for us, for there are many students who come to this point of realizing that they have treated other people in inhumane ways. And it is very difficult for them to admit this without allowing another spirit that they have created in past lifetimes to take over their reaction to this realization. Many times they snap into a spirit that can only react with guilt and self-blame because the spirit was created based on this matrix.

The fallen beings are experts at creating this catch-22 where you create one spirit to react in inhumane ways and you create another spirit to blame yourself for reacting in inhumane ways. The effect of this is that it is extremely difficult to recognize the first spirit because then you know that the other spirit will take over your reaction and make you feel so bad that you cannot deal with it.

When you have come to the seventh level, and have gone through the other six levels, you have received such help, such support, such love from us and the other Chohans that you are able to take our hand and to look at both spirits and see that the self-blame does not come from God because your I AM Presence does not blame you for anything you have done here on earth. It sees that it is all unreal; it is all part of the cosmic sandbox that this planet is. Therefore, there is nothing done on earth that has any permanence that has an reality. And if it has no permanence and no reality, then why do you have to carry

it with you as part of your lifestream? What is it that carries it
with you? It is a spirit in your being that is carrying this with
you.

Erasing the akashic record

This is when we can take you back to my retreat, and you can go
in and have the experience of seeing in the akashic records the
very situation where you created this spirit of self-blame and
where you created the spirit that has kept you in an action-reaction pattern. Then you can, when you have a momentum
on the decrees of the seven rays (which you have built at this
point or you would not have come to this point), then you can
use that momentum to go into the akashic record. And almost
with laser-like precision, by directing a beam of light that is like
a laser beam, very focused, you can erase that original record
from the akashic record.

Then you will see the reality that when something is erased
from the akashic record, you have fulfilled the requirements
whereby God says: "I will remember their sins no more." And
that is when you can dismiss, and in fact shatter, the thought
matrix of the spirit that carries this situation with you in your
memory body, constantly using it to blame you for having
made a mistake in the past. When you have transcended the
consciousness that caused you to make that choice in the past,
then there is no reason for you to carry the memory of it in
your lower being. For the positive lesson of transcending that
level of consciousness is now part of your causal body.

Do you understand? Your causal body does not store the
negative memories. It stores only the lesson learned, the positive
lesson learned. And that is when there is no record, and this
is the ultimate experience we seek to give you at the seventh

level, Saint Germain and I, of having that inner knowing – that direct experience – that it is possible to be completely free of a negative situation from your past. It is possible to completely transcend a so-called mistake that you made and to turn it into a positive, life-supporting, growth-supporting experience.

You may not be consciously aware of this, but there are some of you at this point who will be able to realize that when you think back at your life, you will see that even as a child you may have had a certain optimism, a certain ability to take life lightly, a certain inner sense that nothing could be really bad that nothing really bad could happen to you that you could never have made a really bad mistake from which there was no way back. It is not necessarily a sense that you haven't made mistakes but that any mistake you could have made can be made good again, can be transcended, can be left behind.

You may also recognize that you have had a tendency to blame yourself, for many spiritual students have such a desire to do well that they also have a tendency to blame themselves when they make mistakes. But I am talking about a deeper track – for these reactions are, of course, only spirits – but I am talking about the deeper track where you know because the Conscious You that you are has a connection to the I AM Presence. And therefore, you know that at the level of the I AM Presence, everything that happens on earth can be turned into a positive experience.

Life can be an upward spiral

When you become more conscious of this inner knowing – as, of course, I am seeking to make you conscious by giving you this outer teaching – then you can become more conscious of the fact that life on earth – even in the state that this planet is in

right now – life on earth can become an entirely positive experience. Where you go from positive learning experience to positive learning experience and you keep transcending yourself in
an upward spiral. And indeed, the graduation ceremony from
my retreat, before I can send you on to Lord Lanto's retreat on
the Second Ray, will happen only when you have locked in to
this, when you have some sense – some experience – that life
can be a positive experience.

It doesn't mean that you have cleared your subconscious
minds, the four levels of your mind, from all spirits and all
patterns from the past that make life difficult. But it does mean
that at some level of your being, you have this inner knowing
based on the experience that life can be positive. And of course,
it is the hope of all of us, the seven Chohans and the Maha
Chohan that by the time you come to the 96th level, you will be
completely locked in a knowing that life is an upward spiral. So
that no temptation from the serpents can take you out of this
upward spiral, for you continue to transcend yourself. Because,
after all, you have experienced that nothing the serpent can
throw at you on the seven rays can stop your progress, can
stop your self-transcendence.

It is a great joy for me when the student has reached that
level, when he or she can graduate from my retreat. And I can
then invite Lanto to come and take that student by the hand.
And I stand and look at you walk with Lanto on a bridge of
light from my retreat to his, and I simply see you walk away as
you see in some movies where the hero rides into the sunset.
You are riding into the light with Lanto, and I stand back,
feeling sometimes a tear of joy of knowing I have done my job
as the Chohan of the First Ray. I have taken a student as far as
he or she can be taken in my retreat, and I have lovingly and
joyfully seen that student move on to the next level.

For I am the Chohan of the first retreat. I know I am not the one who takes the student all the way to the ascension point. I am the first Chohan. I am sort of the one who does the most dirty work, for surely by the time you have been through my retreat, you have been somewhat purified. Which is why you are ready for the higher instructions that await you at Lanto's retreat.

I have chosen to be the Chohan of the First Ray. I am completely at peace with my position and the challenges and difficulties it entails. I am completely in love with the First Ray of power and will. But really, I am in love with the creative drive, and there is nothing more joyful for me than helping lifestreams unlock their creative powers, so they are willing to make creative decisions instead of mechanical decisions—that are not really decisions but that are non-decisions, what Jesus has called Death decisions.

Thus, this is enough for this installment. But I shall return with a few more remarks about the First Ray, actually a few more than a few more remarks. For there are still some characteristics of the First Ray that I wish to put into a form where they can be studied at the physical level, at the level of waking awareness. Thus, Master MORE I AM, and I am forever MORE.

18 | INVOKING POWER AND FREEDOM

In the name I AM THAT I AM, Jesus Christ, I call to my I AM Presence to flow through the I Will Be Presence that I AM and give this invocation with full power. I call to beloved Elohim Hercules and Amazonia and Arcturus and Victoria, Archangel Michael and Faith and Archangel Zadkiel and Amethyst, Master MORE and Saint Germain to help me overcome the immediate block to my greater freedom. Help me see and surrender all patterns that block my oneness with Master MORE and my oneness with my I AM Presence, including ...

[Make personal calls]

Part 1

1. Master MORE, I am willing to be free with you, and I am willing to consider the question: "Am I able to be free with Master MORE?"

> O Hercules Blue, we're one with your will,
> all space in our beings with Blue Flame you fill,
> a beacon that radiates light to the earth,
> bringing about our planet's rebirth.
>
> **O Hercules Blue, all life you defend,**
> **giving us power to always transcend,**
> **in you the expansion of self has no end,**
> **as we in God's infinite spirals ascend.**

2. Master MORE, I am willing to consider how free I feel to share with you my concerns about my own growth, and whether I feel free to ask questions or are afraid of what the answer might be.

> O Hercules Blue, your wisdom so great,
> within us a sense of knowing create,
> a new frame of reference we suddenly gain,
> for going beyond duality's pain.
>
> **O Hercules Blue, all life you defend,**
> **giving us power to always transcend,**
> **in you the expansion of self has no end,**
> **as we in God's infinite spirals ascend.**

3. Master MORE, I sincerely want something more than repeating the same old patterns that I have been repeating for a long time.

> O Hercules Blue, we lovingly raise,
> our voices in giving God infinite praise,
> in feeling your flame, so clearly we see,
> transcending the self is the true alchemy.

> **O Hercules Blue, all life you defend,**
> **giving us power to always transcend,**
> **in you the expansion of self has no end,**
> **as we in God's infinite spirals ascend.**

4. Master MORE, help me see that what determines your ability to help me is how free I am in terms of stepping back from my present state of consciousness, my present perception filter, my way of looking at life.

> O Hercules Blue, all life now you heal,
> enveloping all in your Blue-flame Seal,
> we're grateful for playing a personal part,
> In God's infinitely intricate work of art.

> **O Hercules Blue, all life you defend,**
> **giving us power to always transcend,**
> **in you the expansion of self has no end,**
> **as we in God's infinite spirals ascend.**

5. Master MORE, I am willing to step back, freely look at where I am at in consciousness and recognize: "I no longer want to be here, I want to come up higher?"

O Hercules Blue, your Temple of Light,
revealed to us all through our inner sight,
your power allows us to forge on until,
we pierce every veil and climb every hill.

O Hercules Blue, all life you defend,
giving us power to always transcend,
in you the expansion of self has no end,
as we in God's infinite spirals ascend.

6. Master MORE, help me realize that the way I look at life right now is only one possible way to look at life. There are many others—and it is only by considering some of those other ways that I have a chance of ascending to a higher state of consciousness.

O Hercules Blue, I pledge now my life,
in helping this planet transcend human strife,
duality's lies are pierced by your light,
restoring the fullness of our inner sight.

O Hercules Blue, all life you defend,
giving us power to always transcend,
in you the expansion of self has no end,
as we in God's infinite spirals ascend.

7. Master MORE, help me see that if I continue to look at life the way I look at life right now without questioning it, then I cannot rise. It is that simple.

O Hercules Blue, we set all life free,
from the subtlest lies of duality,

the prince of this world no more has a bond,
for with you we go completely beyond.

**O Hercules Blue, all life you defend,
giving us power to always transcend,
in you the expansion of self has no end,
as we in God's infinite spirals ascend.**

8. Master MORE, I am willing to step back, look at my present state of consciousness and ask: "Master MORE, show me where I am in consciousness. Show me what it is that is holding me back right now that prevents me from taking the next step to a higher level."

O Hercules Blue, in oneness with thee,
we open our hearts to your reality,
your electric-blue fire within us reveal,
our innermost longing for all that is real.

**O Hercules Blue, all life you defend,
giving us power to always transcend,
in you the expansion of self has no end,
as we in God's infinite spirals ascend.**

9. Master MORE, help me see how personally I take everything that happens to me in life. I am willing to look at my life and see the situations where other people say or do something and I take it very personally.

O Hercules Blue, you fill every space,
with infinite Power and infinite Grace,
you embody the key to creativity,
the will to transcend into Infinity.

**O Hercules Blue, all life you defend,
giving us power to always transcend,
in you the expansion of self has no end,
as we in God's infinite spirals ascend.**

Part 2

1. Master MORE, help me see where I feel that other people are personally attacking me, ridiculing me, seeking to put me down, seeking to embarrass me, seeking to make me angry. And therefore, I go into a reactionary pattern.

Beloved Arcturus, release now the flow,
of Violet Flame to help all life grow,
in ever-expanding circles of light,
it pulses within every atom so bright.

**Beloved Arcturus, your Violet Flame pure,
is for every ailment the ultimate cure,
against it no darkness could ever endure,
earth's freedom it will forever ensure.**

2. Master MORE, help me see where this pattern of reaction comes from. Help me see that it comes from the spirits that I have allowed to enter my lower being or that I have created within my lower being.

Beloved Arcturus, thou Elohim Free,
we open our hearts to your reality,
we have no attachments to life here on earth,
we claim a new life in your Flame of Rebirth.

**Beloved Arcturus, your Violet Flame pure,
is for every ailment the ultimate cure,
against it no darkness could ever endure,
earth's freedom it will forever ensure.**

3. Master MORE, help me see that the Consciousness You, which is pure awareness, cannot take anything on earth personally. Because it knows that it is not the body, it knows it is not the lower mind, it knows it is not the spirits.

Beloved Arcturus, be with us alway,
reborn, we are ready to face a new day,
expanding our hearts into Infinity,
your flame is the key to our God-victory.

**Beloved Arcturus, your Violet Flame pure,
is for every ailment the ultimate cure,
against it no darkness could ever endure,
earth's freedom it will forever ensure.**

4. Master MORE, help me see that the Conscious You does not take anything personally. I take things personally only when I look at a situation through the filter of a certain spirit.

Beloved Arcturus, your bright violet fire,
now fills every atom, raising them higher,
the space in each atom all filled with your light,
as matter itself is shining so bright.

**Beloved Arcturus, your Violet Flame pure,
is for every ailment the ultimate cure,
against it no darkness could ever endure,
earth's freedom it will forever ensure.**

5. Master MORE, help me see that the first line of reaction is the spirit. But the spirit was created out of a particular thought matrix. It is not real. It is only a thought matrix created in the mind, and it is created based on a selective view of life.

> Beloved Arcturus, your transforming Grace,
> empowers us now every challenge to face,
> with your Freedom's Song filling the ear,
> we know that to God we're ever so dear.

> **Beloved Arcturus, your Violet Flame pure,**
> **is for every ailment the ultimate cure,**
> **against it no darkness could ever endure,**
> **earth's freedom it will forever ensure.**

6. Master MORE, help me see that when a given spirit was created, it was based on this particular view of life. This was a view that I either accepted because of something that happened to me here on earth, or that I chose to create in order to deal with certain situations on earth.

> Beloved Arcturus, we surrender all fear,
> we're feeling your Presence so tangibly near,
> as your violet light floods our inner space,
> towards the ascension we willingly race.

> **Beloved Arcturus, your Violet Flame pure,**
> **is for every ailment the ultimate cure,**
> **against it no darkness could ever endure,**
> **earth's freedom it will forever ensure.**

7. Master MORE, help me see that from the moment I embodied here and dared to express my creative drive, I have been

ridiculed, put down and attacked in various ways: physical, emotional, mental and even at the identity level.

Beloved Arcturus, bring in a new age,
help earth and humanity turn a new page,
your transforming light gives us certainty,
Saint Germain's Golden Age is a reality.

**Beloved Arcturus, your Violet Flame pure,
is for every ailment the ultimate cure,
against it no darkness could ever endure,
earth's freedom it will forever ensure.**

8. Master MORE, help me see that I came as a new lifestream with the best of intentions and feeling like an innocent child. I was viciously attacked by people, who wanted to put me down or destroy me in order to keep me from expressing my creative drive.

Beloved Arcturus, illusions you pierce,
no serpent can stand against angels so fierce,
no forces of darkness can stop Violet Flame,
all discord on earth it will instantly tame.

**Beloved Arcturus, your Violet Flame pure,
is for every ailment the ultimate cure,
against it no darkness could ever endure,
earth's freedom it will forever ensure.**

9. Master MORE, help me see that I didn't know how to deal with this, and therefore I created a spirit to deal with this situation. This spirit was created based on the limited sense of self that I had at the time.

Beloved Arcturus, we love Saint Germain,
and therefore we call forth again and again,
your Violet Flame to flood all the earth,
so Saint Germain's eyes are filling with mirth.

Beloved Arcturus, your Violet Flame pure,
is for every ailment the ultimate cure,
against it no darkness could ever endure,
earth's freedom it will forever ensure.

Part 3

1. Master MORE, help me see that I was not able to look at the situation with the same clarity with which my I AM Presence looked at the situation. I had forgotten that I am a Conscious You that is pure awareness and therefore does not have to react to anything on earth but can allow the Presence to react.

Michael Archangel, in your flame so blue,
there is no more night, there is only you.
In oneness with you, we're filled with your light,
what glorious wonder, revealed to our sight.

Michael Archangel, your Knowing so strong,
Michael Archangel, oh sweep us along.
Michael Archangel, we're singing your song,
Michael Archangel, with you we belong.

2. Master MORE, help me see that I had come to believe that I had to react to things on earth based on my present level of self-awareness.

Michael Archangel, protection you give,
within your blue shield, we ever shall live.
Sealed from all creatures, roaming the night,
we remain in your sphere, of electric blue light.

Michael Archangel, your Knowing so strong,
Michael Archangel, oh sweep us along.
Michael Archangel, we're singing your song,
Michael Archangel, with you we belong.

3. Master MORE, help me see that because I did not know
how to react, I did not want to react and I thought there was
no constructive or purposeful way to react, I created a spirit to
react for me.

Michael Archangel, what power you bring,
as millions of angels, praises will sing.
Consuming the demons, of doubt and of fear,
we know that your Presence, will always be near.

Michael Archangel, your Knowing so strong,
Michael Archangel, oh sweep us along.
Michael Archangel, we're singing your song,
Michael Archangel, with you we belong.

4. Master MORE, help me see that the spirit was created based
on my level of consciousness, based on the way I looked at
life through the self I had taken on at the time. Thus, it is by
nature a limited spirit. It only has limited options for reacting
to certain situations.

Michael Archangel, God's will is your love,
you bring to us all, God's light from Above.

God's will is to see, all life taking flight,
transcendence of self, our most sacred right.

**Michael Archangel, your Knowing so strong,
Michael Archangel, oh sweep us along.
Michael Archangel, we're singing your song,
Michael Archangel, with you we belong.**

5. Master MORE, help me see that once the spirit is created, it is locked by the matrix that defined it. It does not have the self-awareness to transcend that matrix, so it can only continue to react to these situations based on the same pattern.

Michael Archangel, you are the best friend,
from all worldly dangers you do us defend,
the devil no match for your power of light,
and therefore our souls can freely take flight.

**Michael Archangel, your Knowing so strong,
Michael Archangel, oh sweep us along.
Michael Archangel, we're singing your song,
Michael Archangel, with you we belong.**

6. Master MORE, help me see that a spirit can only take this pattern towards an extreme, so that if the pattern is to become angry, I can become more and more angry, until I am constantly angry, constantly ready to lash out at anything that irritates me.

Michael Archangel, as children we play,
we're bringing the earth into a new day,
we raise it from all of the patterns so old,
our planet's life story is by us retold.

Michael Archangel, your Knowing so strong,
Michael Archangel, oh sweep us along.
Michael Archangel, we're singing your song,
Michael Archangel, with you we belong.

7. Master MORE, take me to the retreat of Saint Germain at the Cave of Symbols and show me visually how certain spirits are reacting when I take things personally.

Michael Archangel, God's power you show,
that you are invincible, this we do know,
you are undivided and thus can withstand,
anything coming from serpentine band.

Michael Archangel, your Knowing so strong,
Michael Archangel, oh sweep us along.
Michael Archangel, we're singing your song,
Michael Archangel, with you we belong.

8. Master MORE, help me see if I have a sense of being embarrassed or ridiculed in many situations where I do not feel I am being accepted by others.

Michael Archangel, come raise now the earth,
giving her thus a complete rebirth,
collective the mind that we do now raise,
for this we do give our infinite praise.

Michael Archangel, your Knowing so strong,
Michael Archangel, oh sweep us along.
Michael Archangel, we're singing your song,
Michael Archangel, with you we belong.

9. Master MORE, show me how my reaction is not a creative reaction where I make a choice about how to react. I am reacting automatically by stepping back – essentially giving up my self-awareness – and allowing a spirit to take over my reactions.

> Michael Archangel, the earth is now new,
> covered in Blue-flame as the morning dew,
> our planet now sparkles throughout all of space,
> as we are receiving your infinite Grace.
>
> **Michael Archangel, your Knowing so strong,**
> **Michael Archangel, oh sweep us along.**
> **Michael Archangel, we're singing your song,**
> **Michael Archangel, with you we belong.**

Part 4

1. Master MORE, show me how this spirit is reacting and what the spirit looks like. Show me that what is coming at me is not a creative reaction because anytime someone is attacking me, it is not a creative reaction from the other person or the dark forces.

> Zadkiel Archangel, your flow is so swift,
> in your violet light, we instantly shift,
> into a vibration in which we are free,
> from all limitations of the lesser me.
>
> **Zadkiel Archangel, encircle the earth,**
> **Zadkiel Archangel, with your violet girth,**

Zadkiel Archangel, unstoppable mirth,
Zadkiel Archangel, our planet's rebirth.

2. Master MORE, help me see that other people have also allowed spirits to take over their minds, and thus it is this aggressive spirit that is attacking me. And I am now reacting to it with a spirit of my own.

Zadkiel Archangel, we truly aspire,
to being the master of your violet fire,
wielding the power, of your alchemy,
we use Sacred Word, to set all life free.

Zadkiel Archangel, encircle the earth,
Zadkiel Archangel, with your violet girth,
Zadkiel Archangel, unstoppable mirth,
Zadkiel Archangel, our planet's rebirth.

3. Master MORE, help me see whether I react with an aggressive spirit that fights back, or with a passive spirit that submits to the attack and deals with it by taking it inwards.

Zadkiel Archangel, your violet light,
transforming the earth, with unstoppable might,
so swiftly our planet, beginning to spin,
with legions of angels, our victory we win.

Zadkiel Archangel, encircle the earth,
Zadkiel Archangel, with your violet girth,
Zadkiel Archangel, unstoppable mirth,
Zadkiel Archangel, our planet's rebirth.

4. Master MORE, help me see if I either blame myself, or feel stupid, ridiculed, embarrassed or angry at myself for not defending myself and not attacking back.

> Zadkiel Archangel, the earth is now free,
> from burdens put on her by humanity,
> all people are free from their inner strife,
> embracing the freedom to start a new life.

> **Zadkiel Archangel, encircle the earth,**
> **Zadkiel Archangel, with your violet girth,**
> **Zadkiel Archangel, unstoppable mirth,**
> **Zadkiel Archangel, our planet's rebirth.**

5. Master MORE, help me see that my reaction is a spirit, but the attack is also a spirit. So there is one spirit attacking me and there is another spirit reacting to the attack.

> Zadkiel Archangel, the earth will now spin,
> much faster as we Christ victory win,
> for in Christ the captives are truly set free,
> bathed in Christ Light the earth now will be.

> **Zadkiel Archangel, encircle the earth,**
> **Zadkiel Archangel, with your violet girth,**
> **Zadkiel Archangel, unstoppable mirth,**
> **Zadkiel Archangel, our planet's rebirth.**

6. Master MORE, I see that it is completely meaningless to allow my life to be eaten up by these spirits attacking each other or defending themselves from the attacks of other spirits.

Zadkiel Archangel, the forces of night,
are bound by your penetrating Freedom Light,
the earth is now cleared from forces so dark,
as your Violet Light provides a new spark.

Zadkiel Archangel, encircle the earth,
Zadkiel Archangel, with your violet girth,
Zadkiel Archangel, unstoppable mirth,
Zadkiel Archangel, our planet's rebirth.

7. Master MORE, I see that this is eating up my attention, it is
eating up my life, and I have the determination to say: "Stop!
I will no longer allow my freedom to be taken away by these
spirits."

Zadkiel Archangel, we truly love you,
and to Saint Germain we will always be true,
help us now see our plans so Divine,
so we on this planet our full light can shine.

Zadkiel Archangel, encircle the earth,
Zadkiel Archangel, with your violet girth,
Zadkiel Archangel, unstoppable mirth,
Zadkiel Archangel, our planet's rebirth.

8. Master MORE, help me look at the spirit that I am dealing
with right now, the main spirit that I am allowing to take over
my reactions to life or specific situations in life.

Zadkiel Archangel, there is no more night,
a new day is born from your great Violet Light,
transforming all manifestations of fear,
we know that the Golden Age is now here.

Zadkiel Archangel, encircle the earth,
Zadkiel Archangel, with your violet girth,
Zadkiel Archangel, unstoppable mirth,
Zadkiel Archangel, our planet's rebirth.

9. Master MORE, I hereby make the decision that I no longer want this spirit to control my reactions to this particular type of situation. I am willing to use my power and my will to make a creative decision about how to react to these situations.

Zadkiel Archangel, your violet flame,
the earth and humanity, never the same,
Saint Germain's Golden Age, is a reality,
what glorious wonder, we joyously see.

Zadkiel Archangel, encircle the earth,
Zadkiel Archangel, with your violet girth,
Zadkiel Archangel, unstoppable mirth,
Zadkiel Archangel, our planet's rebirth.

Part 5

1. Master MORE, help me see that a creative decision is where I am free to react in a way that I have not done before. I am free to react based on how I want to react, not letting a spirit take over my reactions.

Master MORE, come to the fore,
we will absorb your flame of MORE.
Master MORE, our will so strong,
our power centers cleared by song.

**Master MORE, your Sacred Heart,
from this we will no more depart,
we are forever in your flow,
of Diamond Will that you bestow.**

2. Master MORE, I see that I have created a spirit. I see that I have in the past reacted in certain ways many times in this kind of situation. But why should I be bound in the now by the way I have reacted in the past? This is not free will. I am not exercising my willpower when I am allowing a spirit to take over my reactions because I do not want to choose.

Master MORE, your wisdom flows,
as our attunement ever grows.
Master MORE, we have a tie,
that helps us see through Serpent's lie.

**Master MORE, your Sacred Heart,
from this we will no more depart,
we are forever in your flow,
of Diamond Will that you bestow.**

3. Master MORE, I take back my will power. I take back my power of will, and I am willing to choose. For I realize that the spirit that I created many lifetimes ago, was created based on the sense of self I had at the time. But I have grown. I have expanded my sense of self. Therefore, I am able and willing to react in a more mature, conscious and more aware way now than I did in the past.

Master MORE, your love so pink,
there is no purer love, we think.

Master MORE, you set us free,
from all conditionality.

**Master MORE, your Sacred Heart,
from this we will no more depart,
we are forever in your flow,
of Diamond Will that you bestow.**

4. Master MORE, help me see that freedom can be lost by not making decisions. But freedom cannot be won without making conscious, willful, deliberate decisions.

Master MORE, we will endure,
your discipline that makes us pure.
Master MORE, intentions true,
as we are always one with you.

**Master MORE, your Sacred Heart,
from this we will no more depart,
we are forever in your flow,
of Diamond Will that you bestow.**

5. Master MORE, help me see that freedom is an active force. It requires power to be free, and power can be unleashed only through will. I cannot be free by being passive and hoping for a point where no one will attack me. For that point will not come on planet earth.

Master MORE, our vision raised,
the will of God is always praised.
Master MORE, creative will,
raising all life higher still.

Master MORE, your Sacred Heart,
from this we will no more depart,
we are forever in your flow,
of Diamond Will that you bestow.

6. Master MORE, help me start to depersonalize my life by realizing that the people who are attacking or ridiculing me are not actually ridiculing me personally. They are not even seeing me, for they are seeing me through the filter of the spirit that is dominating their consciousness.

Master MORE, your peace is power,
the demons of war it will devour.
Master MORE, we serve all life,
our flames consuming war and strife.

Master MORE, your Sacred Heart,
from this we will no more depart,
we are forever in your flow,
of Diamond Will that you bestow.

7. Master MORE, help me see that what such a spirit sees is based on the matrix that defined the spirit, the spirit sees only the matrix. It is not seeing the reality of who I am. It is simply seeing the pattern that is created in the mind of the spirit when this spirit encounters me, or even the spirit that is running my life.

Master MORE, we are so free,
eternal bond from you we see.
Master MORE, we find rebirth,
in flow of your eternal mirth.

Master MORE, your Sacred Heart,
from this we will no more depart,
we are forever in your flow,
of Diamond Will that you bestow.

8. Master MORE, help me see that the spirit in the other person is not seeing me. The other person is not conscious, is not aware. Nobody can attack me if they are fully aware of who they are as spiritual beings. For then they would also be aware that I am a spiritual being.

Master MORE, you balance all,
the seven rays upon our call.
Master MORE, forever MORE,
we are the Spirit's open door.

Master MORE, your Sacred Heart,
from this we will no more depart,
we are forever in your flow,
of Diamond Will that you bestow.

9. Master MORE, help me see that one spiritual being would not put down another. But one spirit would indeed put down another spirit or another spiritual being, but they are not seeing the spiritual being that I am. They are only seeing a mirage created in their own minds by their perception filter encountering who I am.

Master MORE, your Presence here,
filling up the inner sphere.
Life is now a sacred flow,
God Power we on all bestow.

**Master MORE, your Sacred Heart,
from this we will no more depart,
we are forever in your flow,
of Diamond Will that you bestow.**

Part 6

1. Master MORE, help me see that if they are not attacking me personally, why am I taking it personally? It is not really about me. Why am I then feeling that I am personally attacked?

Saint Germain, your alchemy,
with violet fire now sets us free.
Saint Germain, we ever grow,
in freedom's overpowering flow.

**O Saint Germain, your Golden Age,
sets people free from psychic cage,
the earth is raised to starry height,
as we project with Freedom's Sight.**

2. Master MORE, help me realize that the Conscious You – the pure awareness – is not feeling personally attacked. It is the spirit through which I am looking at the situation that is feeling personally attacked.

Saint Germain, your mastery,
of violet flame geometry.
Saint Germain, in you we see,
the formulas that set us free.

**O Saint Germain, your Golden Age,
sets people free from psychic cage,
the earth is raised to starry height,
as we project with Freedom's Sight.**

3. Master MORE, help me see that my spirit was created to feel personally attacked and to deal with this kind of situation in a specific way. I am not the spirit, and I do not need to feel what the spirit is feeling. Even though the spirit takes it personally, I do not need to take it personally.

Saint Germain, in Liberty,
you give the love that sets all free.
Saint Germain, we do adore,
the violet flame that makes all more.

**O Saint Germain, your Golden Age,
sets people free from psychic cage,
the earth is raised to starry height,
as we project with Freedom's Sight.**

4. Master MORE, I see that the "I" that is reacting to the situation is not the same "I" that is giving this invocation. Because I have the ability to ask myself which I is reacting to the situation, there is an I that is the Conscious You and there is an I that is only the spirit—and the I that thinks it is the spirit has no reality to it. The spirit has no reality to it.

Saint Germain, in unity,
we will transcend duality.
Saint Germain, the self so pure,
your violet chemistry so sure.

O Saint Germain, your Golden Age,
sets people free from psychic cage,
the earth is raised to starry height,
as we project with Freedom's Sight.

5. Master MORE, help me see that I am not bound by the way this spirit reacts. I am not bound by the matrix. I now make a creative decision to look at the matrix, see how it is limiting me, and say: "I do not want to look at this situation through this matrix. I want to look at it in a more creative way. I want to be more free to look at this situation from a higher perspective and therefore react from the higher vision."

Saint Germain, reality,
in violet light we are carefree.
Saint Germain, our auras seal,
your violet flame our chakras heal.

O Saint Germain, your Golden Age,
sets people free from psychic cage,
the earth is raised to starry height,
as we project with Freedom's Sight.

6. Master MORE, help me see that the spirits I have created are limiting my power. They are saying that I cannot react in a creative way to a certain situation, I have to react the way I have always reacted because I have to react through the spirit.

Saint Germain, your chemistry,
with violet fire set atoms free.
Saint Germain, from lead to gold,
transforming vision we behold.

O Saint Germain, your Golden Age,
sets people free from psychic cage,
the earth is raised to starry height,
as we project with Freedom's Sight.

7. Master MORE, help me see that this is not expressing my creative power. The more spirits I have created, the more I will limit the amount of creative power that will stream through me from my I AM Presence.

Saint Germain, transcendency,
as we are always one with thee.
Saint Germain, from soul we're free,
we so delight in knowing thee.

O Saint Germain, your Golden Age,
sets people free from psychic cage,
the earth is raised to starry height,
as we project with Freedom's Sight.

8. Master MORE, help me see that the fallen beings knew that if they attacked me with enough viciousness and injustice, then I would feel so traumatized that I could be deceived out of my innocence by thinking that I had to react to the attack from a similar level of consciousness.

Saint Germain, nobility,
the key to sacred alchemy.
Saint Germain, you balance all,
the seven rays upon our call.

O Saint Germain, your Golden Age,
sets people free from psychic cage,

the earth is raised to starry height,
as we project with Freedom's Sight.

9. Master MORE, help me see that in order to remain innocent, I have to allow the fallen beings to continually attack me by being transparent so that it passes right through me. Ultimate innocence is transparency where whatever they direct at me from the fallen consciousness passes right through me.

Saint Germain, your Presence here,
filling up the inner sphere.
Life is now a sacred flow,
God Freedom we on all bestow.

O Saint Germain, your Golden Age,
sets people free from psychic cage,
the earth is raised to starry height,
as we project with Freedom's Sight.

Part 7

1. Master MORE, help me see that the dark forces could not force me to react to them. I had to choose to react at the same level. I now look calmly at the spirit that is holding me back at this level and say: "You have had your day. You are not going to control my life any longer. You are not going to control my reaction to this particular type of situation, and thus I am willing to make conscious decisions about how to react here."

Master MORE, come to the fore,
we will absorb your flame of MORE.

Master MORE, our will so strong,
our power centers cleared by song.

Master MORE, your Sacred Heart,
from this we will no more depart,
we are forever in your flow,
of Diamond Will that you bestow.

2. Master MORE, help me see how to deliberately change my reaction to specific situations or specific other people. Help me see that if the relationship is to change, which is what I want, then I am the one who must do something to change the dynamic. And that means I must change my reaction and I must change the way I treat the other person.

Master MORE, your wisdom flows,
as our attunement ever grows.
Master MORE, we have a tie,
that helps us see through Serpent's lie.

Master MORE, your Sacred Heart,
from this we will no more depart,
we are forever in your flow,
of Diamond Will that you bestow.

3. Master MORE, help me accept that I have exercised my free will by changing my reaction. I will not allow myself to be deceived by the serpentine mind into thinking that it is my responsibility to change the other person. I am continuing to react in an impersonal way to the other person.

Master MORE, your love so pink,
there is no purer love, we think.

Master MORE, you set us free,
from all conditionality.

**Master MORE, your Sacred Heart,
from this we will no more depart,
we are forever in your flow,
of Diamond Will that you bestow.**

4. Master MORE, help me see that one of the primary ways in which the serpents tempt me to enter this action-reaction pattern is by making me believe that there is a certain outcome that *must* be attained. They often do this with the epic mindset that there is some superior cause that demands the manifestation of a certain outcome.

Master MORE, we will endure,
your discipline that makes us pure.
Master MORE, intentions true,
as we are always one with you.

**Master MORE, your Sacred Heart,
from this we will no more depart,
we are forever in your flow,
of Diamond Will that you bestow.**

5. Master MORE, help me free myself from this action-reaction pattern by seeing that there are always two extremes in the duality consciousness, and I need both in order to be trapped in this consciousness.

Master MORE, our vision raised,
the will of God is always praised.

Master MORE, creative will,
raising all life higher still.

**Master MORE, your Sacred Heart,
from this we will no more depart,
we are forever in your flow,
of Diamond Will that you bestow.**

6. Master MORE, help me recognize my own higher humanity – my spirituality – and see the specific spirit that is causing
me to react in a way that is inhumane towards others and also
inhumane towards myself.

Master MORE, your peace is power,
the demons of war it will devour.
Master MORE, we serve all life,
our flames consuming war and strife.

**Master MORE, your Sacred Heart,
from this we will no more depart,
we are forever in your flow,
of Diamond Will that you bestow.**

7. Master MORE, help me see this spirit, see that it is not me,
see that it is unreal, and thereby decide to completely let it go
without going into the reaction of feeling guilty for having created that spirit in the first place.

Master MORE, we are so free,
eternal bond from you we see.
Master MORE, we find rebirth,
in flow of your eternal mirth.

**Master MORE, your Sacred Heart,
from this we will no more depart,
we are forever in your flow,
of Diamond Will that you bestow.**

8. Master MORE, help me see a particular spirit without going into another spirit that can only react with guilt and self-blame because the spirit was created based on this matrix.

Master MORE, you balance all,
the seven rays upon our call.
Master MORE, forever MORE,
we are the Spirit's open door.

**Master MORE, your Sacred Heart,
from this we will no more depart,
we are forever in your flow,
of Diamond Will that you bestow.**

9. Master MORE, help me transcend the catch-22 where I create one spirit to react in inhumane ways and I create another spirit to blame myself for reacting in inhumane ways. The effect is that it is extremely difficult to recognize the first spirit because then I know that the other spirit will take over my reaction and make me feel bad.

Master MORE, your Presence here,
filling up the inner sphere.
Life is now a sacred flow,
God Power we on all bestow.

**Master MORE, your Sacred Heart,
from this we will no more depart,**

**we are forever in your flow,
of Diamond Will that you bestow.**

Part 8

1. Master MORE, I am willing to take your hand and look at both spirits and see that the self-blame does not come from God because my I AM Presence does not blame me for anything I have done here on earth. It sees that it is all unreal; it is all part of the cosmic sandbox that this planet is.

Saint Germain, your alchemy,
with violet fire now sets us free.
Saint Germain, we ever grow,
in freedom's overpowering flow.

**O Saint Germain, your Golden Age,
sets people free from psychic cage,
the earth is raised to starry height,
as we project with Freedom's Sight.**

2. Master MORE, help me see that there is nothing done on earth that has any permanence that has an reality. And if it has no permanence and no reality, then why do I have to carry it with me as part of my lifestream? What carries it with me is a spirit in my being, but I am *more* than the spirit.

Saint Germain, your mastery,
of violet flame geometry.
Saint Germain, in you we see,
the formulas that set us free.

O Saint Germain, your Golden Age,
sets people free from psychic cage,
the earth is raised to starry height,
as we project with Freedom's Sight.

3. Master MORE, help me use my momentum to go into the akashic record and with laser-like precision direct a beam of light to erase that original record from akasha.

Saint Germain, in Liberty,
you give the love that sets all free.
Saint Germain, we do adore,
the violet flame that makes all more.

O Saint Germain, your Golden Age,
sets people free from psychic cage,
the earth is raised to starry height,
as we project with Freedom's Sight.

4. Master MORE, help me see the reality that when something is erased from the akashic record, I have fulfilled the requirements whereby God says: "I will remember their sins no more." And that is when I can dismiss and shatter the thought matrix of the spirit that carries this situation with me in my memory body, constantly using it to blame me for having made a mistake in the past.

Saint Germain, in unity,
we will transcend duality.
Saint Germain, the self so pure,
your violet chemistry so sure.

O Saint Germain, your Golden Age,
sets people free from psychic cage,
the earth is raised to starry height,
as we project with Freedom's Sight.

5. Master MORE, help me see that when I have transcended the consciousness that caused me to make that choice in the past, there is no reason for me to carry the memory of it in my lower being. For the positive lesson of transcending that level of consciousness is now part of my causal body.

Saint Germain, reality,
in violet light we are carefree.
Saint Germain, our auras seal,
your violet flame our chakras heal.

O Saint Germain, your Golden Age,
sets people free from psychic cage,
the earth is raised to starry height,
as we project with Freedom's Sight.

6. Master MORE and Saint Germain, help me have that inner knowing – that direct experience – that it is possible to be completely free of a negative situation from my past. It is possible to completely transcend a so-called mistake that I made and to turn it into a positive, life-supporting, growth-supporting experience.

Saint Germain, your chemistry,
with violet fire set atoms free.
Saint Germain, from lead to gold,
transforming vision we behold.

O Saint Germain, your Golden Age,
sets people free from psychic cage,
the earth is raised to starry height,
as we project with Freedom's Sight.

7. Master MORE, help me connect to the childlike innocence where I know that any mistake I could have made can be made good again, can be transcended, can be left behind.

Saint Germain, transcendency,
as we are always one with thee.
Saint Germain, from soul we're free,
we so delight in knowing thee.

O Saint Germain, your Golden Age,
sets people free from psychic cage,
the earth is raised to starry height,
as we project with Freedom's Sight.

8. Master MORE, help me see that I have such a desire to do well that I also have a tendency to blame myself when I make mistakes. Yet the Conscious You knows that at the level of the I AM Presence, everything that happens on earth can be turned into a positive experience.

Saint Germain, nobility,
the key to sacred alchemy.
Saint Germain, you balance all,
the seven rays upon our call.

O Saint Germain, your Golden Age,
sets people free from psychic cage,

**the earth is raised to starry height,
as we project with Freedom's Sight.**

9. Master MORE, help me become conscious of the fact that life on earth – even in the state that this planet is in right now – can become an entirely positive experience where I go from positive learning experience to positive learning experience and I keep transcending myself in an upward spiral.

Saint Germain, your Presence here,
filling up the inner sphere.
Life is now a sacred flow,
God Freedom we on all bestow.

**O Saint Germain, your Golden Age,
sets people free from psychic cage,
the earth is raised to starry height,
as we project with Freedom's Sight.**

Sealing:

In the name of the Divine Mother, I fully accept that the power of these calls is used to set free the Ma-ter light, so it can outpicture the perfect vision of Christ for my own life, for all people and for the planet. In the name I AM THAT I AM, it is done! Amen.

19 | THE OUT-BREATH AND THE IN-BREATH OF GOD

Master MORE, I AM. And I come to give you an impression of what the First Ray really is. Not as you see it when you first begin the Path of the Seven Veils where you start at the 48th level and work your way up through the seven initiations in the First Ray retreat. But I wish to give you an impression of what the First Ray is seen from the perspective of an ascended being and even the Creator itself.

The levels of the material realm

You should know that life has a hierarchical structure. You may start at your present level of awareness where most people are focused on the physical body and the material realm, what they can detect with the senses. Yet if you are a spiritual person open to this teaching, you know, of course that there are other realms, other dimensions. You know that there is an emotional realm where you find your feelings. This has a higher vibration than the material, as seen by the fact that it is not as dense that feelings are easier to change than physical matter.

When you go beyond the emotional level, you reach the mental where you have thoughts. And thoughts are even more fleeting and easier to change than feelings. Once a feeling is set on a track and qualified with a certain vibration, such as anger, it is harder to change that feeling than to change the thought that often precedes the feelings. Once you are angry with a person, it is harder to change this than if you are just thinking about what the person did or did not do.

Of course, you can go beyond the mental into the etheric where you find your sense of identity. And here you also find that your identity is actually much easier to change, once you get to the point where you are tuned in to the identity level rather than looking at it through the filter of the conscious mind, the emotional mind and the mental mind. Once you use the Conscious You's ability to project itself into the identity realm, then it is easy to switch your sense of identity. In fact, you can instantly switch from believing you are a human, material being to knowing and experiencing that you are spiritual being that you are pure awareness.

Likewise, you can potentially instantly shift to not identifying yourself as a being in embodiment but as a spiritual being. I admit that at your current level of consciousness it would be difficult to make that shift instantly, but as you rise on the path toward the 144th level of consciousness, you learn to consciously master the process of switching your sense of identity. And when you come to the 144th level, it is but a small switch – a small step – to shift from there to the ascended state.

The levels of the spiritual realm

If you keep going up, you now – after you ascend – you enter the spiritual realm. At first you might enter the realm that is closest to the material world in vibration. But again, there are many levels of the spiritual realm. And how do you work your way up through those levels? By, again, experiencing a certain sense of self until you have had enough of that experience and want more. And therefore you switch into a higher sense of self.

You may start seeing yourself as a newly ascended master, and you can choose to stay with the earth and help other unascended beings. Or you can chose to move on to other realms in the ascended world where you can be of a different kind of service or have a different kind of experience. But then you will grow towards higher levels. You will come to a point where you can serve in one of the higher offices. You can even become worthy to hold the office of an Archangel or Elohim or God or Goddess and therefore fulfill still higher offices in the hierarchical structure of the one mind of God.

We have given a teaching that you might be familiar with that there are different spheres that the Creator first created one sphere and then, when the self-aware extensions of the Creator had brought that sphere to its ascension point, a new sphere was created. And this has continued through seven levels, so that you are now in the seventh – unascended – sphere whereas the six previous ones have all ascended.

As you work your way up to the ascended state, you will first enter the lower levels of the spiritual realm, which is represented by the sixth sphere, the one most recently ascended. In that sphere there is a hierarchical structure. You can work your way up through that structure until you come up to the highest level of the sixth sphere. Then you can transcend, going up to the fifth, work your way up through that and continue this process until you reach the first sphere where you will work your way up to the point where you attain the level of awareness held by the Creator, the Creator who created this world of form out of its own Being.

This is your long-term potential, and it is open to any self-aware being that is an extension of the Creator. This does not necessarily mean every human being currently embodied on earth, but it does mean the majority of them. What does creation – what does the world of form – look like from the viewpoint of the Creator itself? Why did the Creator create anything? Why did the Creator start the process of creation?

Why the Creator created

Well, the First Ray is the first ray because it embodies the basic vision, desire, driving force that made the Creator start the process of creating this world of form. It is something that cannot easily be translated into the words you use on earth, which is why we have described the First Ray in various ways, such as the ray of God power, the ray of God will or the ray of the creative drive.

But truly, you can also describe it as the desire to be more because the Creator is in a state of being completely self-contained, completely self-sufficient. A being who has attained the Creator consciousness can indeed be completely content for what you on earth would call a very long time, almost eternity, without creating anything. A Creator has no obligation or duty to create.

Why does a Creator decide to create—and thereby essentially tie itself to its own creation until that creation has gone through the process of reaching its fulfillment? Well, a

Creator does this out of this love to be more, out of this drive to be more. And you may say, with the earth consciousness: "Well where did this drive come from? Where did it start? Who started everything? Who created the first Creator?" These are questions that can be asked from the linear mind but cannot be answered by the linear mind. I cannot give you an answer that works for the linear mind because the linear mind cannot fathom that everything cannot be put on a scale with a beginning and an ending.

Your world of form has a beginning when your Creator said: "I will create. I will be more. I will express." It will have a logical conclusion when all self-aware extensions of the Creator have reached the Creator consciousness. But the process of life itself never had a beginning and never will have an end. It is on-going, ever-transcending and there is no limit.

This is something the linear mind finds impossible to deal with, but there is no limit for creativity. This is an important concept for you to ponder, somewhere in the back of your mind because it will help you fully integrate the lessons you are meant to learn from these First Ray instructions, but it will also help you integrate the lessons you will learn from the other Chohans.

No creative limits

There truly, my beloved, is no limit to creativity. Why is this so? Why is the First Ray often called the ray of will? Because creativity, creation, starts with a will to create. And what drives creativity is the will to be more, the will to create something that is more. You are part of the co-creative process because you have been given free will. One of the hardest things to understand for the students who come to my retreat – and who in many cases have just risen beyond the 48th level or to the 48th level – is precisely that free will is FREE.

I have students that are dear to me because they have faithfully studied ascended master teachings and practiced our decrees for 30-40 years or more. But many of them still find it difficult to understand the reality that free will is always free. To help you – perhaps – grasp this, let me ask you to consider the situation of the Creator, a being with the Creator consciousness, who has just made the decision: "I will to create."

As we have explained *[The Power of Self]*, the Creator first defines a spherical boundary around itself to separate itself from the Allness in which no separate form can exist. After having created this void by concentrating itself into a singularity in the center of the void, the Creator then projects out what we have described as the first sphere inside the void. This sphere will have certain structures and forms in it, so that there is a platform for the newly created self-aware extensions of the Creator.

Why is this so? Because when you are a new being, who has not reached the level of the Creator consciousness, you cannot handle standing there with all creative possibilities open to you. It would simply be impossible to be in the same situation as the Creator because you would not know where to begin creating. So consider the situation faced by the Creator when it has withdrawn itself into a singularity, has projected the Ma-ter light out as the first sphere and now it is facing the situation of creating structures in the sphere.

There is nothing in this sphere that is manifest. There is no form. But now consider this. The Creator has not created anything before this point. The Creator has not made any previous choice except the choice: "I will to create." But it has not made any choice about forming, designing, envisioning specific forms. This means that when your Creator created the very first sphere, all possibilities were open. The Creator could create this sphere in absolutely any way it wanted. There was no previous choice that could limit the Creator's choices.

The mechanics of creation

My beloved, try to still the analytical mind and just focus on the Conscious You who is witnessing you as you are sitting here, listening to or reading this dictation. Try to become aware that you have the ability to mentally step outside of yourself and actually be aware that you are sitting here taking in these words. This is the part of your being that we have called pure awareness or the Conscious You. You can mentally be aware that you are engaged in an activity. When you are aware of this pure awareness, you have some sense of co-measurement of what the Creator faced. All choices were open. There was no previous choice that could in any way set a direction for the succeeding choices.

Now imagine what happened when the Creator made a choice in its mind to focus its attention on a specific design, certain principles and certain ideas. You see the mechanics, do you not? What the Creator was doing was creating a world of form. This is a world where there are different forms that are set apart by their differences. This does not necessarily mean that they are separate, as the ego sees everything as separate, but it does mean that the Creator was creating forms that had differentiation.

There are an infinite number of differentiated forms that could have been created in that first sphere. Nevertheless, by the very mechanics of creating something that has differentiation, it is impossible to create forms that embody all possibilities. In other words, the Creator could not create everything at once. The Creator had to make a selection, had to make a choice, had to limit the infinite possibilities to a certain range.

This means that when the Creator started out the creative process, it had to narrow down from an infinite number of possibilities, until it had focused on a specific range of possibilities that it wanted to use as the foundation for your specific world of form. Once the Creator had made the choice to narrow down the range of possibilities that initial choice then set the stage, set a matrix, for everything that the Creator designed after that point—and everything that the self-aware extensions of the Creator could design within the sphere created by the Creator.

Setting a matrix for co-creation

The nature of making choices is that you are selecting from an infinite number of possibilities, but you are focusing on a few and you are choosing to carry those out. That is not to say that you, on earth, have an infinite number of possibilities for your creative efforts. For you are creating within the framework set not only by your Creator in the original decision, but also by the whole hierarchy of co-creative beings starting in the first sphere, then going to the second sphere.

But you see, the first sphere, as it ascended, set a certain matrix. And when the beings in the first sphere created the structures of the second sphere, they made choices within the matrix set by the first sphere. So the co-creators in the second sphere could only make choices within that range. You now see how the different levels of hierarchy work. For each level that you go down from the Creator, you are in a sense narrowing the range of possibilities, the range of possible creative choices.

When you go all the way through this hierarchy of the six previous ascended spheres to the unascended sphere in which you are focused, then you see that you are making choices within the hierarchical structure. And in a sense, each of the levels of hierarchy have narrowed down the potential creative choices that can be made.

When you get to a planet like earth, you will see that in its original design the Elohim made certain design choices for the earth, for the design of this planet, for how life would unfold on this planet. And they were certainly within the hierarchical structure of the entire creative hierarchy, reaching back to the Creator. But even so, the seven Elohim had many more possibilities for creating a planet, but they again narrowed down the selection.

The out-breath and the in-breath

You see now that this creative process of going out from the point of the Creator who has infinite possibilities – but going through different levels in a hierarchical structure that gradually narrows the creative possibilities – this entire structure can be seen as the out-breath of God where the Creator is breathing out. And what it is breathing out is the creative drive itself.

But as the out-breath happens, the creative possibilities, the range of creative possibilities, is gradually narrowed, until you reach the latest level in the creative process, the unascended sphere where it reaches its narrowest point. And this is the situation that you face when you embody on earth at the 48th level.

You are starting out your co-creative efforts in the most dense, the most narrow, environment so far created through the hierarchical process of co-creation. Your original task

– in the ideal scenario where you embody at the 48th level of consciousness – is to begin the process of the in-breath of God where you start out with a limited range of creative options but you gradually expand your sense of self.

What does it mean to expand your sense of self? Well, when you are at the 48th level, you can see a certain range of creative options, a certain range of ways you can express your creativity. When you express your creativity at that level and learn from it, there will come a point where you begin to ask yourself: "But are these really my only options? Is this really the limit to my creative drive, my creative force?"

Then you can realize: "Yes, these options are the limits to my creative options at my current sense of self." And that is when you can connect – whether people do this consciously or unconsciously – to the fact that you are at your core pure awareness. You do need a certain sense of self in order to express yourself in a dense environment like earth. This is why the Maha Chohan has said that you need to create a sense of self, or a certain spirit, through which you express yourself.

But the entire point of the in-breath of God is that you have the intuitive sense that you are not the outer self. You are not the spirit. You are not the physical body. You are not the mental body. You are not the emotional body. You are not the identity body. You are more than this. You are pure awareness. Thus, you can shift into a higher sense of self where you now open up a more vast array of creative options. You can co-create more at the 49th level than at the 48th level because you can see more options than you could see at the previous level.

All possibilities are open

We could say that in essence, in principle, all creative options are open to you at this moment but you cannot conceive of these options. And even if you could conceive of them, you could not believe that you have the power to manifest them. The in-breath of God is the process whereby you gradually raise your self-awareness, until you begin to see more and more options and you come to believe and accept that you can choose these options. You can express them. You can bring them into manifestation.

To give you a simple example, Jesus had raised his self-awareness to where he could see the possibility of having a certain mastery of mind over matter. He could believe it was possible that through him, through his outer self and form, God could manifest the transformation of water into wine. And he was willing to let the power of God flow through him because he accepted that this was possible.

Right now your sense of self determines how much of the power of God you can accept flowing through you and what you can accept that that power of God can do through you. And the entire process of the in-breath of God is that you gradually raise your sense of self through many levels of the hierarchical structure, until in the end you come to the process of realizing that the creative power that you see being expressed through your Creator is not limited to the Creator. It is the creative power of life itself, and it can express itself through any being with a sufficient level of consciousness, a sufficient sense of self. Thus, you have the potential to attain the Creator consciousness, be a Creator, and create your own world of form where you can make different choices, a different selection of possibilities, than what was done by your Creator.

The test of creativity

What is it that I want to teach you by giving you this somewhat abstract teaching? It is that, in principle, at any point you are at in your level of self-awareness, you are facing the challenge, the test, which we can call by different names. You may call it the serpentine consciousness, the devil, satan, the prince of this world, Mara—whatever you want to call it. But it is a simple test: Will you allow your previous choices to limit your future choices?

Think about this. Think about this in the context of what we have told you about the difference between the ideal scenario and what you face on earth right now. We have told you that it is possible to start at the 48th level, make choices, express your creative abilities, but you can do so in a way that does not limit yourself or any part of life. You are doing it from the sense that you are a connected being that you want to raise all life, including yourself. Thus, it is possible to express your creative powers in such a way that it uplifts all life. This means that it does not create for yourself what in many spiritual teachings is called karma. There is no residue of your past choices that you are carrying with you and that can limit you in the future.

What is it, then that has happened to those beings who went into the consciousness of separation, descended below the 48th level of consciousness? Is this just part of the out-breath of God where you might say: "Well, they have just taken the out-breath further by limiting the creative choices even more?" But nay, my beloved, it is not. This is not part of the out-breath. This is an entirely different process where people use their free will to actually separate themselves from the out-breath of God.

What God has done in the out-breath – or what the creative hierarchy has done in the out-breath – is to define a certain matrix for the range of creative choices that can be made on earth. The Elohim, as I said, defined the original planet, the original matrix for this planet, and it was much more pure than what you see today. They had a certain range of creative choices that could be made by the first beings that embodied here.

Leaving the out-breath

Now, notice that I say that the Elohim had defined a range of creative choices. With that I mean choices that would help raise all life and would eventually raise planet earth from the level at which it was created by the Elohim – which was the low range that the Elohim envisioned – to the highest level that the Elohim envisioned. Where the earth would then ascend to a higher level and could eventually ascend with the rest of the sphere.

Yet because of the nature of free will, it is possible that beings can choose not to engage in this creative process of building up from what the Elohim have created. They can choose to separate themselves from that process. They can chose to rebel against that process. They can choose to believe in the serpentine lie that they will become as gods who can define their own range of creative choices. They can even chose to believe in the lie that this is how they won their creative freedom and this is how they are really helping to co-create God's creation.

There are all kinds of lies. There are all kinds of subtle temptations for justifying this choice. But the fact is that this was not part of the out-breath. And the reason for this is very simple: The process of the out-breath continually defines a more narrow range of creative choices, but no matter how low this range of choices has been taken, you can always go up from there. Any creative choice you make, will take you up and will raise the whole. Thus, even at the lowest point of the out-breath, the entire purpose is to help self-aware beings start the process of the in-breath.

But when you separate yourself from the creative process, you are no longer part of the out-breath leading to the in-breath. You have separated yourself from the process, which means that now you cannot start the in-breath. Well, you can, but you can only do so by reversing the former choices. And those choices – when you make the choices from the consciousness of separation, from the consciousness of duality – will not facilitate your shift into the in-breath. They will keep you in separation, and you will actually continue to make choices that will create consequences, or karma, which will limit your future options.

You know, probably, by experience that when you have a karmic return, such as an illness or accident or whatever it may be, you feel powerless to do anything about it. You feel like you can do nothing to escape the situation. You have no creative options. You can only endure this and wait and see how it plays out. But this is a perception that is only true when you are looking at the situation from inside the sense of self, the spirit that made those limiting choices that made the choices out of separation.

The linear view of karma

If you can shift into pure awareness, you can see that even in the most dense karmic situation, you do have choices. Even if you cannot in the short term change the outer physical circumstances, you can always change the way you react to those circumstances. You can change your state of mind. This choice is always open to you, when you are willing to shift out of the separate self, out of that separate spirit, out of the death consciousness. You see, the death consciousness does not lead you back into the in-breath. It only leads you into a downward spiral that ends up becoming self-destructive. In order to shift into the in-breath where you move back towards having more creative options, you need to realize that you are more than the separate self because you are pure awareness.

What is the essential difference between pure awareness and the sense of being a separate being? Well, when you are in the sense of separation, when you are focused on the separate self, you will feel that outer situations, your karma, other people, God, fate, destiny, bad luck, or even your own past choices, are limiting the choices you can make in the present.

What does this mean? It means that many people get trapped in this kind of linear thinking, and you will see, if you look honestly at the spiritual people on earth that many of them are trapped in this kind of linear thinking. Where they think: "Oh yes, I recognize that I have lived before and in past lives I have created karma for myself. How can I escape this?" And then you think, with the linear mind that you actually have to go back in time to the situation where you made that choice that set you on this karmic course. You think you have to go back there and change something, and then you will be free of the choice.

You will see, if you look at popular literature and movies that there has been, for a long time, this dream of creating a technological device called a time machine where you can physically travel back in time. In other words, you enter a machine, you set a certain destination in time, there is burring and whizzing and noises of all kinds, and suddenly you open the machine and step back. And now you are, in your present physical body, back in prehistoric times, perhaps running around among medieval people or dinosaurs or whatever people envision.

But do you see that when you think about this logically, what would be the purpose of going back in time with your present physical body? The karmic choices you made ten lifetimes ago were not made with your present, physical body. They were made when you were in another physical body. Even if your physical body could be transported 500 years back in time, how could your present physical body change the choices you made when you were in a different physical body? Again, I am simply trying to use the linear mind to show you the illogical way of reasoning of the linear mind.

Beyond linear thinking

It is, of course, far better if you can shift into pure awareness and realize that there is no point in thinking that in order to be free of your past and your karma from the past you have to go through a linear process. Do you understand how technology and science have given you this concept that there is a linear process of evolution? You have all been brought up to think that the present species that you see on earth can all be put on this giant structure, like a family tree where at the current level of species you see a great variety. But if you go to lower levels of the tree, then you see that the current variety is an expression of previous levels that were more simple. And thus from the many branches and leaves you get few bigger branches. Eventually you connect to the trunk, you go back to the root where you supposedly had one event that initiated life on earth as a single cell. This is the image you have been given by science and it is an image that is constructed from the linear mind. It has very little connection to how the current species were actually created because many of the current species do not have a common ancestor; they were created simultaneously. Scientists have even seen this as something they call the Cambrian explosion, when enormous amounts of different species appeared in a very short period of time.

What I am trying to tell you here, my beloved, is that when you consider how to be free of your past, you cannot look even at your past embodiments as an entirely linear process. You cannot think that in order to change the effects of a choice you made 500 years ago, you have to somehow go back there and make a physical change. This is not how life works.

I admit that we have given certain teachings that can be interpreted in a very linear way, and we did this out of simple necessity because people were not ready to accept a more spherical, non-linear teaching. But as you climb the Path of the Seven Veils, the other Chohans will gradually take you towards a more spherical form of thinking. And I wish to at least give the initial impetus to this shift by giving you the teaching I am giving you here.

Your karma boat

What I would like to do now is to have you envision that you are sitting in a little boat that has a rudder with a little rod that you can use to turn the rudder with your hand. You are sitting in this little boat out in the middle of the ocean. The ocean is completely calm. There is no wind. The ocean is like a mirror. Now, as you are sitting there in your boat, you may think that you are not moving at all that your boat is sitting still. Yet you will know that in the ocean there are currents, and thus even if you are sitting in the middle of an ocean that is completely still, your boat is not sitting still because it is being carried along with the ocean current. So you are still moving.

However because you are not moving relative to the water, you cannot steer the boat. In other words, in order for the rudder on your boat to work and actually turn the boat, the boat must be moving relative to its surroundings. Otherwise, you can turn the rudder all you want but your boat will not change direction. Because even though it is moving along with the ocean current, it is not moving relative to the water around it.

I wish to take this image to a different situation. I wish you to now envision that you are still sitting in the same boat, but now you are on a river. And you can see that the river has a current because you can see that the boat is moving relative to the banks of the river. Thus, you will know that when your boat is drifting with a strong current in a river, your rudder will actually have an effect because by changing the angle of your rudder, you can change the angle that the boat is moving downstream. And this means it is possible for you to change the direction of the boat so that it will move, for example, towards one shore.

Now let me ask you to envision that you are drifting down the river and you are looking forward and you are seeing that your boat is headed straight for a cliff. And you can see that if you continue going in this direction, you will hit that cliff. Naturally, you attempt to turn the rudder, but you find that it is stuck. You cannot turn it.

What does this symbolize? It symbolizes that in past lifetimes you made choices from a certain level of consciousness. This has created what we normally call karma. This karmic return is now coming due, and this means that your boat that is being carried along with the River of Life, is now heading for a cliff. Now you could say to yourself: "When did I make the choice that set my rudder at this angle, taking me towards the cliff?" And you could then, if you were able to look back, you could see that back there, 20 miles upriver, you made a choice to turn your rudder in a certain direction and that is why you are now heading for the cliff. You could then reason to yourself: "I need to start rowing my boat back up against the current, until I get back to the point where I changed the angle of my rudder, and then I will change it to a different direction that takes me away from the cliff."

My beloved, this is how the linear mind would think. This is how you think when you are in the consciousness of separation. Because you think that in order to change the consequences of a choice made with the separate self, you have to make a different choice with that separate self. But the reason why your rudder is stuck is that you still have not transcended the state of consciousness in which you made the original choice.

Life is about moving on

What I am telling you is this: The only way to change course in the River of Life is to transcend the consciousness that made the choice that locked your rudder in its current angle. When you transcend that level of consciousness, you see that your rudder is not locked because you have other options. And that means you can now change your rudder to at least a slightly different angle. And if you can change your rudder enough, you can avoid the cliff. It may be a close brush with death, but you can change the angle just enough that you can avoid the cliff. And this means that you can, as I have actually explained before, avoid a karmic return by changing your consciousness enough whereby those who oversee the karmic return for earth might say: "This person has learned his or her lesson

434   *The Mystical Initiations of Power*

and therefore does not need to have the lesson of the physical return of the karma."

You see the deeper point I am seeking to make here? You are sitting in a boat, you realize you want to change direction, but it seems like your rudder is stuck. But the rudder is stuck only because you look at the situation from a limited perspective, a limited sense of self, a limited awareness. You are looking at the situation through a specific spirit that was the same spirit through which you made the original choice that created the karma.

That is why you think you cannot turn the rudder. You cannot see the options for how you can change the angle. And therefore because you cannot change the angle of your consciousness, you cannot change the angular momentum of how you are moving with the current of the River of Life.

You can always change your sense of self

There are several things you can ponder here. You can ponder that you are an individual, yes, and that you are currently embodied on earth. Therefore, you are part of the collective consciousness created by all of the individuals that embody on earth, and even those who are tied to the earth in the emotional, mental, and lower etheric realm. You are part of this whole—no man is an island.

This can be seen as the stream of the collective consciousness. It isn't necessarily the River of Life in its purest form, but it is certainly the stream of the collective consciousness. And as an individual, you do not have the power to row your boat up against that stream. And it would, in effect, be futile to attempt to do so. Many people have, over the years, gone into a prideful sense of wanting to dam the river or control its flow, and you have seen how they have set themselves up as dictators who have attempted to do this. But eventually, their reign, no matter how powerful, was overturned. Time ran out. Time ran away from them.

You can be in the separate consciousness and you can continue in the separate consciousness and think that you have to row against the current, you have to control the current, you have to dam the river, you have to do this and do that to control the flow. Or you can simply accept that as long as you are in embodiment, you are carried along with this current.

What you can do is you can change the angle of your rudder, so that you move in the direction in the river that you want to go. In other words, you are not on an ideal planet. Yes, the collective consciousness has limited your creative options. You cannot currently do absolutely anything you want or make any choice you want. But what you can do at any point is choose to do something different than what you have done before. You can choose to do something that is more. This option you always have.

What I am saying is: Even though you might have separated yourself from the creative flow of the out-breath and the in-breath and gone into the dead end of the death consciousness, you are still not limited by the choices you made in the death consciousness in the sense that you can never choose to rise above them. You *can* choose to rise above them. Ponder this, for it is an essential teaching for those who will be free of their own past choices.

When you are focused on the death consciousness in the separate spirit, you will be limited by your past choices. In other words, your past choices have limited your creative options far beyond what the Elohim did when they designed the earth. The collective choices of humankind have limited the creative options for human beings in embodiment far beyond what was the original design of the Elohim. If you are focused in that separate self, you cannot see the reality that you can still exercise your free will by choosing to transcend the separate self. The false teachers, the dark forces, your ego, want you to believe in one simple lie: You are bound by your past choices. Once you made the choice to eat the forbidden fruit, you are condemned forever and only an external savior can save you.

But the external savior – that is external to your separate self – is the pure awareness of the Conscious You, which realizes: "Oh yes, I did enter that separate self; I have looked at life through that separate self, but I did not become that separate self. I am not bound by it. I can step out of it. I can choose to be more than the separate self." And when you choose to be more, you will see at least a few more options than you can see right now. And that means you can change the angle of your rudder at least a degree or two.

Small changes with big results

You will know, if you have ever been on a boat in the ocean, you will know that when you are traveling far, changing your rudder by just one or two degrees can make a very big difference concerning where you will land when you reach the shores of the ocean. The further you travel, the more of a difference there will be in the destination point by just a change of one degree on your rudder.

You see, even now you have the option to choose something that is more than you have chosen before. And even a small change will alter your course, so that in the long run you will end up in a very different place. And that is why even the smallest choice to be more will have a dramatic positive effect on your future.

Of course, once you choose to be more, you can choose to be more than that, to change your angle another degree. And you can continue to do this until you truly move out of the death consciousness and then move back into the in-breath of life. Where you are now no longer going further way from oneness, but you are part of the flow of going back towards oneness, the flow that the Maha Chohan has called the Holy Spirit. Which is the upward momentum created by all self-aware beings in all spheres who have chosen to move closer to oneness. This is what we have called the River of Life, the true River of Life, not the current of that underground river that leads you to the realm of the dead, as you see in certain mythological teachings.

I know that I have given you a teaching that may be beyond your capacity to grasp at your present level, but nevertheless this is part of who I am. For am I not Master MORE? So how could I fail to give you more than what you can grasp? For it is only by giving you more than you can grasp that you become able to grasp more. And this is the creative process itself.

Thus, I thank you for your attention, and I thank you, this messenger and all people who have been part of making it possible for me to give this teaching by embracing the teachings we have given previously, by embodying, internalizing those teachings. And therefore advancing the process of progressive revelation where we of the ascended masters can reveal more and more advanced teachings as people raise their consciousness and raise the collective consciousness.

Truly, you may think that this teaching on the seven rays is fairly basic. But I tell you, the teaching we are giving on the seven rays now could not have been brought forth 5 or 10 or 30 years ago because the collective consciousness was not there. The collective consciousness is there because of the many people who have embraced ascended master teachings in some form and used them to raise their consciousness and to raise the collective. And for this you have my undying, everlasting, ever-expanding, ever-transcending gratitude.

For I AM MORE.

DECREE TO ELOHIM HERCULES

In the name I AM THAT I AM, Jesus Christ, I call to my I Will Be Presence to flow through my being and give these decrees with full power. I call to beloved Elohim Hercules and Amazonia to release flood tides of the Light of Power and Will to help me see through an overcome all abuses of power, including…

[Make personal calls]

1. O Hercules Blue, we're one with your will,
all space in our beings with Blue Flame you fill,
a beacon that radiates light to the earth,
bringing about our planet's rebirth.

**O Hercules Blue, all life you defend,
giving us power to always transcend,
in you the expansion of self has no end,
as we in God's infinite spirals ascend.**

2. O Hercules Blue, your wisdom so great,
within us a sense of knowing create,
a new frame of reference we suddenly gain,
for going beyond duality's pain.

**O Hercules Blue, all life you defend,
giving us power to always transcend,
in you the expansion of self has no end,
as we in God's infinite spirals ascend.**

3. O Hercules Blue, we lovingly raise,
our voices in giving God infinite praise,
in feeling your flame, so clearly we see,
transcending the self is the true alchemy.

**O Hercules Blue, all life you defend,
giving us power to always transcend,
in you the expansion of self has no end,
as we in God's infinite spirals ascend.**

4. O Hercules Blue, all life now you heal,
enveloping all in your Blue-flame Seal,
we're grateful for playing a personal part,
In God's infinitely intricate work of art.

**O Hercules Blue, all life you defend,
giving us power to always transcend,
in you the expansion of self has no end,
as we in God's infinite spirals ascend.**

5. O Hercules Blue, your Temple of Light,
revealed to us all through our inner sight,

your power allows us to forge on until,
we pierce every veil and climb every hill.

**O Hercules Blue, all life you defend,
giving us power to always transcend,
in you the expansion of self has no end,
as we in God's infinite spirals ascend.**

6. O Hercules Blue, I pledge now my life,
in helping this planet transcend human strife,
duality's lies are pierced by your light,
restoring the fullness of our inner sight.

**O Hercules Blue, all life you defend,
giving us power to always transcend,
in you the expansion of self has no end,
as we in God's infinite spirals ascend.**

7. O Hercules Blue, we set all life free,
from the subtlest lies of duality,
the prince of this world no more has a bond,
for with you we go completely beyond.

**O Hercules Blue, all life you defend,
giving us power to always transcend,
in you the expansion of self has no end,
as we in God's infinite spirals ascend.**

8. O Hercules Blue, in oneness with thee,
we open our hearts to your reality,
your electric-blue fire within us reveal,
our innermost longing for all that is real.

O Hercules Blue, all life you defend,
giving us power to always transcend,
in you the expansion of self has no end,
as we in God's infinite spirals ascend.

9. O Hercules Blue, you fill every space,
with infinite Power and infinite Grace,
you embody the key to creativity,
the will to transcend into Infinity.

O Hercules Blue, all life you defend,
giving us power to always transcend,
in you the expansion of self has no end,
as we in God's infinite spirals ascend.

Sealing:

In the name of the Divine Mother, I fully accept that the power of these calls is used to set free the Ma-ter light, so it can outpicture the perfect vision of Christ for my own life, for all people and for the planet. In the name I AM THAT I AM, it is done! Amen.

DECREE TO ARCHANGEL MICHAEL

In the name I AM THAT I AM, Jesus Christ, I call to my I AM Presence to flow through the I Will Be Presence that I AM and give these decrees with full power. I call to beloved Archangel Michael and Faith to shield me in your wings of electric blue light, and shatter and consume all that limits my willpower, including...

[Make personal calls]

> 1. Michael Archangel, in your flame so blue,
> there is no more night, there is only you.
> In oneness with you, we're filled with your light,
> what glorious wonder, revealed to our sight.
>
> **Michael Archangel, your Knowing so strong,**
> **Michael Archangel, oh sweep us along.**
> **Michael Archangel, we're singing your**

song,
Michael Archangel, with you we belong.

2. Michael Archangel, protection you give,
within your blue shield, we ever shall live.
Sealed from all creatures, roaming the night,
we remain in your sphere, of electric blue light.

Michael Archangel, your Knowing so strong,
Michael Archangel, oh sweep us along.
Michael Archangel, we're singing your song,
Michael Archangel, with you we belong.

3. Michael Archangel, what power you bring,
as millions of angels, praises will sing.
Consuming the demons, of doubt and of fear,
we know that your Presence, will always be near.

Michael Archangel, your Knowing so strong,
Michael Archangel, oh sweep us along.
Michael Archangel, we're singing your song,
Michael Archangel, with you we belong.

4. Michael Archangel, God's will is your love,
you bring to us all, God's light from Above.
God's will is to see, all life taking flight,
transcendence of self, our most sacred right.

Michael Archangel, your Knowing so strong,
Michael Archangel, oh sweep us along.
Michael Archangel, we're singing your song,
Michael Archangel, with you we belong.

5. Michael Archangel, you are the best friend,
from all worldly dangers you do us defend,
the devil no match for your power of light,
and therefore our souls can freely take flight.

Michael Archangel, your Knowing so strong,
Michael Archangel, oh sweep us along.
Michael Archangel, we're singing your song,
Michael Archangel, with you we belong.

6. Michael Archangel, as children we play,
we're bringing the earth into a new day,
we raise it from all of the patterns so old,
our planet's life story is by us retold.

Michael Archangel, your Knowing so strong,
Michael Archangel, oh sweep us along.
Michael Archangel, we're singing your song,
Michael Archangel, with you we belong.

7. Michael Archangel, God's power you show,
that you are invincible, this we do know,
you are undivided and thus can withstand,
anything coming from serpentine band.

Michael Archangel, your Knowing so strong,
Michael Archangel, oh sweep us along.
Michael Archangel, we're singing your song,
Michael Archangel, with you we belong.

8. Michael Archangel, come raise now the earth,
giving her thus a complete rebirth,

collective the mind that we do now raise,
for this we do give our infinite praise.

**Michael Archangel, your Knowing so strong,
Michael Archangel, oh sweep us along.
Michael Archangel, we're singing your song,
Michael Archangel, with you we belong.**

9. Michael Archangel, the earth is now new,
covered in Blue-flame as the morning dew,
our planet now sparkles throughout all of space,
as we are receiving your infinite Grace.

**Michael Archangel, your Knowing so strong,
Michael Archangel, oh sweep us along.
Michael Archangel, we're singing your song,
Michael Archangel, with you we belong.**

Sealing:

In the name of the Divine Mother, I fully accept that the
power of these calls is used to set free the Ma-ter light, so it
can outpicture the perfect vision of Christ for my own life, for
all people and for the planet. In the name I AM THAT I AM,
it is done! Amen.

DECREE TO MASTER MORE

In the name I AM THAT I AM, Jesus Christ, I call to my I AM Presence to flow through the I Will Be Presence that I AM and give these decrees with full power. I call to beloved Master MORE, the other Chohans and the Maha Chohan to release flood tides of light, to consume all blocks and attachments that prevent me from freely exercising my free will by making more aware choices, including...

[Make personal calls]

1. Master MORE, come to the fore,
we will absorb your flame of MORE.
Master MORE, our will so strong,
our power centers cleared by song.

**Master MORE, your Sacred Heart,
from this we will no more depart,
we are forever in your flow,
of Diamond Will that you bestow.**

2. Master MORE, your wisdom flows,
as our attunement ever grows.
Master MORE, we have a tie,
that helps us see through Serpent's lie.

Master MORE, your Sacred Heart,
from this we will no more depart,
we are forever in your flow,
of Diamond Will that you bestow.

3. Master MORE, your love so pink,
there is no purer love, we think.
Master MORE, you set us free,
from all conditionality.

Master MORE, your Sacred Heart,
from this we will no more depart,
we are forever in your flow,
of Diamond Will that you bestow.

4. Master MORE, we will endure,
your discipline that makes us pure.
Master MORE, intentions true,
as we are always one with you.

Master MORE, your Sacred Heart,
from this we will no more depart,
we are forever in your flow,
of Diamond Will that you bestow.

5. Master MORE, our vision raised,
the will of God is always praised.

Master MORE, creative will,
raising all life higher still.

**Master MORE, your Sacred Heart,
from this we will no more depart,
we are forever in your flow,
of Diamond Will that you bestow.**

6. Master MORE, your peace is power,
the demons of war it will devour.
Master MORE, we serve all life,
our flames consuming war and strife.

**Master MORE, your Sacred Heart,
from this we will no more depart,
we are forever in your flow,
of Diamond Will that you bestow.**

7. Master MORE, we are so free,
eternal bond from you we see.
Master MORE, we find rebirth,
in flow of your eternal mirth.

**Master MORE, your Sacred Heart,
from this we will no more depart,
we are forever in your flow,
of Diamond Will that you bestow.**

8. Master MORE, you balance all,
the seven rays upon our call.
Master MORE, forever MORE,
we are the Spirit's open door.

**Master MORE, your Sacred Heart,
from this we will no more depart,
we are forever in your flow,
of Diamond Will that you bestow.**

9. Master MORE, your Presence here,
filling up the inner sphere.
Life is now a sacred flow,
God Power we on all bestow.

**Master MORE, your Sacred Heart,
from this we will no more depart,
we are forever in your flow,
of Diamond Will that you bestow.**

Sealing:

In the name of the Divine Mother, I fully accept that the power of these calls is used to set free the Ma-ter light, so it can outpicture the perfect vision of Christ for my own life, for all people and for the planet. In the name I AM THAT I AM, it is done! Amen.